Demons in the Age of Light

Demons in the Age of Light

A MEMOIR OF PSYCHOSIS AND RECOVERY

By Whitney Robinson

PROCESS

A PROCESS MEDIA ORIGINAL PAPERBACK
ISBN: 978-1-934170-27-4
ALL RIGHTS RESERVED.

Printed on recycled paper

Process Media
1240 W. Sims Way Suite 124
Port Townsend, WA 98368
www.ProcessMediaInc.com

Design by Bill Smith | designSimple

Author's Note

This is a memoir, subjective by nature but bound by certain standards of truth. The time-line of some events has been altered, usually by condensing for the purpose of narrative flow. Names of others have been changed and dialogue reconstructed where memory fails, but in the end this book reflects a genuine attempt to describe a real experience . . . the interpretation is all yours.

PART I

Self

From childhood's hour I have not been
As others were—I have not seen
As others saw—I could not bring
My passions from a common spring.
From the same source I have not taken
My sorrow; I could not awaken
My heart to joy at the same tone;
And all I lov'd, I loved alone.
Then—in my childhood—in the dawn
Of a most stormy life—was drawn
From ev'ry depth of good and ill
The mystery which binds me still:
From the torrent, or the fountain,
From the red cliff of the mountain,
From the sun that 'round me roll'd
In its autumn tint of gold—
From the lightning in the sky
As it pass'd me flying by—
From the thunder and the storm,
And the cloud that took the form
(When the rest of Heaven was blue)
Of a demon in my view.

—

"Alone", Edgar Allan Poe

Stained Glass

I believe it was church windows that caused my conviction that the soul exists to linger when reason declared the absurdity of such concentrated meaning in the universe. If mere patterns of colored glass could stir in me, heathen gum-popping brat, emotions as rich and subtle as the wine tones of their many facets, it seemed there must be something here that was more than a byproduct of chemicals and their collision. Darwin has explained many things, but not the mechanism by which small hairs stand on our arms when light falls through the rippled panes of a stained glass Eden, concentrating in the ruby eye of a forbidden apple until it is an all-seeing and all-knowing point of flame.

I had ample opportunity to ponder the aesthetics and metaphysics of church windows in my youth, because Orthodox liturgies are a good two hours and change, never mind vespers and feast days. My parents were active in the church and so, by default, was I, home-schooled and raised in a peaceful anachronistic world of Sunday school, coffee hours, fast days, and holy weeks. For the first decade of my life, my parents managed to shield me from most of the things they found wrong with the world. They could not protect me from myself. I had the disposition of a stagnant lake…brooding, opaque, wanting to seep inside things and break them to their elements. One of my favorite games was to take a jar of marbles and sit cracking them on the molten blacktop of our driveway, then hold them up against the sun. The goal was to produce a marble that had shattered inside, but remained whole, a small planet of broken pieces held together by surface tension.

I broke some things that breathed, too, mostly by keeping them in jars and admiring them until they died. I ate pickles and jam constantly, just for the jars. I kept them in the attic of our rotting barn, where cobwebs thick as jungle vines hung from the rafters and the air was tinged with the bitter dust motes of several decades. Dozens of glass containers lined the room, arranged on hay bales and broken furniture, each containing some unfortunate creature that had caught my possessive eye. Stick insects, field mice, fuzzy yellow caterpillars, freakishly large moths, and the fat toads that ventured out of our garden to eat them. I was impervious to the object lesson that a wild-born creature kept in a concord grape jelly apartment with some wilting leaves and a bottle cap of water will not lead a long or happy life. I simply caught them, stored them until they desiccated, and began the process again.

In my serial killer phase, I read that this is not an uncommon obsession of young psychopaths, the persistent jarring of small life forms. On the other hand, Nabokov was a lepidopterist; he drowned his butterflies in ether. He wrote *Lolita*; he did not act it out. Humanity is full of darkness and words are its sanctioned release. The problem is when they turn on us, when they will not be tamed.

In the Eastern religions which put forth reincarnation as truth, and to which many disenchanted seekers are drawn from more jealous faiths, a human birth is the rarest of gifts. We alone among the gods and demons and animals and hungry ghosts are granted with insight, the ability to deviate from instinct for better or worse. As each soul traverses the weary circle of learning and forgetting, life and death, it may be cast into any realm, and the human world is the point where all paths intersect on the journey to that final destination in which you have no further actions to play out on the universal stage.

That's the ideal, anyway—most of us are simply learning to become a little less like prideful gods or empty ghosts or animals reacting blindly to circumstance. But coyly I've avoided the category with personal relevance, the realm my soul best remembers and to which the universe would call it back, given its way. This is the world from which representatives have been sent to entreat my return. *Things fall apart, this is the natural order of the world, embrace it* . . . demons love chaos theory.

But I am not a demon, and this, I would like to think, is the story of my unbecoming.

The professor is stirring now. He goes to the blackboard and writes *Philosophy 101* in fine copperplate script, then returns to his desk corner roost and begins to speak.

"Imagine yourself in a dark cave, chained to the wall."

"Kinky," someone murmurs, followed by snickers, which the professor ignores.

"You have been there a very long time, long enough that you can remember nothing else. There are others with you—who they are and how many is immaterial now. The entrance to the cave lies behind you, so your only impression of the world is the shadows that fall upon the ancient wall. Maybe the shadows of trees blowing in the wind, of animals or people passing by the mouth of the cave. This is all you have ever known.

"Now imagine that one day, a sharp rock is pitched into the cave and lands at your feet. You cut the ropes that have bound you to the cave. The others cry for you to free them also, but in your haste to leave your prison, you abandon them. You go out to see the world."

Blackjack Girl's cell phone begins to play "Mambo No. 5." She reaches down to turn it off and there are a few uneasy giggles.

"What falls upon your weary eyes is unlike anything you have experienced," says the professor, ignoring the interruption. "Imagine, color for the very first time, depth, sunlight. You return to the cave to tell the others what you have seen. But they don't believe you, they don't understand. All they have ever known are shadows on the wall. They think you are a liar, or worse, insane. They will probably kill you in the end. This is Plato's allegory of the cave, in which all the things we have seen or touched or tasted are only fallen replicas of the perfect forms we strive hopelessly to imitate. In philosophy we attempt to move closer to these universal truths, even to question whether truth itself dissolves on contact with a mind. Philosophy is the art of taking nothing for granted, of finding the path that leads us out of the cave. Philosophy is coming into the light."

One would think we'd be tweeting snidely about this by now, or at least smirking at this pallid and socially moribund man who declares that through philosophy we can achieve some druglike bliss. But the students are pensive, as pensive as eighteen-year-olds of mixed gender in a room can be, and no one is laughing. Without dismissing the class or looking at us, the professor takes up his briefcase and walks out the classroom door. The students wait uncertainly for a moment, then some critical mass of decision is reached and we scrape back our chairs and leave quietly without speaking.

My senses, grateful to return to the natural world, interact vividly with my surroundings. How the sun dazzles, how the chips of quartz in the sidewalk glitter. The air rings with the greeting calls of students and an occasional fearful cry followed by the cackle of geese on the campus green. And yet, I remind myself, this is only the world of objects. Bright shadows though they are, we can't quite trust them. I notice I am walking oddly, with light tentative steps on the balls of my feet. The way I used to walk in the woods over uncertain footing, down slick leaf-covered slopes and over damp logs fallen across streams. Ready for sudden movement in any direction, for the ground to give way at any moment.

After a quick lunch of Cheetohs and Gatorade from a nearby vending machine, I chew my pen into a shapeless wad of plastic as I listen to my first abnormal psychology lecture, all neuroimaging studies and diathesis stress models and serotonin reuptake inhibitors. Where are the defense mechanisms, the wandering uteri, the oral fixations? The instructor is now showing us what I first take to be a Rorschach blot but is actually an MRI scan of a brain. It looks like a butterfly encased in frost. But the butterfly is the cerebral ventricles, the snowflakes convolutions of brain matter. You are here to be a scientist, not a poet, I remind myself.

After psychology, physics. Most of the students already look defeated, slumped apathetically in their seats, and I can't blame them. I wouldn't be here myself if it weren't a requirement for pre-med majors. I wanted to take the comp lit course in the same time slot, but doctors have to make a lot of sacrifices so I figure I might as well get used to it.

"Wait a minute, this is *math*," one of the students cries indignantly when syllabi have diffused throughout the room. "I thought we were going to be learning about wormholes and, like, strings."

"This is an introductory physics seminar," says the professor, a tweedy man with an abstract pouf of white hair atop his shining head, a veritable cartoon academic. "Our focus is on classic or Newtonian physics, which covers principles of matter and motion in the everyday world. What you're thinking of is quantum mechanics, which I also teach in my advanced seminar. Something to look forward to," he says with a twinkle in his eye, and continues: "The most basic concept in physics is that of matter. What is matter?"

"Strings!" the student cries hopefully. "They're even smaller than atoms, right? Aren't they like tiny gateways to other universes? How does that work?"

The professor looks annoyed, then sighs and begins to scribble a lengthy equation on the board. Surrendering the rest of the lecture to quantum theory, he explains that it's the Heisenberg interpretation of the Uncertainty Principle, which is that thing where particles exist only as abstract probabilities until they're observed. It's pretty trippy if you think about it, but the math that goes along with it is difficult and boring. After class I linger to take a closer look at the formula, hoping that if I stare long enough, it will start to sparkle inspirationally and form meaning in my mind. But ten minutes later it still looks like math, and graduate students are starting to drift into the room for a lecture on things I couldn't begin to understand.

And now, suddenly, it's four in the afternoon and I'm wallowing in freedom. I feel like I should be socializing in some way, but I've passed the age where you can park yourself next to someone and say, "Hey, let's be friends." Plus I was never very good at that to begin with. In the end, I find a bench next to a fountain in the campus center and crack open *The Trial and Death of Socrates*, which I read when I was ten. A girl with tripartite platinum-purple-pink hair plunks down next to me and says hello.

"Oh, hi," I say, looking up from Athens, 399 B.C. The girl gives me a weird look and continues her cell phone conversation. I get up and buy an overpriced chai latte from a nearby café, Socrates drinks his hemlock, and I'm not sure why college is supposed to be such a priceless experience.

Later, on my way to the bus stop, I see one of the students from my physics class, her hand resting too casually on the back of a bench. Conjecture, but it seems she is unwilling to put too much faith in gravity. With the equivocations of philosophy on one hand and the uncertainties of science on the other, what can we be principled in except our uncertainty? A student on a skateboard veers down a stairway railing and crosses in front of me, airborne at high velocity. But a crash is just avoided by my reflexive feint to the left; I'd been walking on my toes again.

Ornithologist

I grew up in a backwater Massachusetts town of abandoned mills, pizza parlors, and churches. The Fourth of July fireworks were generally the high point of the year. Otherwise, there were several defunct factories to explore, an expanse of gray river where interesting things sometimes washed up on the banks—giant blobs of algae, bottles with fish trapped inside, once a dead baby—and a liquor store that also sold candy and was easy to shoplift from because the teenagers behind the register were always high.

Before I was born, my parents had bought a shambling Victorian house, painted it the color of blue-green sea glass, and restored it to nearly its original magnificence. My mother cultivated gardens full of rose trellises and iridescent gazing balls, and when kids from town came over to play they used to ask if my dad was a drug dealer or in the Mafia (he was, in fact, an attorney). Our front door, affixed with a sign declaring "No Solicitors" and another, "Trespassers Will Be Prosecuted," opened into a hall of cherry-red wood and stained glass with a spiral staircase to the second floor. The rooms were heated by metal radiators that hissed and groaned and made the house seem like a convention of arthritic ghosts. My room had a fireplace into which bats occasionally dropped and swooped in dizzy orbit above my bed, and I spent many nights chasing them sleepily around my room with a shoe box.

In the attic, formerly the servants' quarters, there was a cubby lit by a bare bulb that I called "the murder room" because it contained a slashed leather chair and a mysterious stain on the rough-hewn floor. I used to shut myself in and wedge the chair under the door when my parents argued—three stories up was generally sufficient to block out the noise. There I would eat from my forbidden bag of Skittles and read Sherlock Holmes mysteries and crawl into the piles of cotton-candy colored asbestos fiber insulation in the heating ducts and fall asleep.

In the back yard there was a rotting barn and behind it, a stone wall that separated our yard from the municipal park, a hundred-acre tangle of woods with a venous system of overgrown trails running through it.

I wasn't supposed to play there alone, but I was often left to entertain myself while my mother was painting and my father was engaged in dull lawyerly phone calls in his study. I had an uncanny sixth sense that allowed me to slip over the wall and explore the woods for a few hours, then return just as my parents were starting to wonder where I was.

I felt like the woods were an extension of my soul, full of shifting patterns of light and shadow, places where you could lie in the sun and pull petals from the heads of yellow flowers, one by one, to discover if you were loved. There were cold pockets of evergreen where the ice didn't melt until nearly summer, shy watersnakes, noisily foraging squirrels, and the occasional dismembered deer or rabbit. In addition to supplying me with endless scurrying, swimming, and slithering pets, the park was the ideal location to play my favorite game, which I called The Last Person on Earth, in which I would go deep into the woods and pretend that everyone else in the world had turned into zombies, and I had to flee civilization and survive on my own in the wilderness.

Since the local school system was based mostly on D.A.R.E classes and sex education, my parents home-schooled me in all subjects required by state law, as well as a few that weren't on the official curriculum. My father took me to the gun range as soon as my little hands could hold steady a semi-automatic, and I was educated in chess and Latin by a pair of Orthodox monks who lived in a moldering wedding cake of a mansion in the middle of the woods. They always plied me generously with sweet cakes and vodka before lessons began, which may explain why in the span of four years I managed to learn maybe six Latin phrases and a handful of extraneous vocabulary. This was a significant source of tension in my early years—as far as I was concerned, the language wasn't nearly dead enough—and indeed, I was hardly what you'd call a model pupil in any subject. Hopeless at math, foggy on geography, I possessed the kind of mind that wandered into irrelevant details and stayed there, feeding carrots to Robert E. Lee's horse while the Battle of Gettysburg raged on for an undetermined reason at some hazy point in time.

My father, a self-described ecofascist, never imposed his politics on me, but I was always peripherally aware of them. Often he held long coffee-and-cake diatribes with other disgruntled white men in our living room, leading them on frequent field trips to the basement to admire his guns. I would sometimes feign interest in these discussions while stealing bits of pastry whenever no one seemed to be paying attention.

". . . In the end," my father would say, casting me a disapproving glance as I eased another strawberry tartlet from the communal plate, "we can't escape the fact that 95 percent of the human population has no value as anything but high-protein fodder for our animal friends."

"Chop them up, can them in factories!" I'd declare, spewing crumbs. "Let the noble feline grow fat and sleek on the flesh of the *untermenschen!*" This idea came from a Hindu-Nazi mystic named Savitri Devi whose complete works graced my father's library, and it delighted me for some reason—probably because I had an innate love of both cats and violence. As a visual aid to my secondhand rhetoric, I grabbed my fat gray patchwork cat who was sleeping on a nearby chair and held him Simba-like, aloft. Everyone in the room chuckled and commented on my adorableness. The more bloodlust I showed, the more it pleased my father. Except I had noticed this sort of conversation only took place in certain company. For example: not at Girl Scout meetings, not at church, not at gatherings of my mother's family, not in the middle of the K-Mart toy aisle.

But like most children exposed to a contradictory set of morals— radical fascism pitted against the ideal of Christian love—I learned to hold nothing as sacred and to embrace the proffered ideologies of the moment. Thus my father was left with a listless, dreamy child who was neither a Nazi nor a Christian, and he inadvertently instilled in me the relativism of the liberals he despised.

In my relatively innocent preteen years, my main interest was stalking and capturing small animals. Indeed, the recent passing of Tobias the garter snake had left me with an empty 5-gallon aquarium and a pet-shaped hole in my life. There was an excellent frog pond in the park, a ten-minute stumble through a riot of ferns and chokecherry bushes. I waited until I knew my parents would be at one of my mother's art shows all afternoon, then grabbed my net and bucket and slid on my jelly sandals with images of leaping amphibians doing a veritable Dance of the Sugar Plum Fairy in my head.

At the playground, some kids called out to me to join their game of Capture the Flag, but I ignored them and slipped into the tangle of green. As I approached the pond I heard frogs splashing into the water, which was ringed with spreading ripples by the time I reached the algae-dappled bank. I kicked off my jellies and waded in, stirring clouds of silt through which silver minnows swam to peck black specks of decay from my feet. It felt like many reverent kisses, like I was the god of little fish. Everything was cast in a nostalgic golden hue, a pretty, polluted dream world which I deliberately blurred still further by unfocusing my eyes. Frog hunting was a mental exercise, like one of those magic dot pictures at the optometrist. You couldn't look for the hidden image directly; you had to make your gaze abstract and wait for it to be *revealed*. Soon my sight shifted and I saw a mottled brown frog where moments before had been only mud and rotting leaves.

The water grew murky and opaque as I poised my net to strike, blending the frog back into its camouflage. I looked up and saw a man standing at the edge of the pond, casting his shadow over me.

"Hi," he said.

"Hi." It was hard to see his face with the glare from the sun behind him. Other times I might have run away, but I was not playing The Last Person on Earth today, so he was not a zombie, just a man. There was a moment of silence in which I still couldn't properly see his face. Then he said, "What are you doing?"

"Looking for frogs."

"Oh, really? I'm looking for something myself. I'm kind of an amateur ornithologist. Do you know what that is?"

"Studies birds."

"Right . . . that's exactly right. So what's your name, Miss Frog Hunter?"

"Chelsea Summers," I said, using the name of a kid in my Girl Scout club because I didn't know who the man was or how he'd come to be here. Then a cloud drifted across the sun and I saw he had an ordinary face and his shirt was from L. L. Bean, which was where my father bought his shirts.

A flurry in the water captured my attention, and I pounced instinctively. Urine-colored water streamed from my net and something struggled in the webbing. I splashed ashore and shook a juvenile leopard frog into my bucket. As frogs go, it was not a lovely specimen—in fact its bug-eyed appearance was unsettling enough to make you wonder what chemicals had been leaching into the groundwater. I looked up to find the man still watching me.

"Caught one," I said conversationally, perhaps even flirtatiously.

"Won't the other frogs miss it?" he asked as the frog flopped against the side of the bucket with a rubbery sound.

"Frogs don't really have families the way people do. The other frogs are probably glad. 'More mosquitoes for us! Mosquito pie, mosquitoes 'n' gravy!'"

He laughed like this was a really clever thing to say, and I could feel his entire awareness on me, the kind of interest you normally only get from an adult if you do something very clever like recite the Declaration of Independence from memory, or else something very bad like climb up the fireplace flue in your bedroom to get onto the roof. And he was a scientist.

"How old are you, Chelsea?"

"Nearly eleven."

"You seem like a bright girl."

"Well, I'm home-schooled."

"I see." His eyes trailed over my mud-splattered legs, my candy-stained mouth, and the pond weeds trailing across my arms like henna tattoos. "You must spend a lot of time here. Maybe you can help me."

"With what?"

"I'm taking pictures of birds for my collection." He held up a small camera that hung by a cord from his neck. "Maybe you could help me identify some of the birds around here."

"Well, there are ducks down by the river, but I'm not sure if they count as birds. They sort of remind me of poodles, which are like technically dogs but really *not*, you know? And if you get lucky you might see a hawk. There's usually chickadees all over the place, but I don't see any today."

"Really? I was hoping to see a chickadee. Maybe we can find one together, if we look hard enough."

I pointed to some black birds squabbling over a dead minnow on the far shore. "Those are crows—you can tell because they're smaller than ravens. Edgar Allan Poe wrote a poem about a raven . . . I had to memorize it for school. I don't know what you call a bunch of ravens, but the collective noun for a group of crows is a murder." I looked at him sideways and smiled, full of a darkness I couldn't express.

"Is that so."

"I know another poem with a bird in it."

"Oh?"

"It's called *The Second Coming*, by W. B. Yeats. Would you like to hear it?" I had never seduced anyone before, but it seemed to come so naturally, poetry and coy glances.

"Yes." The man's voice was hoarse.

"Turning and turning in the widening gyre, the falcon cannot hear the falconer. Things fall apart, the center cannot hold . . ."

As I spoke, I trembled with all the things I understood while my body remained pale and contracted, too incipient to respond in kind. There was a smell radiating from his body, clean white soap and a little sweaty beneath. I could feel the restlessness inside him even though he strolled casually beside me, as careful to speak softly and avoid sudden movements as if he were taming a wary cat.

Did he want to kill me? A delicious shudder ran through my body. Here was my Dr. Lecter, the closest thing I might ever have. It was late at night, at a sleepover, when I found my first love object. My friend asleep beside me on a cot that smelled like cat pee, the television playing out the terrifying and blessed confirmation that I was not alone in seeing the world as I did, full of words like scalpels and jars of eyes and freezers full of human hearts. Sometimes I'd wonder, what if I'd been born into a different body, cast into a different life? What if I'd not been a little girl with golden hair whose mother read her fairy tales? What if I'd been a boy with crooked teeth and a slimy nose, a bastard child no one wanted? What if I'd had an *excuse*?

Nothing that entered my eyes escaped without coming to consciousness, nothing died without a dissection. But the one standing here, he was just a shadow puppet—he didn't understand the dark matter coursing through him. Maybe I was Dr. Lecter after all. I moved closer, close enough to touch. But before contact came a black-capped bird landed on a dead tree at the edge of the pond.

"Aren't you going to take a picture of it?" I asked.

"What?"

"It's a chickadee." I pointed again to the bird, still twittering its heart out to some unseen mate.

"Oh, yes." The ornithologist lifted the camera and snapped a few shots. "That's a chickadee, all right. I'm glad you spotted it for me, Chelsea." He let his camera fall around his neck and reached out to put a hand on my shoulder. Meanwhile, sense had got the better of me and I shied away out of reach. I didn't really want to die today, it was just the idea of it that intoxicated my blood. The birdwatcher's smile remained fixed, but the agitation reached his eyes.

"What's the matter?"

"I have to go—it's my dinner time, I can tell by the sun. Maybe I'll see you again sometime." As I spoke, I stepped backwards at the same rate he was walking toward me. I was strangely fixated on my shadow on the ground, on not letting him step into its radius. Then the game gave way to something like pursuit and I ran in earnest, but it was so weightless and free that I forgot I was doing it because I was afraid.

Now I was safe on the playground with a mother pushing a baby in a swing, and the group of kids still playing tag, and some teenagers trying to ride the yellow dog on a spring. There used to be a skunk on a spring too, but the teenagers, or at least some teenagers, broke it. I almost wished the ornithologist had kidnapped me and put me in his basement full of taxidermy birds so I could have stabbed him with my Scout knife and escaped. Maybe there would have been live birds in cages too, and I could have freed them. I was heroic, full of the excitement of running for my life, and in that short life *It* had never tagged me.

I scaled the stone wall and was stealing across the lawn when I realized I had left the bucket with my poor mutant leopard frog behind. I almost went back—maybe for the frog, maybe for some other reason. But my parents' car was pulling into the driveway, so I hurried inside and parked myself in front of "The Simpsons" (which my father considered a work of high comedy and was one of the few shows I was allowed to watch). And then, because I knew my parents would be suspicious if I'd behaved while they were gone, I dribbled chocolate sauce down the sides of the kitchen counter and lit a match so the house would smell faintly of burning when they opened the door.

Chapter Two

The biology lab is lit by blinding fluorescent strips that make people look dehydrated and sleep deprived, which most of the students are if the noises from the frat houses last night are any indication. Today we are dissecting a sheep's eyeball. My lab partner, Scott, watches equably as I slice away the gummy fat surrounding the eye but makes no attempt to join the festivities. He is cute enough to get away with not really doing any work, and he always manages to look busy when the teacher comes near.

"It's weird not having Wilbur today," says Scott, who appears to be sketching a comic strip in the margin of our lab sheet. "I'm starting to feel like he's our child."

Wilbur is our fetal pig, pallid and rubbery with an eerie smile on his snout, but our specimen today is a golfball-sized eye surrounded by a hunk of white adipose tissue.

"Sheep have bigger eyes," I say. "Easier to work with."

Scott issues a respectfully grossed-out noise as I pierce the sclera and vitreous humor dribbles onto the dissecting pan.

"That's so horrible," he says. "And, um, I was wondering, would you like to go out sometime, like on Friday?"

"OK. But . . . why?"

"I'm impressed that you can do this without puking all over the place, for one thing. And I don't know, you seem different from most girls. Less brainless or something."

"Um, thanks," I say, keeping my attention on the eyeball to avoid having to exude charisma and wit. Scott diagrams as I strip away the tough membranes and waxy fats and gleaming jellies. At the back of the eye is a milky iridescent film that shimmers under the harsh lights.

"What is it?" I breathe, transfixed by the glistening membrane, as arresting among the soggy tissue as rainbow scum on a parking lot puddle.

"That's the *tapetum lucidum*," says Scott, consulting the study guide. "It reflects light back to the retina, helping the sheep see in the dark."

"Isn't it the most beautiful thing you've ever seen?"

For a ridiculous moment I want it, want to take it home and keep it, just to have it to look at whenever I want. Distract Scott and slip it into my pocket. Well, I'll be, I just don't know where that darn sheep's eye could have gone. The moment passes.

The teacher circles the lab, demonstrating proper scalpel use and identifying mysterious bits of tissue impaled on forceps. When she reaches our table, she only says, "Nice work, Whitney. You have a surgeon's hands."

Scott radiates warmth and approval from his comfortable position several yards away, although I noticed he scooted his chair closer when the teacher approached so that she would assume he was taking an active role in the dissection. Later, as we scrape the leftovers from our tray into a biohazard bag, Scott says, "So where should I pick you up?"

"What?"

"You know, on Friday. Say, nineish?"

I murmur an agreement and give him my address—my parents did not want to surrender me to the wilderness of a coed dorm, and are paying for me to rent a room in the home of a wholesome family paying off their mortgage. Some part of my brain directs me toward my next lecture, but I still have not transitioned away from the world inside the sheep's eye. *Tapetum lucidum*: "bright tapestry" in the mostly unlearned language of my youth. We are so ugly inside, every living creature from humans to sheep to baby pigs . . . yet sometimes you come across something so heart-stoppingly beautiful you can hardly imagine it came from inside a humble case of gristle and bone. Sliding into a seat as the philosophy professor drones about some upcoming test, I touch the bulge of my eyelid with a probing finger and wonder if there is a rainbow behind my eye also.

As the light fades from my room on Friday evening, I set down *A Groundwork to the Metaphysics of Morals* and turn my attention to matters of the passions. I am skeptical of human relationships in general because it seems they are all predicated on a single truth: People consume each other. I could have as meaningful a relationship with a packet of cheese snacks. Sex, you say? That's the difference? Well I've tried it (fifteen, community college) and it was right up there with putting on wet socks and eating a cafeteria sloppy joe. *Love*, you dare to venture? Well there's got to be something that transcends the pain and fumbling, or else I can't see how this species has perpetuated itself.

Don't get me wrong, I want to form some meaningful connection with the people around me . . . It's just that talk across genders forms expectations, and bodies are a problem for me. Pale, quivering sacks of blood and bones—they do not compel me to perpetuate the species, or pretend to. Animals have poetry in their shape and motion, but people never really stop looking half-formed, still fetal even as they begin to decay. There are many words in English for dead bodies, yet none to distinguish one that is specifically alive. I think that's telling.

However I've already agreed to this date, so I guess there's no backing out now. I'm pretty sure it's important to smell nice, so I spray myself liberally with some amber-colored perfume an aunt gave me last Christmas. It's called *Scorpio's Passion*, tailored to my astrological sign. According to the bottle, I am powerful, sensual, and magnetic, and these qualities will be exquisitely enhanced while I am wearing the perfume. I start to put on a pair of earrings, but I wear them so rarely the holes have healed over. In order to look feminine and attractive I'm pretty sure I need earrings, so I grit my teeth and stab my way into a pair of amethyst studs.

As I'm wiping blood from my ears with a piece of toilet paper, the doorbell echoes jarringly through the house. I call out that I'll answer it and make my stately way downstairs. I read in one of those teen fashion magazines that it's good to make your date wait at the door instead of answering right away. Apparently a studied indifference has aphrodisiac properties. Well good, because that at least comes naturally.

Scott greets me with a smile as I open the door, startlingly cute in a leather jacket. "How does the Black Sheep sound?" he asks as we get into his car.

"Sure," I say, although I have no idea what the Black Sheep is. Maybe some kind of bar. Maybe one of those places where you need a hand stamp to get in, shaped like a cartoon character and visible only under blacklight. I wonder if he realizes that I'm not old enough to drink and I probably wouldn't do harder drugs.

"You look pretty tonight," says Scott. "Nice earrings."

The Black Sheep turns out to be the kind of café you only find in college towns, with black-and-white photos of abandoned factories on the walls and some guy in a rainbow scarf plucking morosely at a guitar. Scott orders ginger tea and I get a chai and a pastry filled with raspberry goo.

"Ginger is soothing for the stomach, right?" says Scott. "I've been nauseated since we started that horrible pig dissection. The smell of formaldehyde, the oozing noises the organs make when you prod them with the poker thing—"

"The forceps."

"Yeah. The only blood and guts I like are in zombie movies, and I'm pretty sure that stuff is all fake."

"Actually it's probably pig viscera too. Pigs are physiologically similar to humans. You can even fool the experts sometimes. Like snuff films, you know, where they supposedly kill someone on camera? There have been a lot of fakes. Some were so convincing that the FBI got involved, but they were uncovered as staged in the end. I think it turned out that the blood and guts were mostly from pigs."

Scott is looking at me oddly. "And you know this how?"

"I dunno, some documentary on the Internet. Haven't you seen it?"

"Actually, no," he says, and I realize that snuff films are one of those subjects you're probably supposed to avoid on a first date.

I start to pick out the jam from the center of my pastry, then hesitate. Are girls on dates supposed to eat? Maybe I should be gazing insipidly into his eyes. My attempt at smoldering contact is abortive, though. When our gazes meet I feel a cardiac jolt, not a romantic one but the kind that makes concerned doctors order EKGs. Scott smiles and I pluck skittishly at my pastry again. The jam has the color and texture of congealed blood, although not the taste, but at least I know better than to point this out. I clear my throat. "So, um, it's too bad you hate our biology class so much. That really sucks."

"It's the highlight of my day now that I have a lovely lab partner to look at instead of a dismembered pickled pig," says Scott.

"If you could bring yourself to look at the pig once in a while, perhaps our lab report would contain something other than the latest episode of *Sparkle Unicorn and Death Kitten* . . ."

"Oh, sorry about that. I do this webcomic and I'm always afraid I'll forget my ideas if I don't write them down. But you're right, I should totally help out with the dissection more."

"It's OK, I like cutting stuff up. Platonically, I mean . . . "

"A girl who like snuff films and dissecting things . . . disturbing, yet oddly hot."

So many people say things like that, and so few of them mean it. For Scott it's just rhetoric; there's no darkness in him. One senses these things.

"So, ah, where are you from originally?" I ask.

"Vermont." He doesn't elaborate and is looking expectant, like the burden is now on me to provide the entertainment.

"And what other courses are you taking?"

"Econ, social psych, and intro to political science."

"What do you plan to do when you graduate?" Ugh, I sound like I'm interviewing him for a scholarship.

"Dunno, really. I'd love to be an artist, like for graphic novels, but it's tough to make a living doing that. I've got some connections in D.C., so I'll probably end up being the guy who brings coffee to the mayor's aide. But who knows, maybe I'll become President of the United States, and *Sparkle Unicorn and Death Kitten* will be syndicated in every major paper nationwide." He flashes a smile and flecks of amber glint in his eyes. I can't hold his gaze for long, but I preserve the image.

"So what about you? Other than platonically cutting stuff up, what compels you to rise for 8 am lectures?"

"I . . . also dunno. I kind of want to be a surgeon, but when I was younger I thought I'd be an FBI agent. Like Clarice Starling, profiling serial killers."

"Oh, yes," says Scott, straight-faced. "What child doesn't dream of growing up to profile serial killers?"

"But now I'm not sure. I feel like there are too many paths open to me—I haven't even declared a major yet. And according to my philosophy professor, human beings intrinsically hate freedom, or at least too much of it. Who knows, maybe I'll drop out and go to Africa to study tigers like Jane Goodall."

"She studied gorillas."

"I know, it was an analogy. I will be to tigers what Jane Goodall was to gorillas. Except, you know, I probably won't. Most likely I'll end up being, god, an accountant or something. Or a librarian, with horn rimmed glasses—"

"A *hot* librarian," interjects Scott.

"—something terrifyingly ordinary, anyway."

"Yeah, I know what you mean."

The conversation has become so painless that I'm surprised when a barista comes over to tell us the place is closing.

"I should probably get you home," says Scott, "Or my roommates will accuse me of lascivious activity." He looks hopeful that I might extend the invitation, but when I don't he doesn't press the matter. When we reach the house, he gets out of the car to walk me to the door.

"You're a strange girl, Whitney," he says as we stand together on the doorstep in that awkward hovering moment of parting.

"Is that bad?"

Scott leans over and kisses me, a fleeting ephemeral kiss that barely brushes my lips, then bounds down the steps to his car. I could not say what I feel. In the absence of everything I decide that it was beautiful, because I very much want that to be true.

CHAPTER THREE

"*Schizoid personality disorder is characterized by a persistent withdrawal from social relationships and a lack of emotional responsiveness in many situations. A person with schizoid personality disorder may be described as "cold" or "aloof" and may show a marked preference for solitary activities, an indifference to praise or criticism, and a lack of interest in sexual activity. They are often perceived by others as socially inept . . ."*

With a grunt of annoyance, I slam my abnormal psychology textbook shut. "Maybe they just have a low tolerance for idiots," I mutter to no one in particular, since my room is barren of life except for myself and a fat black spider on my ceiling. But of course the book is not personally insulting me. All psychology students have every disorder in the *DSM-IV*. Last week, I diagnosed myself with Cotard's Syndrome after we talked about it in class.

As I turn my attention to the reproductive system of the fetal pig as described and lavishly illustrated in my lab manual, the sound of hip hop music revs up from nearby frat houses. It's Saturday night, when everyone who isn't perceived by others as socially inept is out partying and getting drunk. Suddenly I can't bear another evening spent with impossible equations, psychiatric disorders, and dividing cells. Also, the spider is starting to creep me out. It's the kind with squishy guts, I can tell. I'm afraid it will disappear and leave me in existential terror, but I'm too chicken to go after it with John Stuart Mill's slender pamphlet on utilitarianism.

Instead I put on a hoodie and slip out into the moist night, balmy for late October, and zigzag along the residential streets on the outskirts of campus proper. Many of the houses are ablaze with light and noise. Now a front door is thrown open and people are streaming inside. I find myself cutting across the crisp autumn lawn to join them, an orbiting insect unable to resist the heat and glow.

"Five-dollar cover," says a guy sitting on a folding chair by the door. I fish around in my pocket and hand him a crumpled bill. Inside, I find myself in a large den with the furniture pushed to the periphery, tables with feed tubs of chips and pretzels. Kegs dripping onto the floor and rows of foam-capped plastic cups. More cans and bottles beading up in bins of ice below. I grab a can of beer and crack it, sipping at the unappealing sour fizz. Alcohol was never forbidden when I was growing up—a good Russian child should hold her liquor, my father always said, and perhaps for this reason it never appealed to me as a vice of excess.

People are still flowing through the doors, but once inside they clot into couples or small groups. Everyone seems to know everyone else. Everyone has a reason to be here but me.

"You seem lost," says a voice behind me as I sip awkwardly at my drink. I glance around and see a tall, unnaturally blond boy with that aura of sleepy confidence acquired via popularity in high school. At 5' 10" I rarely have to look up at anyone, but he's got four or five inches on me. Skinny but not drug-addict skinny, sporting a blue shirt with only the middle two buttons buttoned, revealing a well-segmented trapezoid of abdomen.

"Are you looking for someone?" he says. I shrug and take another gulp of cheap beer. It doesn't seem like the sort of party you have to have been invited to, but the fact is I don't know anyone here. The boy's eyes flick down, up, down—I think I've just been Checked Out—then he puts a hand on my elbow and says something I can't hear because someone just put on Fall Out Boy at max volume. The guy tugs at my sleeve and I follow him down a sardine-packed hall into a kitchen in which the unwashed dishes appear to have allied and staged a democratic revolution.

"I said you shouldn't bother with that crap." The boy takes the beer from my hand, can't find an empty surface to set it down, balances it on a plate of bacon scraps. He rummages in the refrigerator and produces two Jell-O shots, one red and one green.

"Stop or go?" he asks with a nuance-laden grin. I take the green shot because I hate cherry-flavored anything, which the red one is sure to be. I knock it back—like an alcoholic lime slug, yet not unpleasantly so—and find the boy pouring me what appears to be an iced tea glass full of bourbon. "I hid this puppy under the sink," he says, "for VIPs only." He hands it to me with a conspiratorial wink. Desiring to prove that I'm not a total mousy wallflower, I down the bourbon in two gulps and hand him back the glass. He raises an eyebrow and is about to say something, but a gaggle of coeds with Oompa-Loompa tans froth into the kitchen and begin to distribute Jell-O shots. One of them asks the boy how to make them, and he launches into an enthusiastic discourse. I notice a bathroom at the end of a deserted hall and shoulder through the crowd. When I close the door behind me, the sudden quiet is a relief. The speckled mirror is adorned with a shaving cream smiley face and a set of male genitalia—I sense the hand of two different artists—pointing toward it. As I'm sitting on the toilet, someone thumps briefly against the door, then it opens.

"The room is occupied," I say. It's the blond boy again, but he doesn't seem alarmed that he's just walked in on me. He oozes through the door and kicks it shut, then swaggers over and crouches down on his haunches in front of me, setting an empty shot glass unsteadily next to the toilet. He puts his first two fingers in his mouth and then presses them between my legs. He glances up at me, smirking eyes contacting startled eyes, and penetrates. I'm speechless because I never expected to encounter a situation where someone walks in on me in the toilet and randomly sticks his fingers in my vagina. It hurts a bit and I should probably be horrified, but instead I start to laugh.

"You like that?" he says, pushing deeper. I shrug and emit a stupid, equivocal, girlish giggle which I am instantly ashamed of.

The fingers slither out and the guy grabs my wrists. "C'mon," he says. "S'go upstairs." Sheeplike and a little drunk, I stumble up an unlit stairway into a shadowy bedroom that smells of old laundry and citrus air freshener. He pushes me down onto a bed and lets his weight fall on me, seals off my mouth with his own. His saliva tastes of high-proof liquor. He strips me in the rough, sticky-fingered way that little boys undress Barbie dolls. He slips off his own shirt, and even in the poor light it's clear that from the perspective of evolutionary biology,

I lucked out. His body has the cut of an artist's model. Now he's taking off his jeans and putting on a condom . . . that's good, although not from the perspective of evolutionary biology. A solitary beam of moonlight frames a poster on the wall—some rock star I can't immediately name stares down, bored and brooding in black and white. He's seen it all before.

The boy finds his way into me and commences the most overrated act in human history. About every minute and a half he prods me into a new position, as if I were a lazy heifer. Finally he grips me hard and lets out a mewling cry, then lies still, twitching slightly, on top of me. When he rolls away he leaves beads of sweat on my chest and stomach.

"Well, fuck *me*," he says with a kind of restless contentment, and reaches into the pocket of his crumpled jeans for a cigarette. He offers me one and I shake my head.

"You remind me of my ex-girlfriend's cat," he says, although I have no idea in what context he means it, and he doesn't elaborate.

"What's your name?" I ask.

"Calder."

"Like Alexander Calder?"

"Who?"

"He was a mid-twentieth-century artist. He made mobiles."

Calder shrugs, rolls toward the side of the bed again, and begins to struggle languidly into his clothing. "Listen," he says, "I've got this thing going on in the morning, so . . . "

"Yeah," I say, sitting up, "I should go."

My underwear comes arcing through the air and lands on top of me, followed by my bra, shirt, and one sock. I put these on and hunt around for the remaining articles in the semi-darkness.

"You've got a *great* ass, you know," says Calder sincerely and apparently in lieu of a goodbye as he escorts me to the bedroom door. Picking my way through the strewn bottles and sprawled bodies to the exit, I realize that he never even asked my name, nor how I got here, nor anything about me at all. Clearly he is, in common parlance, a douchebag. But the funny thing is, I don't mind. Actually there is a wonderful lightness in my step as I walk home alone in the dark, an anonymous figure on the drunken streets. Bodies crash together; they pull away. This seems no more or less violent than using words to the same effect. I feel connected to everything now—I am one with the girl in a miniskirt puking on the sidewalk, one with the comet of a black cat streaking across the road, one with the shadow couple of indeterminate gender making out in the streetlight's glow. Whatever sign is taped to my back that warns people off, it can't be seen in a dark room through a bourbon and Jell-O shot haze. For the first time in a long time, I feel young and alive.

CHAPTER FOUR

The world of the morning after seems sullen and hostile, the soft ebullience of the night replaced by a glowering sky and bare claws of trees striking melodramatic poses against it. In class, I stare dully as my physics professor spins around the room swinging a ball on a chain. His classroom demonstrations have become increasingly aerobic—last week, he shot a stuffed monkey out of a pressure cannon for some reason I don't recall. Clearly, he's trying to convince us that real physics are as interesting as the highfalutin quantum stuff, but he doesn't seem to be having much luck.

"So, as you can see," says the professor, massaging his heart region as the class flips languorously through its handout on acceleration, "the net force required for an object to move in a circle is directly proportional to the square of the speed of the object."

One of the students raises a hand. The professor nods.

"Will you tell us about Schrödinger's cat?"

The professor looks exasperated. "That's really not relevant to today's lesson."

"But they made a joke about it on *House* and I totally didn't get the reference. Please?"

The professor, resigning himself to the fact that Newton just isn't cool enough for undergrads, spins out a dramatic tale of a scientist who sealed a cat in a box with a flask of poison so that the flask would only be broken if someone opened the box and observed the cat. The scientist posited that the cat was simultaneously alive and dead inside the box, but his colleagues thought he was insane so he was denied tenure and eventually driven to suicide. Then some kids snuck into his abandoned lab, years later—on Halloween, I think—and opened the box, and the cat was still warm like it had *just* died, meaning the Uncertainty Principle was true. Actually, I just made that up because I wasn't really listening and there was math involved and I think I had a seizure reaction to the sound of chalk scraping against the blackboard.

When the class is over, I linger to take a closer look at the blackboard full of grad student equations by the lectern. Some minds probably see something beautiful in the scrawled symbols, like good poetry. I stare at them without blinking until the numbers run together and flashes of light streak across my visual field. But try as I might, I can see only the surface elegance, not the deeper significance. I take a piece of chalk and start scratching away, trying to simplify where I can and make it mean something, but after ten minutes I've just ruined the equation and I have no idea how to fix it before the next class starts, and they're probably going to come in and be like, what retard was fucking with our equation for whatever the hell this equation is.

Your mathematics are appalling . . . destroy yourself at once.

I snort and stare at the chalk tray, because it seems like it's the silver edge that's spoken, the words being synonymous with a feeling of cold metal pressed against skin unable to pull away. But I'm not touching the tray, and they're words.

You've divided yourself by zero . . . now you can't exist at all.

Chalk dust sucking the moisture out of my mouth, dehydrating every cell in my body until the membranes rupture. It could be either the sensation or the words, whichever I want, but I don't want either and I find that I am pressed against the wall for support. The porous cinderblock digs warning grit into my skin and threatens to become as spongy as a muffin. All the matter in the world is unhappy with its form. It lusts for transformation, it wants to be liberated into energy, it *desires*.

I feel like my limbs ought to be in violent motion, but I'm having trouble getting them to move at all. I hear voices down the hall, grad students coming for their class. I don't want them to catch me in front of the wrecked formula, so I slip quietly out the door and take the bus to my apartment. My homework for tomorrow's classes is incomplete and expresses its preference to stay that way. I want to write a poem, but there are too many words to choose from and the right ones shy out of reach. Instead, I go back to bed until I feel the acid stab of hunger. But the kitchen seems impossibly hostile, so full of knives and fruit that does not belong to me. Instead, I pour tap water from the bathroom into a glass and add ramen. The shrimp kind isn't bad, mostly because it tastes strongly of salty chemicals and nothing of shrimp.

As night falls, I have the disconcerting sense of being the last person alive on the planet, the way you feel if you find yourself on an empty street or in a deserted waiting room, half-afraid but sort of hoping in your heart that it's the Rapture, because how *cool* would that be, at least until you were consumed by tongues of fire or dragons of the apocalypse. But the others are still here . . . I can hear them all around me. I can hear their drunken cries and feel the beat of their atrocious music in my bones.

A day passes, and another, moving patterns of light and shadow across the floor. But it's OK—as a bright and questioning college student, I am duty-bound to be stricken by a metaphysical nausea that will prompt me to mark this world as my own during my brief time here. It's normal to meet my own eyes in the mirror and stir with desire to tear into the egg-white sclera until the third eye finds the rainbow behind it all. I must try to write that poem, the one that hides in the dusty heating vents and grows like mold in the throat of the bathroom sink, just out of reach. Oh, language, you wary cat, I will not throw you at hapless passersby like a weapon. I only want to use you to adorn my otherwise unexceptional self. I have no desire to chain you to the mundane task of describing the mammalian digestive system. We will not go to class today, you and I.

And for that day and the next, I write lovely, incomprehensible things in notebooks and eat the provisions I have stored in my room: mixed nuts, sugar abstractly inspired by fruit and wrapped in shiny foil. As I contemplate my final packet of ramen, someone approaches the door and calls my name. A moment later it opens, and daylight from the hall streams into the soupy mid-tones around me. My muscles tuck and gather, ready for fight or flight, and I stand quickly as my mother enters the room.

"Oh, Whitney—I didn't think anyone was home. Didn't you hear me knock?" And without pausing for my reply, "It's stuffy in here, why don't you let in some light?" She grabs at the string of the window-shade, startles it into a defensive coil, and picks up a piece of granola bar foil with a *tut*. "I'd hoped that living on your own would teach you cleaner habits. How was school today?"

"School?"

"Yes, your classes. How are they going?" My mother pauses to observe me in finer detail: hair unbrushed, decked out in fuzzy slippers and horse-head pajama bottoms. "Why aren't you dressed? Are you sick? Did you even *go* to class today?"

A jarring question to which I have no parentally acceptable response.

"Of course I did," I say at last, coldly.

"Well, I've been trying to reach you all day. You didn't lose your cell phone, did you?"

"Of course not," I say with conviction. Cell phone? What the hell is a cell phone? The schema comes back after a moment of bewilderment, and then I am not at all sure I haven't lost my cell phone.

"Hurry up and get your things," says my mother. "Your dentist appointment is at three and then your birthday party's at five. I hope you haven't been eating too much sugar. Your skin is looking oily . . . are you using that special face wash?"

I grab some clothes from the floor and stuff them into my backpack, kicking aside stray ramen exoskeletons. When I follow my mother out to the car, I am surprised by how cool and fresh the air feels.

"You know," says my mother after the vehicle is in motion, when I am unable to escape the conversation without sacrifice of life or limb, "I wonder if it was the best idea for you to move out on your own. Do you think maybe it wasn't such a good idea?"

"I don't know."

"Is everything going okay at school?

"Wonderful. I love my classes." For some reason I can't keep a belligerent edge from my voice. My mother starts to say something else, then falls silent. The dentist's office is close to our house, so when we get there I tell her that there's no need to wait, I'll walk home.

The receptionist says, "Brrr, where's your jacket?" when I enter, and I look at her blankly. *Jacket?* What an odd woman . . . Polish, maybe. I take a spool of complimentary dental floss and spend ten minutes in the bathroom carefully flossing my teeth to make up for all the times I didn't. Blessed be those who come even unto the eleventh hour.

On my way back to the waiting room, I pause in front of the machine that dispenses plastic bubbles filled with small toys for children who didn't try to bite the dentist's face. Near the bottom is a rubber bouncy ball, a cooling blue with flecks of glitter suspended inside. I wish I could get it, but I believe I am too old now to be given a token. Back in the waiting room, I lean down to examine the aquarium of zebra fish. They are lethargic today, gills working in labored rhythm as they drift toward the sucking filter. I flick a fingernail against the glass, but they seem to be in a state of suspended animation, as if they too were trapped inside a rubber ball.

I grab an issue of *Highlights for Children* and take a seat. Inside, I find a garden in which thirteen butterflies are hidden.

Can you find the butterflies?

Can, or will die trying. Three etched into the back of a garden bench, two yellow ones camouflaged among the flowers, three more fluttering in plain sight through the sky, one cloud shaped like a butterfly—ha, they think they're so clever—a butterfly on a smiling kid's shirt, two blue butterflies in the reflecting pool . . . wouldn't they drown? But there is no thirteenth butterfly. I scan the picture again, looking for more tricks like the cloud-butterfly, but I am sure I've found them all. OK, three on the bench, three in the sky . . .

A shadow passes across the hallway door, gone by the time I look up. Maybe it was my imagination, but the figure that crossed my peripheral vision seemed furtive and distorted. It might have been carrying some kind of sharp instrument. Possibly one with a gleaming metal blade. Something in the room seems to curdle. The receptionist clacks at her keyboard with her back to me. The tapping has an unsettling rhythm, mathematically wrong. I am fairly certain that if she turns around, she will have no face. I glance warily down at the magazine. They are liars; there are only twelve butterflies. The last butterfly is a fabrication designed to make small children go insane. The fish tank gurgles in amusement, a wet choking sound.

I drop the magazine and jump to my feet as the receptionist calls my name. It is my turn to see the dentist. I follow her to the examination room. She motions me to sit in the sticky plastic chair and shines a light into my face. The lamp has a frosty quality, emitting as much chill as illumination. Drops of ice crystallize on my forehead and I wish I had brought a jacket. She turns on a hissing drain, the one you spit into, and leaves the room. A poster on the wall shows the four stages of tooth decay. The accompanying pictures are gruesome, the last one black with necrotic tissue. A tacit threat? The machine makes a patient gargling noise, waiting to be spat into.

Soon the dentist comes in wearing a paper mask, which annoys me. It seems like he should put it on in my presence, like how at restaraunts they uncork wine bottles in front of you so you know they haven't poisoned it. I can only see his eyes, and eyes are always sinister out of context.

"Good morning, Ms. Robinson. I see it's been a year since your last checkup and you are cavity-free. Let's take a look." He snaps on a pair of white gloves. How does he know I have no cavities? Is there some kind of background-check system for dental patients? I open my mouth so he can poke inside with forceps identical to the ones I have used to plumb Wilbur's pickled depths. A dental hygienist lurks in the background, also wearing a mask.

The dentist clucks with disapproval. "Dear, dear. We've got a 19DO."

The hygienist's eyes flash understandingly. "I'll prepare the filling."

Without seeing their mouths move, there is a disconcerting feeling that the words come from nowhere. This, more than anything, makes me feel that whatever they put in my mouth will not be a simple silver amalgam, but some kind of experimental alloy containing a time-release neurotoxin or silent carcinogen. The dentist is preparing a syringe of clear fluid. When the pair steps out of the room, I seize my chance and slip quietly away. The waiting room is empty and the receptionist is still typing ominously with her back turned. Only the zebra fish, hanging motionless in a rubber blue ocean, see me leave.

Off-White Cat

In the barn attic, my caterpillars were roasting in their dill pickle penthouses. The field mouse panted in its wooden crate, and the praying mantis would not eat. I poked a blade of grass between his pincers and it hung there limply. Only the ladybugs seemed unaffected by the heat, crawling in endless *mobius* figures from the bottom of the jar, across the lid, and down again. My parents had gone to the funeral of some distant relative, and the possibilities for this afternoon were nearly paralyzing. I could go anywhere—the park, Harper's convenience store with its bags of cheap candy, the abandoned mills that had all sorts of mind-expanding graffiti on the walls—*anywhere*. But as usual, my greed for amphibians took precedence. At the playground, the metal skeletons of jungle gyms shimmered in the heat. A group of children were clustered around the merry-go-round, poking something beneath it with a stick.

"What is it?" I asked, approaching with caution.

"A cat," said a redheaded girl with a snub-nosed face. "Jordan tried to catch him, but he ran under here."

"He won't come out," said the girl with the stick, tall and nearly a teenager.

"Then poke him harder, Cassidy," whined the boy.

The girl obliged, sweeping the stick from side to side beneath the merry-go-round. A liquid growl issued from the depths.

"He's too far under. I can't reach him."

"Then let's go home, it's too hot out here. And *Pokemon* starts at four."

"Jordan's right, I'm roasting." The girl tossed away her stick and they left the playground. When I crouched down to look under the merry-go-round, X-Files-green eyes glinted from the darkness. Immediately, I decided that whatever was under there was mine and its name was Snickers. I made encouraging here-kitty noises and drummed my fingers on the ground. The eyes never moved or blinked, but I hesitated for only a moment before plunging my hand into the shadows. I groped until I felt fur, then clamped down like the electric claw on those stuffed animal vending machine games. The owner of the fur yowled and lacerated my arm, but I held on grimly and dragged my new pet out by inches into the light of day.

It was a dirty cat that might have been white if it were clean, but in its present state was more of a spoiled cream color with grass-stain accents, grown past the cuteness of kittenhood into sullen and angular adolescence. Its ear was torn and its fur had the coarseness of a wild animal, but its eyes were luminous blue, like a baby doll's. The glint of green was only an illusion created by the reflective membrane at the back of its eyes. The cat continued to scratch and squirm and froth in my arms, but I have always had an uncanny ability to hold on to a struggling cat. It's not as useful as, say, virtuosity with quadratic equations or string instruments, but we all have our small areas of genius. Thus I sustained only minor injuries transporting Snickers to his new home in the barn loft, where he immediately hurtled out of my arms and began batting at a toad in a pickle jar, tail lashing hungrily from side to side.

Realizing Snickers would need private quarters and that a five-gallon aquarium would not serve this purpose, I stacked four bleached straw bales into a square and folded a rose-printed hand towel stolen from our guest bathroom inside. I found a sheet of plywood to serve as a roof, and eight dusty volumes on the geography of the world to weigh it down. When completed, there was just room enough to drop in the cat and slam the plywood ceiling. A few knotholes in the wood provided necessary oxygen, and Snickers would remain safe and secure in his new home.

I brought him bits of steak and salmon hidden in napkins, dangled sparkly hair elastics above his head. But he wasn't the sort of cat that liked to play. After a week of kinetic rebellion during which my arms and ankles took on the look of an abstract painting titled something like *Meeting of Flesh and Rose Garden*, Snickers yielded limply to my clumsy affection and collars woven from embroidery floss. His doll-blue eyes never left my face once I let him out of the enclosure, and he swirled around my ankles with his mouth open in a silent meow.

I hoped that if I could teach him some cute tricks, maybe to walk on his hind legs or play chopsticks on a keyboard like the trained Abyssinian on *Animal Planet*, my parents would find him so cultured and entertaining that they'd let me keep him. We already had two cats, but one spent most of its time hiding among boxes of winter clothing in the attic, and the other was a massive sedentary creature who benevolently tolerated my attempts to adorn him in *haute couture* of the baby doll variety, but was not otherwise very entertaining. Snickers was the sort of cat that could be a girl's best friend, I was sure, the kind you could carry on your shoulders and tell secrets to.

But one morning I entered the attic room to find that the sheet of plywood covering my feline soul mate's enclosure was knocked askew. The interior smelled strongly of urine, and piles of white fur had drifted into the corners. Snickers had been shedding a lot recently. The glass jars lining the room were shattered and there were cat droppings scattered across the floor.

As I stood surveying the wreckage, Snickers streaked out from under a broken dresser and bolted through the door. By the time I ran outside, he was already scaling the stone wall to the park. I cringed at the thought of coyotes, whose tracks I often saw crossing the trails, or of a strange car gliding silently to a halt on the road—*want some fish, little kitty?*—and whisking him off to start life anew as Frisky or Paws or some other undignified name that stupid people are always giving cats (although, in retrospect, this may have been the pot calling the kettle black).

Then I saw a flash of white at the edge of the playground. Snickers was sitting by the path to the pond, washing his paws. He looked up when I called his name, and a static blue shock passed through me with the thought: *That is not my cat.* His eyes were full of things that don't exist in animals, the complexities that make human gazes so difficult to bear. It stopped me in my tracks, that stare, and I felt as though I had fallen through the looking glass, that I was the dumb animal in the pair of us and I'd best be on my way now as he was late, because of me, for a very important tea party . . .

But Snickers—or whatever it was—only turned and flitted away into the cattails, and as children are programmed to do, I ran after him, branches snapping under my feet. I came to a breathless halt as I reached the clearing, searching out anything white and in motion. Nothing . . . he seemed to have disappeared entirely. Then a branch snapped that wasn't under my feet.

"Snickers?"

"Chelsea."

CHAPTER FIVE

Outside the dentist's office, I pause to take in the familiar small town scenery: comic book shop, pizza parlor, defunct movie theater with the display of candy still visible behind the darkened glass like the sword in the stone, waiting for some kid who is brave enough to throw a rock through the window and make off with the treasure. I am struck by the feeling that only the surface of these buildings are real, that if I tried to walk into them, the doors would simply open into an abyss.

I know I should go home . . . people are expecting me, there may even be a dinner of some kind. But when I reach my house, it seems to warn me off like an animal that by its watchful stillness commands you not to come any closer. There are cars in the driveway and the sky is portentous, an infected greenish light suffusing the purple clouds, like it's ready to hemorrhage and something less expected than rain might fall.

I continue up the street until I reach the stable where my family keeps my horse, Apollo. My golden snowflake Appaloosa, blaze-faced with a dusting of white like powdered sugar across his hindquarters. I haven't seen him since I left for college, and I miss him—I used to show every weekend, 4-H and hunter jumpers, but he's nearly twenty and has earned his pasture years. The barn, built into the side of a hill, was once part of a working New England farm. There is a network of underground storage rooms in which you can still find bits of old harness and machinery. The owner used to breed Arabians back in the '80s, when you could still make money doing that, but now only an ancient mare and gelding remain in testament to the rows of dusty ribbons above the stalls.

When I enter the barn, Apollo snaps up his head and snorts at me as if he's never seen me before. But I find a few carrots in his brush box and suddenly he remembers me, nuzzling orange slime down the front of my shirt. I tack him up and we head through the overgrown fields, into the park. When we pass the playground, I turn him down a wooded trail lined with hundreds of white button mushrooms. I wonder why they grow here and nowhere else in the park, if it has something to do with the acidity of the soil. Apollo is flighty today, jumping in his skin at falling pine cones. I feel uneasy too, as if wolves were stalking in the shadows and some oily predator smell has alerted my limbic system before I see the shine of eyes.

Something crashes in the trees behind us and Apollo bolts, cutting sideways into the woods. I hit the ground with a breathless gasp and a sound of cracking plastic as the casing on my helmet breaks. For a moment the world goes grainy and gray, and points of light streak across my visual field. When my head clears, the woods are silent and Apollo is gone. I get stiffly to my feet and track the path of flattened underbrush through the woods. My blood pressure rises with every step when I see where the trail is leading.

The pond is waiting like a Japanese still life, bare and ominous and poetic. The water is dark and silent, moodily reflecting the sky. There is no sign of my horse, or of anything alive. I don't know how the universe orchestrated my return to this place, only that it was inevitable. The will is the weakest particle of all because its charge is borrowed and drained so we can have light when no one is there to observe it. The thought arises in my mind from some place of spontaneous generation, like the larvae you find in decomposing meat. Except a scientist proved that all agents of rotting come from the outside world, that food sealed off from the environment will not decay. That's how it feels, like the *dura mater* protecting my brain from pathogens and parasites has ruptured, like a maggot has fallen into my ear and is thinking strange thoughts that I am reluctant to claim as my own.

The silence is broken by two squirrels chasing each other around a rain-blackened tree. One is fat and glossy, the other lean with a tail as ratty as an old chicken feather. The bedraggled squirrel has gotten a piece of bread from somewhere and the fat one wants it, advancing with beady, greedy eyes as the other clutches its bread protectively.

The poor hungry fellow will win this,
but he'll die before winter . . .
a rodent's life is unusually tragic.

I turn quickly, but the woods are empty. I'm not even sure if the woods are the right place to look. The words don't seem to come from any direction, and the voice, now that I think about it, could almost be the sound of dead leaf husks scraping on the ground.

Something much larger than me seems to exhale, a fresh lifeless breeze that raises goose bumps on my arms and makes the dry leaves rattle. The sleek squirrel charges, the other squeaks in alarm and drops the bread. Another frenetic chase around the tree trunks ensues. At some point the tables must have turned, because only the starving squirrel returns to the bread. He stuffs it into his mouth and flits away to the bare winter treetops, disappearing in that uncanny way of forest animals—he might as well have ceased to exist. *A rodent's life is unusually tragic . . .*

I am alone now, or was I always? Now that the squirrels have gone, the pond is again devoid of life, dangerously so—animals have instincts for this sort of thing. What sort of thing? Not quite as agile as I used to be, I find myself tripping over roots and branches in my haste to escape from between the nuclear sky and its reflection.

The playground is deserted, and seems even more desolate because a child's winter jacket is draped carelessly across the monkey bars. Where is the child? It is much too cold for a child to be outside without a coat in this weather. The playground equipment looks absurdly small from an adult perspective, frail shapes slick with rain under the bruised sky.

I find Apollo nosing distastefully at the dead grass in his pasture, his broken reins trailing on the ground. I lead him back to his stall and put Betadine on his scratches. In the tack room, cats emerge from every orifice and writhe around my feet until I find a sack of dry food and pour some into a saddle soap tin. Then I go out and stand under the chipped sign that says Sugar Hill Arabians, listening to the chain creak in the wind until I remember the way home.

When I get there, people are gathered for my birthday. They ask where I have been. My old friends Evie and Alexis are here. We were in 4-H together, and in summertime, we used to tear up the park like the four horsemen of the apocalypse in cutoff shorts and bikini tops. We'd race across the playground, scattering small children, and chase down the ice cream truck as it bounced down the road toward a Little League game.

I smile and eat cake and otherwise try to behave like a normal human being, maybe even one who is happy to see her friends. When everyone has left, I go up to my room and look carefully over my personal effects, particularly the things that are shiny or fragile. I have a feeling that if something were taken, it would be small and useless and of apparent value to me. Nothing is missing, but on everything lingers the ghost of a foreign touch. Something has been here.

Night has fallen, and I look out the window and see the moon's crescent grin over the black border of trees. I let the shade fall and rummage through my desk drawers until I find it, my old Swiss Army knife. The cherry-red metal feels warm and alive, like a familiar pet, and I fall asleep with it clasped in my hand.

Skull and Promise

"helsea."

I turned and he was behind me, close enough to touch.

"I thought I might never see you again. I was starting to think you weren't real, that maybe something so beautiful couldn't be real."

A choke in his voice, and I knew that whatever spark of madness and danger I'd felt before had ignited and consumed him. My hand groped for my Swiss Army knife, but it wouldn't open—I'd used it to slice up a lemon Airhead for breakfast, and the taffy had stuck to the blade and sealed it shut.

"You ran off so quickly, but I tried to find you. Did you know there's another Chelsea Summers who lives in this town? She has blond hair too, but she's nothing like you. I thought maybe I had dreamed . . ."

He was crying. I couldn't bear to look at him—it was like looking at the face of God, terrible and unpredictable and *loving*. In fact, it seemed like he had no face at all, just a tearful tilted expression you might call a smile, but with everything bleeding through. His eyes were no particular color I can recall, but they were *shining*.

I knew that to move would shatter everything, but my sneakers still edged away a few pine needles' width at a time. He noticed at once.

"No, don't go. Don't leave me again." There was a regressive whine in his voice.

"I'm not leaving," I said quickly. In his eyes, I saw that somewhere beneath their plasticine sheen he knew I knew, but they begged me not to call out whatever it is that children say when games must end. I swallowed hard, but nothing went down. "Actually, I'm looking for my cat," I said, my voice betraying me. "Maybe you could help me find him. He's white, with um . . ."

But he was not listening. "Love is a cruel thing, Chelsea. If you don't know that now, you will someday." It didn't seem like his feet moved, rather that he was just suddenly closer, like some magnetic force was closing the gap between us. "Do you even know about love?

What do you think love is, Chelsea? What do little girls think love is?"

I didn't know what to say. And I began to realize, it doesn't matter what I say, there is no way out of this. His eyes moved up to mine again and I did not look away. No barrier between dark abyss and dark abyss of dilated pupil, no distinction between us. I felt his desire; I *was* his desire. The black space between us closed, wet and writhing like white skin pushing through rain-soaked soil, surfacing from dream to action for the first time. Through his eyes, I became the object. His hands on cold ivory, the form of innocence.

"I love you . . . you know that, right?"

He was so alone and god, I was so beautiful. Everything past this moment is decay . . . never again will I be so beautiful. And then the fear, the contraction from the blaze, the eternal truth that the object must be destroyed when it has been corrupted. I saw before he did.

"Why are you crying, Chelsea? You know I would never hurt you."

You don't know it yet, but you will.

A rustle in the underbrush—some white animal streaked across our field of vision. His eyes flickered away from mine. The spell was broken, my perfection gone. I fell back into myself, saw my scabbed knees and the chocolate pudding crusted around my mouth because I was a heathen child who did not wash my face unless reminded several times a day.

The spell had broken him too. He grabbed for my arm, but my arm was no longer there. I didn't look, just ran with my heart furious to bursting that I betrayed it so willingly, offered it so freely for sacrifice.

The ground sloped steeply upward, littered with sharp rocks. The undergrowth grew thicker, stabbing defensive branches into the soil. I had never been so far into these woods before—I had always grown afraid and turned back at the point where every direction seemed to lead into the same endless tangle of wilderness. But now I burrowed deep and deeper into the thorns and vines until I reached a small clearing with a jagged rock formation in the center. I pressed myself into a crevice and stayed there a long time. I could hear water running nearby, but that was the only sound. Even the birds seemed to have gone. I closed my eyes and thought of bodies, how they were dumped in water on television crime shows. I imagined being left to float in the golden pond, the weeds extending delicate tendrils to welcome me, and the minnows picking my body clean, feeding pieces of me to their young.

But fear has such a short half-life in children, or maybe I was something different from the beginning. I soon found myself uncoiling, like a caterpillar relaxing into a warm hand, and getting up to explore the clearing. Flowers grew among the scattered rocks, purple in sunlight and blue in shadow. A breeze tossed the canopy above so the flowers shimmered and rippled from color to color, falling in and out of the light. Suddenly and irrationally, I wanted them more than I had ever wanted anything. My fear forgotten, I hurried forward and made a greedy bouquet of them in my fist. I scrambled around an axe-sharp boulder to find more and met accusing eyes.

A skull, waiting here in this uncultivated garden, gazing into me with empty eyes that were not empty at all, that pulsed with awareness and life. I dropped the flowers and they seemed to scatter very quickly, like someone had blown them away in a breath. Delicate shards of bone swirled through the skull's exposed nasal passages, like coral shell. I imagined the creature it belonged to as something sinuous and dappled and shifting like the leaves, even in life wearing a knowing grin.

You have walked in my garden. You have taken what does not belong to you.

The message seemed to spontaneously generate, half-language and half-image inside me. Flaky dead fish swirling in black water, white fungus on a fire-blackened log. The brutal half of nature, light or dark? I did not think of running. The trees would not let me leave these woods. They were witnesses as I beheaded small purple-crowned flowers. If I tried to escape, they would catch me and bind me and eat me in their slow way, breaking me down to carbon for their roots.

My flowers, gather them. Every petal.

Most of the blossoms had blown into a patch of chokecherry briars. My face and arms were stained sticky red as I plunged my hands into thorny crevices wherever I saw a flash of purple-blue. After a while, everything looked purple-blue. I looked up and the sky was purple-blue. I took the flowers, gone limp in my hand, and set them down before the skull, which was resplendent in the gloomy twilight.

Put them inside.

Inside where?

Inside me.

I crushed the flowers into a ball and pushed the mass into the skull's cranial cavity. The black eyes looked into me, thoughtful, and I gazed back, pleading. It was dark. Late. I did not know the way home, or if there was a way home.

Follow the water.

I heard a stream gurgling somewhere in the tangled night. I turned and ran, tripping over stones and ripping through foliage until I found the source. After a purgatory of walking on slippery wet rocks, I emerged onto the playground, eerie without children and silver in the moonlight. When I reached the stone wall of my back yard, I kept my hand on the rough stone for a minute. Base. I am home now. *It* can't tag me. Across the lawn, the house was lit up brightly, and I ran to it in the gathering night. It occurred to me then that I must have missed dinner. And dessert. And the new episode of *The X-Files*, worst of all.

As I crouched beneath the kitchen window, trying to gather my wits to connive, the door opened and a sliver of light fell across the yard. I had never noticed how golden indoor light was, how warm.

"... Never stays out this late. She doesn't *have* any friends she would visit and forget to call. Maybe she ran away. I think you upset her earlier. You shouldn't have been so cross about the declensions. She's ten years old, not a classical scholar."

"She translated *veni vidi vici* as '*wine makes life rich*'. Maybe we should just put her in the public school system and abandon her to the wolves. It's not too late to have another child."

I must have made a noise, because the door opened the rest of the way and my parents saw me in the shadows.

"Whitney! Where the *hell* have you been?"

I looked up at my parents, their silhouettes framed by the doorway. They were separated entities whose lives only incidentally crossed mine, three meteoric rocks accidentally pulled into the gravity of the same planet. It no more occurred to me to confess the night's events to them than to the garden bird feeder.

"There was a cat. I chased it. I got lost."

"A *cat?* Jesus Christ, don't you know there are serial killers and pedophiles out there? A girl went missing from the park just last year. You can't even imagine . . ." The yelling and gesticulating went on for a long time, and eventually I was coated with iodine and dropped into a bath that was far too hot. It made me sick to look down and see my white legs like a cadaver under the water, but I didn't dare use the pink bubble bath to cover them. When I climbed out of the tub, I noticed something floating on the surface of the water, and caught it in my hand before it swirled away down the drain. A small purple flower. It must have stuck in my hair. A trembling fear passed over me, the kind that is compounded by being wet and warm and naked, surrounded by peach wallpaper and steam. I pressed my palm against the steamy windowpane and peered through the clear handprint in the glass.

The yard was empty and quiet, lit by a sliver of waxing moon. It had been there other nights, I was sure of that, but now it seemed to carry a message, to shine with malicious intent. Acknowledging a favor owed, a thing taken but not paid for, a grinning void between an action and its equal and opposite consequence. I let the shade fall and went to bed, but kept my bedside lamp burning.

For days I stayed in the house, lurking behind drawn shades and looking increasingly wan and Victorian until even my mother encouraged me to play outside. In the yard, that is, and not setting a toe outside the yard unless I wanted to be locked in my room until the sun burned out and the sky rained ash, et cetera. So I drifted moodily across the yard, turning over rocks with my toe, but even when I found a feathery crimson centipede nearly three inches long, I didn't have the heart to put it in a canning jar and gaze at it with affection until it died quietly of captivity.

Finally, unable to stand it, I climbed the stairs to the barn attic and surveyed the glittering wreckage on the floor. The jars were shattered and the creatures had crawled their slow way to freedom. Then a flutter of motion caught my eye. One jar remained unbroken among the others. I picked it up and saw that the chrysalis inside had hatched. The air around the fuzzy-headed moth seemed to shimmer as its wings beat against the sides of the jar. I leaned in closer and saw my eyes reflected in the glass. They were *shining*.

I wanted to drop the jar, shatter the image, but instead I went outside and unscrewed the lid with trembling hands. The moth seemed not to know it was free, and hovered for a moment in willing captivity. I tipped the jar until the moth found the opening, and my heart did not settle until its flight had carried it up out of reach. It settled on the floodlight above the barn and crawled inside the plastic shell. Stupid moth, it would fry now. I thought about getting a ladder to rescue it and put it back in its jam jar, safe. But the jar was like a mirror reflecting the glassy bulge of my eyes, so I left it in the light.

CHAPTER SIX

"Please take a seat around the lab stations, and we will commence the written portion of the exam," says my biology professor. "I can take one student at a time for the practical examination. Otherwise, do not leave your places until you have finished the test."

"Lazy French Tarts Lie Naked In Anticipation," I mutter, wiping my sweating palms on my jeans.

"Excuse me?" says Scott from across the table.

"Lacrimal, frontal, trochlear, lateral, nasociliary, internal, abducens. The order of nerves that pass through the superior orbital fissure."

"What's a superior orbital fissure?"

"It's a cleft between the lesser and greater wings of the sphenoid."

"Oh." Scott looks miserable. "What's a sphenoid?"

"Part of your skull. Just anterior—in front of the temporal bone. You'll do fine." The teacher starts handing out exams. "Lazy French Toast Lies Cooling In Expectation," mumbles Scott. I lean over to correct him, but the teacher clears her throat.

"No talking once the exams have been passed out. On the third page, the photocopier cut off question twenty-two. Answer choice D should read, "Occipital, parietal, frontal, temporal, ethmoid, and sphenoid."

"Old People From Texas Eat Spiders," I recall, flipping to question twenty-two and marking D. Then, deciding to get the practical over with, I follow the professor to a table where a fetal pig, not Wilbur, has been laid open, numbered markers stuck like golf course flags in its innards. A microscope and a tray of slides are set out beside it, and our skeleton model is watching from the end of the table, wearing a festive bow tie for the occasion.

"Please identify the superior vena cava," says the professor.

"Thirteen," I say, indicating a wormy blue protrusion threading its way through some gummy tissue above the pig's heart.

"Please show me a patella."

I walk over and tap the skeleton's knee, feeling a bit like a trained seal. You'd think at the college level they'd challenge us a little, maybe have us culturing recombinant DNA or transplanting monkey heads. Obediently, I identify a section of transverse colon, a parietal bone, an anaphase cell, a hyoid, a flagellum, a metacarpal bone, a microtubule, a femur, and an epithelial cell. The cell is as pretty as a church window, the nucleus stained royal blue, the cytoplasm bubblegum pink with dots of minty mitochondrion. For a moment, adjusting the power of the microscope, there is an optical illusion that makes it seem as though the lacy shapes of chromosomes are doing their dividing dance inside the dead cell. But when I show the professor the slide, she appears to see nothing unusual. "Thank you," she says, her face expressionless as a character in a Far Side cartoon. "You may sit down."

I return to my exam, which does not appear to be written in English. The markings on the page are alien, unfamiliar. My own brain is sabotaging me. The test is so easy, but still I fail by forgetting how to read. The other students are circling merrily away. I cast a fleeting look at Scott's test. His pencil hovers uncertainly near the bottom of the page. I crane my neck to read the question—if I see what Scott sees, maybe his comprehension will be imposed on the aspect of the world he is observing, and I can borrow his cogence to complete my exam.

Scott glances up and notices me. He gives me a look I don't know how to interpret and makes an odd motion with his head. Oh, shut up, Scott, I've bailed you out a thousand times in lab when you didn't know an aorta from an alveolus. I ignore him and concentrate on the upside-down letters of his exam, trying to focus on them in a peripheral and nonthreatening manner. It works for frog ponds and dot pictures, and it works for exams. The words shift into meaning: *"True or false: The Golgi apparatus packages lipid and protein macromolecules for consumption by the cell . . ."*

"Excuse me, what do you think you're doing?" says an unhappy voice behind me.

I glance briefly down at my own page and see, *"The Golgi apparatus packages lipid and protein macromolecules . . ."*, then look away to find the professor standing over my shoulder.

"Come with me. Bring your exam."

She leads me to a solitary chair in the corner and points to it the way you'd point out a mess on the floor to a naughty dog. "Sit here," she says, "and finish your test. Don't go anywhere when you're done."

"Why? What's wrong?" It hits me. "Oh . . . Scott . . . no, I wasn't looking at his answers." My voice rises indignantly above a test-time murmur. The teacher holds a finger sternly to her lips.

"After class."

The professor turns and escorts a waiting student to the fetal pig, but he knows nothing of its inner mysteries. The words on my page are plainly legible now, but the sentence still sounds empty when I say it in my head: *The Golgi apparatus packages lipid and protein macromolecules for consumption by the cell.* The words could mean whatever I wanted them to mean, really. Perhaps realizing this is the test, that the statement's truth value cannot be determined because it is too free with precepts.

One by one, the students bring their exams to the front of the room, darting barbed glances at me from beneath politely downcast eyelashes. Their expressions vary from open revulsion to quiet admiration to smug superiority. Scott takes a long time finishing his test, lingering until everyone else has gone.

"Did you have a question?" asks the professor as Scott hesitates in the doorway.

"Um, no," says Scott, casting me a worried look. "But she wasn't cheating. I mean, she doesn't need to."

"Thank you, but I'll handle this."

"I know she wasn't cheating."

"This really isn't your concern, is it?" The professor arches one eyebrow into a lightly veiled accusation. Scott shakes his head and backs reluctantly out the door.

"He's right," I say, my voice irritatingly stupid and whiny even to my own ears. "I wasn't cheating."

"You've been a good student in this class, Whitney, so I'm not going to report this to the dean. But understand that if I catch you looking at another student's paper again, you will be dismissed from this course with a failing grade."

"I *wasn't* cheating. I was just trying to . . ." To read Scott's exam because he accepted it as an *a priori* truth, so its integrity remained intact when mine ceased to have phenomenological clarity. Right. I shut my mouth.

"Everyone makes mistakes and caves in to pressure sometimes," says the professor. "Even scientists." Her severe mouth quivers slightly at the corners. "That's why you get a second chance. But only the one."

"Yes, of course," I say numbly. "Thank you." I gather my things and stumble out the door, past a gauntlet of smugly preening students, none of whom realize that they are only scratching the surface of the world, swabbing away a few epithelial cells. I am glad to leave the specious, obtuse empiricism of the sciences behind. Thank god we have philosophy to purify ourselves.

But all truths have been corrupted, all knowledge decays into apathy when examined. The classroom is as airless as ever, lit with sickly fluorescent strips that cast everything in jaundice yellow and contusion blue. Light that transforms time into a disrupted insomniac night whenever and wherever it actually is. The exam covers ethics: Aristotle's virtue theory, Kant's categorical imperative, Mill's utilitarianism. Topics about which I suddenly and inconveniently remember nothing. OK, think: Aristotle. Ancient Greece. That was a while ago. 2000 B.C.? Or 4000 B.C.? Maybe less. Maybe like 200 B.C. It doesn't matter. Virtue theory: People ought to be virtuous. Aristotle's virtue theory states that people ought to be virtuous.

It's disconcerting how there is a stained circle on the wall instead of a clock and there isn't one photon of natural light in the room. I can imagine what kind of plant would grow here. You know, everyone's done that grade-school experiment where you put a pot of radish seeds in an airless closet and one on a sunny windowsill. The ones in the closet are the palest green if they sprout at all, and they grow with their little seedling bellies to the ground because they have no sun to seek. The professor, sitting motionless at the front of the room, reminds me of one of those plants. Something in the angle of his wrist as he bobs a piece of chalk between his fingers, waiting to mark down the next increment of time remaining to us on the blackboard. Meanwhile, the sun could have gone out and we'd never know. Conclusion: Radishes and philosophers need light to survive. But I can't for the life of me remember what Aristotle or any of the others thought stupid people should do about their stupid problems. But I have to write something; I can't just turn in a blank paper. That would be existential, and this test concerns the ethical. And yet the words don't come. Then, as the virgin exam passes from my hands, I remember that Aristotle believed that *arête*, translated as virtue or excellence, is the highest good, and that virtue consists in fundamental traits of character such as courage, temperance, and generosity displayed to a golden mean between two extremes of vice. To find *arête*, people should seek those unique forms of excellence that are innate to their nature rather than trying to conform to some universal mold.

Immanuel Kant, 1724–1804, son of a German harness maker, formulated an ethical theory called the categorical imperative in which one creates a maxim for one's every thoughtful action taking the form of: Whenever I am in situation x, I will do y. A given act is morally right if and only if we can imagine a world in which our maxim is followed as universal law and rationally will such a world to come about. Furthermore, our actions should always undertake to use our fellow men as ends in themselves and never as mere means.

John Stuart Mill was the son of James Mill, a utilitarian philosopher. In utilitarianism, one is obligated to create the greatest happiness for the greatest number of people. The most common objection to utilitarianism is that it seems to justify acts of cruelty against a single person for the benefit of the majority; e.g., it would be morally right to kill a lone drifter and harvest his organs to save four productive citizens, or to torture a child for a thousand years if this action would provide absolute peace on earth for the same duration. John Stuart Mill died in France in 1873.

That would have been worth a B- at least, but time rules us with an iron hand and sadistic humor. I am not amused, but a malicious delight charges the atmosphere; even the cartoon cheetah on a nearby vending machine seems to be sharing in the joke. It smiles so sharp and white, and the machine glows with unnatural orange light, humming its amusement in a low steady frequency. I give it a kick and it dispenses a packet of cheese snacks in apology. I eat them, but I do not feel better.

Creeps

By the time I was a teenager, my father had stopped going to church, or insisting that I go. Gradually, the crucifixes and icons in his study had been replaced with Tibetan prayer flags and statues of Hindu deities. I was suddenly allowed to watch whatever I wanted on TV, buy CDs with adult advisory stickers, and for my birthday, I received my very own computer with wi-fi set up. As thrilling as this was, it was at the same time unsettling, like my parents' grand experiment at a Christian life had failed and now it was fine for me to become the spawn of modernity.

The Internet at the dawn of the millennium was a wilderness of unpoliced chat rooms, political extremism, pornography, and awful animated GIFs, still mostly the domain of tech-savvy entrepreneurs, autistic teenagers, and pedophiles. Happy day for the last: There were enough virtual pet games, personality quizzes, and teen-themed sex advice forums to attract actual young girls into this untamed kingdom. I began to frequent the chatrooms on MSN—at the time, any user could create an unmoderated chat on any topic, thus each day saw the emergence of a hundred virtual petri dishes for the angry, the horny, and the otherwise dispossessed. I spent many formative nights bathed in the sickly glow of computer screens at 3 a.m., talking to middle-aged men who exposed me to whole new horizons of vocabulary and filth. Still with shades of Dr. Lecter in me, I'd tease them away from a superficial exchange of words passing for bodily fluids and into a kind of psychoanalysis of their pasts, their desires, their lives as they lived them now. If they became too vulgar or tiresome, I'd tell them I was with the FBI and an agent would be contacting them soon to "continue this illuminating conversation in person." I don't know if I caused any of them to live in fear, but the irony amused me: A seductive child posing online as an FBI agent to freak out pedophiles.

There was one in particular, VENETUYO, that I met in a philosophy chatroom.

LittlePegasus: Hi I'm 13/f/MA and I was wondering, what is nihilism?
BenthamsVote: Oh please mods, kill the zygote
Aristophanes666: This chatroom is 16+
VENETUYO: Let her stay. How else can the young ones learn?

Private Message from VENETUYO: Nihilism is a subject that exists so people can argue endlessly about what it means. That is its purpose. Its definition is an absence of belief in any system of values. The first nihilists were young Russian men who became disillusioned with technology and political progress. I hope that helps you . . . are you writing a paper of some kind?

LittlePegasus: No, I'm not writing a paper, I'm just curious. And thanks . . . you're a lot friendlier than most of the people here. Just because I'm young doesn't mean I'm an idiot, you know?

VENETUYO: In truth I prefer the company of young people. The mind tends to close with the passing of years . . .

LittlePegasus: How old are you?

VENETUYO: Old . . . so old that you'll have to remind me, what is it like to be thirteen?

LittlePegasus: It blows. But seriously, how old are you?

VENETUYO: 33

LittlePegasus: I'm never going to be that old. I don't know how, but I can just feel that it isn't going to happen. I can imagine maybe five years into the future, and then it just stops. There's going to be some kind of apocalypse and the world will end. When I try to imagine farther I just see this blue field—not like sky, but electric blue like that channel between the TV and the tape recorder.

VENETUYO: Maybe you're going to die young . . .

LittlePegasus: No, I know the whole world will stop existing when I do. I created it somehow and it will end with me.

VENETUYO: That's called solipsism . . . I've always thought it was a lovely philosophy. But I'll bet it's not nearly as lovely as you. What do you look like?

This confirmed one of my amateur sociological observations, that the chatroom-dwelling male would take no longer than ten superfluous exchanges to turn the conversation to sex. White pride, gay pride, virtual beach parties, philosophy—these were only diversions.

For weeks, my virtual H. Humbert and I chatted almost every night, and in him I found something I had simply not accounted for: an intellectual superior. Someone who could play as well as be played. I had grown curious about the books in my father's study and I needed someone to decode them. Nietzsche, Heidegger, Alastair Crowley—I could read the words, but their messages were as elusive as alchemical incantations, and I could not turn their base metals into gold. VENETUYO explained their philosophies in words a naïve child could understand, but that were long and rare enough to make her feel special. He told me about his joyless marriage to a Japanese ice sculpture who believed that sex was fundamentally immoral. They had married in Tokyo ten years ago, when she was seventeen and he was teaching English and searching for enlightenment. He showed me his charcoal drawings of beautiful young girls being molested by demonic angels in their sleep. He never told me his name, and I just called him Ven. He was the only one who ever knew mine or anything true about me.

I told him about my crush on Hannibal Lecter and how, when I met the man in the park who was the first to ever touch me, it was like I was seeing the world through his eyes. I masturbated for him for real, and not just saying I did while eating Starburst and playing Minesweeper with the hand that wasn't typing. Whenever someone asks me who my first lover was, it's him I think of. He said that when I was older he would leave his wife and take me to all the places I had never seen: Paris and Vienna and Japan, which he said was like a living poem.

Then one day he didn't show up in the chatroom when we were supposed to meet. He wasn't there the next day or the next. After a time, the chatroom itself disappeared and the links to his pictures went dead. I lurked in my room, ate nothing but drugstore candy, and stared at the pages of my school books without reading a word. I had dreams in which the shadow creatures from his drawings climbed in through my window and pinned me to my bed, then dissolved into black smoke and entered my body through every opening they could find.

I began to sneak into the park again, and developed an obsession with the children on the playground, the happy toddlers playing, falling, crying, being comforted, discovering the world. I wanted to go back there, but time sealed me out. As I sat on the swing set trailing my long gazelle limbs in the dirt, I felt eclipsed by a shadow much greater than myself. Sometimes I imagined luring one of them into the woods and drowning them in the river. Not from malice, I told myself, but to stop them from changing. I was enamored with the idea of symbolism, the notion that certain objects or actions could have a significance beyond their literal meaning.

Yet despite my predilection for the dark and violent, maturity dragged me by relentless degrees. I read at the college level and wrote essays on Dante and Emerson, but I'd often steal away to the attic and leaf through my old picture books for hours at a time. I still kept a herd of My Little Ponies in my room—I'd made two bookshelves into an apartment complex with plastic doll furniture, potted cactus community gardens, and a mixing bowl filled with water that served as a public swimming pool. When my parents suggested I was getting too old for such toys, I refused to talk or eat for several days until the matter was dropped. Selective mutism held an almost fetishistic appeal for me, but it freaked out my parents so much that I abandoned any attempts within days. I had daydreams as guilty and vivid as sexual fantasies about turning into an object, a chair or a plant or a vase on the mantel, observing without the expectation that I move or be changed or relate in any way to the social dramas playing out around me.

Evie and Alexis had been my friends for several years, but sometimes I wondered if this was only because my mother was a leader in our 4-H club. She drove us to horse shows and paid for Evie and Alexis to have riding lessons when their parents couldn't afford them. Later, after I got Apollo, she arranged to borrow two horses from a neighbor with a scruffy herd and paid for their upkeep so that Evie and Alexis could ride with me. In short, she was bribing them with a king's ransom, and I sometimes got the impression that we'd be BFFs no more if they ever stopped getting something out of it.

One night I had a sleepover with both of them and their boyfriend Drake at Alexis's house. I could never figure out to whom Drake belonged, because it seemed to vary from week to week. He was never with me, but that was OK because I found him repulsive. He had cataract blue eyes, facial scruff, and a peculiarly salty body odor that summed to remind me of the fish people in H. P. Lovecraft's story, *The Shadow Over Innsmouth.*

Alexis's parents were considerably more liberal than mine, which was one reason I preferred her house to my own, despite the fact that there were fourteen cats, two Akitas, and a lot of unwashed laundry packed into the cramped apartment. Her parents smoked and drank beer and allowed us to do the same as long as we stayed inside. They bawled at her to clean the litter boxes and she bawled right back that she'd done it last week. She never understood why I liked to spend so much time there. "Your house is so beautiful," she said once. "It's like a mausoleum." By which she meant museum, I think, but both terms seemed applicable.

On this particular evening, Alexis's parents retired to bed after inquiring whether Drake had brought condoms. He had. Alexis and Drake started making out on the couch, agitating several cats who were sleeping in a semi-liquid pile on the cushions. Evie got another Sublime Blue Ice from the fridge and I put on the movie, which was about Jeffrey Dahmer, and which we'd rented at my insistence. Evie was paying more attention to Drake and Alexis, watching them sullenly from the corner of her eye as she sipped her drink, but I experienced a repetition of my *Silence of the Lambs* epiphany as I watched young Jeffrey evolve from awkward misfit into sadist killer. *I could do these things*, I thought. *I could play in blood and shadows.* The only thing stopping me was that sticky clear membrane that holds people in their places, like the one that keeps organs from spilling into the abdominal cavity. *You remember it from that rabbit, don't you? The one you cut open with your knife when you weren't old enough to know any better . . .*

When the movie was over, I went upstairs to Alexis's room and sat on her unmade bed. On her desk, half a dozen bettas swam in jars of cloudy water. I had ten of them at home myself. I'd started the trend, but now Alexis and I walked together to Dave's Pet City every Tuesday, when the owner got new fish from the breeder, and fought bitterly over the prettiest specimens. A few weeks ago, she had seen first what I had not: a stunning purple, white, and blue fish with an iridescent lavender sheen. She called him Indigo and kept him in his own three-gallon aquarium lined with sea glass and fake coral. I'd tried all manner of bribery, begging, and blackmail, but nothing could convince her to part with him. Now, as I watched him puffing and preening at the fish in the jar next to him, I was filled with a toxic, childish, murderous anger. If I couldn't have the fish, no one could.

There was a bottle of gardenia Bath and Body Works perfume lying on the floor, and its pinkness took on a malevolent hue as I unscrewed the cap and poured about half the contents into Indigo's tank. The fish reacted as though it had been electrocuted, darting from one end of the tank to the other, bumping up against the glass with a sharp little sound. The perfume spread throughout the water in a floral atom bomb cloud, and the fish ricocheted from corner to corner in search of safer waters. After a minute it hung listlessly, fins trailing down in ragged strings. Gradually it began to list to one side until finally it floated on the surface of the water, its lovely fins fanned out like flower petals, now translucent and drained of color. The gills were motionless, dilated and bloodshot, and it soon became clear that it was dead.

As this sequence of cause and effect concluded, I thought of Japanese plays and chemistry experiments. *As art, this is over; as science, it has hardly begun,* some invisible narrator declared haughtily within me. I felt like something inside me was physically burning, and I could taste the bitter carbon in my mouth. Heat and death, they are linked somehow. *I'm a pervert, I'm an exhibitionist, I'm a masturbator. And a killer, like you.* The perfume bottle dropped to the floor as objects will do if nothing restrains them, and I became aware of my own reflection in the mirror behind Alexis's desk. Dizzied by a sudden vertigo, it seemed like there were physically two of me in the room and my perspective was trapped between them, a bodiless observer torn between possible selves. One of these creatures was filled with a terrible sadness and the other blazed with savage joy, and I could not have said which one was real.

CHAPTER SEVEN

"**I** guess psychiatrists are more like real doctors these days," says my mother for the third time over the car radio. "They've realized that depression is biological now, not like in Freud's day, where everything was your mother's fault."

I hate having the radio on in cars because something creepily relevant always comes on, like now:

All night, hearing voices telling me to get some sleep,
'cause tomorrow might be good for something.
Hold on, feeling like I'm headed for a breakdown . . .

I lunge forward and jab the radio into silence. Several days ago (and not so coincidentally coinciding with the date when midterm grades were mailed to expectant parents), my mother announced that she thought it would be a good idea for me to see someone, with "someone" being a euphemism for psychiatrist. So now we are driving to see some shrink in Connecticut who deals in Troubled Adolescents.

"Freud was a doctor," I say. "He was a neurologist."

"Oh, well. No one thinks his theories have any value today, do they? Wasn't he a cocaine addict?"

"Yes, and he killed puppies too."

My mother pulls into a parking space at the hospital. I get out of the car and she starts to follow me into the building.

"You can wait here," I say. "I'll find my own way in."

She opens her mouth to argue, then closes it and stands in the parking lot, in the misting rain without an umbrella, making no effort to return to the dry car until I am out of sight. Once inside, I find myself in a waiting area with a table full of magazines for the target demographic: *Autism Monthly, Bipolar Review.* The carpet is that institutional blue-gray color that sucks the joy out of you to look at it. Why do they never decorate these places in sunny peach or invigorating forest green?

I hear someone clear their throat and look up to see a man in a black suit standing in front of me. He says my name, and I nod.

"I'm Dr. Caspian. Will you come with me?"

It seems to me that his suit is a little too black for any profession other than organized crime or mortuary science. He speaks with academic precision, but he has spent at least some time in New York or New Jersey, and I could easily imagine him saying in a grave, elegant voice, "I'm afraid we have an irrevocable difference of opinion regarding the distribution of finances, Vinny."

I follow him into one of the offices lining the hall. The room is full of fussy decorations: vases of plastic flowers, inspirational posters, a framed photo of a dog. That seems pretty stupid to me—if some mental patient got really mad at his psychiatrist but wasn't quite homicidal, of course he would go for the dog.

"I'm afraid this isn't my office," says Dr. Caspian, as though apologizing for the décor. He takes a seat behind the desk and motions me to a chair. "I work on the inpatient unit, so I have to borrow a space to see private patients. Your parents made this appointment for you, didn't they?"

"Yes."

"How old are you?"

"Sev—eighteen."

"You're in college?"

"Yeah."

"Major?"

"Dunno. Some kind of sciency thing, I guess." I know it's dumb, but I don't want to admit to being pre-med because I'm half afraid he's going to start quizzing me on cellular respiration, and I can't handle that right now.

Dr. Caspian glances bemusedly at my black-and-white Converse, and when no explanation is forthcoming, he inquires, "And, ah, what is that written on your shoes?"

"*Tyranny is in greatest danger when it relents, Avoid Russia In Winter,* and *Soylent Green Is People.* Good things to keep in mind, you know.

And there are also a few physics equations, in case I sort of happen to forget them during a test."

"Isn't that cheating?"

"I suppose."

"Hm," says Dr. Caspian, who does not appear to be the most sparkling conversationalist. "Why don't you tell me in your own words why you're here."

"Like, existentially? I haven't really figured that out."

"I mean in this office. What's going on in your life that brings you to see a psychiatrist?"

I consider for a moment. Vague memories of ice-water immersions and electroshock apparatuses from my psychology lecture compel me to take no chances.

"I've been having some trouble at school," I say finally.

"What sort of trouble?"

"I guess I find it difficult to concentrate on the work."

"Particularly in physics class?" says the doctor, glancing at my shoes again.

"Yeah. And I, ah, didn't do as well as expected on my midterms."

"I see. Do you find the material too difficult?

"Not really. It's just . . ." I hesitate, trying to find the words. The clock ticks emptily for a minute. It's a drug clock, but I don't recognize the drug. The doctor appears to be surreptitiously trying to read the abstract of a journal article lying open on the desk. When he has apparently perused the first page, he glances up with a twitch of an inquiring eyebrow. And it seems my options are: Tell him, or deal with it alone.

"Well, a few days ago there was this . . . voice, or something, from . . . I don't know, somewhere."

I sense the doctor's interest in this conversation rising. If he were a horse, his ears would have perked up. I guess if you become a psychiatrist in the first place, truly disturbed people probably interest you more than merely stressed or unhappy ones.

"What did the voice say?" says the doctor.

"That I was bad at math, which is true. And squirrels, they have tragic lives."

"And did it come from inside your head, like a thought you couldn't control, or from outside, like someone talking in a room?"

"Um, both, I guess. Or neither. It's like the language already was embedded within some object in my presence, and my attention somehow released it. But I don't know how or why."

"Did the voice at any point tell you to hurt yourself or someone else?" The mercury level of the doctor's attention is steadily rising.

"No, nothing like that. I just . . . this is a kind of awkward conversation, you know? Voices in my head. It's not a good sign, is it?"

Dr. Caspian doesn't reply, but spends the next ten minutes inquiring about my medical condition, drug use, psychosocial development, and family history, probably running down some industry checklist for potential crazy people. Finally he reaches into his suit pocket and takes out a prescription pad and a pen that bears same drug logo as the clock.

"I'm going to prescribe a medication that is effective in reducing the auditory hallucinations and confused thinking that you've been experiencing," he says. "It might not help right away, and you'll need to call me immediately if you start to feel violent or suicidal. Start with one pill a day. Many patients find it makes them tired, so take it at night."

"Medication? So what's wrong with me?"

"I wouldn't put a label on it at this point, but I think this drug will help with the problems you've described." Dr. Caspian scribbles with practiced flair and hands the prescription across the desk. He says he doesn't know what's wrong with me, but he is willing to provide the cure. This makes me nervous.

"So that's it?" I say, "I just take these? Are they the red pills or the blue pills?" I meant it as a joke, but I guess he hasn't seen *The Matrix*.

"They're white at that dosage, actually. Can you come back a week from today, same time?"

"Yeah." I put the prescription in my pocket and stand up. Dr. Caspian pauses to wipe the fatigue from his face, then follows me to the door. As I step into the hall, it seems to occur to him that some further reassurance is in order.

"You probably feel frightened by what's happening to you," he says, "but try not to worry. Many of my patients are young people like yourself, and many have already reached a much more critical state. The important thing is that you're getting help."

His voice has a cool medicinal reassurance. In my mind, however, I can't help but hear him say, "It's all right, Vinny, everyone makes mistakes, and I'm sure we can reach some kind of understanding," in the same soothing tone. But you know that in the end, Vinny actually winds up somewhere unpleasant, like the bottom of a cement mixer.

I go out to the waiting room and find my mother already there. She drops *Moods* magazine onto the table and says, "So what did the doctor say?"

"I've got a prescription. Can we stop at the pharmacy?" I head for the door.

"Sure. Of course. A prescription. Well, there's no shame in that, you know. Your aunt Gabrielle has been taking Prozac for years. There's no shame in it at all."

"It's not Prozac. I don't know what it is." I allow her to take the prescription from my limp hand when we reach the pharmacy.

"I think I read in some magazine that 20 percent of the population of the United States is taking Prozac," she says when she returns with an orange bottle full of white pills.

"It's not Prozac."

Giving up homework as a lost cause when I get home, I watch mindless sitcoms until my brain begins to ooze out my ears into a gelatinous puddle on the floor. When I turn off the television around 2 a.m., the house vibrates with silence. Already, I have trouble remembering the resonance of the words in my mind, the sensory flashes combining to form an illusion of meaning. But something's wrong. I feel like a cat in the moments before an electrical storm. My mind is a stranger to itself, and its sudden anonymity is malicious, like a photograph that's been scribbled on and the eyes crossed out. *I* . . . the pronoun rings hollow in my head, the way every other word does when repeated to nonsensicality. *I* is supposed to withstand this, but it has become infected and arbitrary. *I* suppose meaningless *I* should take my shiny new pills, but I don't have a glass of water and am too tired to traverse the long hall to the bathroom. I can't swallow pills dry or I choke. Nor do I entirely trust Dr. Caspian with his calm analgesic voice and bizarre undertones of organized crime. Foggy and indecisive, I leave the bottle on the bedside table for morning.

But before morning came the demon.

Shadow & Foreshadow

Around the time my Internet demon lover disappeared, my parents offered my babysitting services to our neighbors across the street who had boys aged six, four, and two point five. Contrary to my expectation, I became wildly popular with the boys, who greeted me by shrieking and crashing against my legs as soon as I entered the house. This was probably because I assumed no authority whatsoever, took a liberal reading of the "one dessert per child" policy, and let them watch TV until ten minutes before their parents were scheduled to get home. Sometimes I felt like more of a child than they were as we built villages out of graham crackers and then smashed them, or raided the garage in search of lost Egyptian treasure.

One day the oldest boy, already the brooding type that would probably wear black nail polish and fishnets in high school, said he wanted to play a game where he was dead and we were at his funeral.

"How'd you die?" I asked.

"I was murdered," he said. "Someone killed me." He went on with the preparations for his mock funeral: emptying the toy bin to use as a coffin, sending his brothers to the garden to snip roses to adorn his casket. He dressed in ironed slacks and white button-down shirt, probably church-and-school-picture-day attire. "I'm dead now," he said to his brothers, who eagerly awaited his next instruction. "You have to mourn me."

They produced a dutiful wailing—the youngest was particularly dramatic, rolling about and beating the floor with his fists, all but ready to throw himself into the funeral pyre. I just stood watching the eldest child in his toybox coffin, face pale and composed, hands clasped vampirically over his chest. And I thought, *You did this. You poisoned him with bleach or drowned him in the bathtub. You imagined doing these things to other children as you watched them revolve on merry-go-rounds, whirling streaks of red shirt, blue shirt, arteries and veins, lives smeared to abstract blobs of color and motion, and you could do it to these boys right now. What do you feel? Nothing. Everything. Whatever you want. That's your gift. Why don't you use it?*

A few minutes later, the deceased got sick of being dead and went with his brothers to see whether the ice pops made from crushed blackberries that we'd picked in the yard had frozen yet. Then they gathered around the television and watched forbidden hours of *Are You Afraid of the Dark?* and *Clarissa Explains It All* on Nickelodeon with unblinking eyes and cyanotic purple lips. The girl who was supposed to be keeping them safe locked herself in the bathroom and confronted a demon that happened to look exactly like herself. She called out for the children to go to bed, and for once, they listened. She waited for headlights in the driveway, collected her twenty dollars, and never went back.

It was then that she . . . that I began to consider the morality of my continued existence. Clearly there was something fundamentally broken in me—in whatever way the brains or souls of Charles Manson and Jeffrey Dahmer were missing some key element, I seemed to have been set down similarly unfinished, a half-formed clay fetish that was animated with the breath of life and the power of speech but was not fully human. There were moments when I felt empathy and sorrow and perhaps even love, but they flitted in and out of their own accord—I could not call them up at appropriate times, and in most situations I found inside me only an unsettling blankness, or sometimes the opposite of what I ought to feel. Wires had crossed somewhere, that much was clear.

And furthermore, I didn't really want to be here, not in this form. The world was interesting and sometimes beautiful, but mostly insofar as I didn't have to interact with it, insomuch as I could be alone and observe. I could stare for hours at the algebraic movements of ants or light shining through church windows, but increasingly I was called upon to be a social, functioning being in the world, to find the right words and express them appropriately, to make friends and keep them, and I wasn't sure I could do it. As one boy I'd met in the park had said after I bragged in adolescent bravado that I'd tasted rabbit blood— *"killed it myself, actually, with my own pocket knife, this one here"*—I was a creep, and creeps should die.

So one day, I went into my father's study when he wasn't home and removed the gun he kept in the drawer of his computer desk. Black pistol, lacking in elegance or mercy, a Rottweiler among guns. I thought about writing a note, but nothing came to mind. If it's come to this, what is there to say?

I pressed the gun behind my ear—I'd read online that it was important to take out the deeper structures. At the temple you risk giving yourself a bullet lobotomy, and in the mouth just seemed gross—and was startled as I heard my mother's voice calling up the stairs, reminding me to get dressed for my riding lesson. This was the only activity I really enjoyed, so I put away the gun, changed into my riding clothes, and stuck a carrot in my pocket for my horse. Tomorrow, I told myself. Wait until no one is home and they'll be sure not to find you until you're good and dead.

We'd just begun to jump in my lessons, and my instructor startled me by telling me what a considerate rider I was, how I yielded to the horse's mouth with my hands. I'm sure it was the first time I'd ever been called considerate in my life. Later, as I was untacking my horse in his stall, I gasped as he shoved his head against my chest and knocked me against the wall. For a moment I was sure that teeth would snap, hooves would fly, and that would be the end of me. But the horse merely rubbed his forehead against my shirt, then began to snuffle at my shaking hands. He had only been scratching an itch, and now he was searching for treats.

It came to me then that as far as this horse was concerned, I was a blank slate. Just one of a dozen teenage girls who rode him in circles each week. I hadn't yanked on his mouth and now I was possibly going to give him a carrot, so life was good. He didn't see me as a dangerous carnivore, he didn't smell the ferment of evil in my blood or psychically sense my black thoughts. His entire concept of me was predicated on how I had treated him so far, a contract extending into the indefinite future.

I finished untacking the horse, fed him a carrot, curried his sweaty saddle spot, and shut him safely in his stall for the night. I went home and did not shoot myself with one of my father's guns. It seemed like I could still feel the horse's eyes on me, calm and trusting. All of literature's meditations on redemption might not have convinced me that my soul was salvageable, but in the wordless gaze of an animal who knew not my sins, nor cared of them, I found some kind of peace.

My life, in fact, changed considerably for the better. Instead of stalking perverts in online chatrooms, I wrote poetry and short stories and posted them on young writer's forums. I entered horse shows, went to 4-H meetings, galloped in mock Kentucky Derbies and ate ice cream on horseback with Evie and Alexis. I stole from my father's liquor cabinet, shoplifted at the mall, listened to subversive music, and became for all intents and purposes a normal teenager. When I was fourteen, my parents bought me Apollo, the stubborn, patient Appaloosa whose watchful pink-rimmed eyes provided me with a new *tabula rasa*, another shot at being human. Apollo the golden sun horse, keeper of my perspective, observer of my small inner light.

In a linear world of logic and reason, lessons and morals, cause and effect, perhaps it would have been enough to master my darkness in this one singular breakdown and redemption in the eyes of a horse. But this is not that universe. Here, we have quantum foam seething in the cracks between the smallest known objects, strange brains of meat pudding and electricity that do not always choose the most elegant solution, and demons that eternally recur. Abandon all hope, ye who enter.

PART II

Self and Other

*Only in spiritual terror can the Truth
Come through the broken mind.*

—

W. B. Yeats

CHAPTER EIGHT

The sentience envelops me while I sleep. I dream of a giant warehouse filled with stacks and boxes and huge freezers full of frozen desserts, the kind they sell in ice cream trucks. I'm holding a mop and unsure of my purpose. Apollo was here a moment ago, running loose among the ominously humming machines, but I could not catch him, and now in the untamed physics of dreams I am suddenly alone.

One of the freezers is leaking an orange puddle and I watch it seep closer to my feet, frozen in that moment when you know you are dreaming but the dream doesn't want to give you up just yet. I feel a revulsion toward the puddle, as if it were some bodily emission we are never meant to see, like synovial fluid. It touches my foot and the dream shatters. I awaken with a gasp in a strange bed. No, it's not the bed that's strange—it's the same one I've slept in since I was a child. My parents have made me leave my attic room and move back home. They say that I'm distracted, that I'm unwell, and I should be with family until someone figures out what is wrong with me.

The strangeness is that I am not alone, here in my bed. I will never be alone again.

I feel it slithering out of the darkness for the first time, the presence that's been whispering its sinister enigmas. A living, breathing thing—cold stars and glittering mathematics with the inhale, hot copper and rotten fruit with the exhale. Foreign from anything I have ever known. Other.

Shhhh, it says, though I have made no sound. A rattling snake noise that brings no comfort.

What's happening?

Awakening.

Awakening from a deep sleep in the dark . . .

Who are you?

I am Lucifer, Legion, Lecter. Machiavelli, Moriarty, Mephistopheles. I am the serpent, the shadow, the swan. The voice is almost giddy. Not quite inside my head, but close. The blood-brain barrier is weak in the area postrema. I feel a moment of nausea in which I am sure that everything I have eaten recently, and then everything I have eaten in any previous incarnation since the beginning of time, is about to be forcefully ejected from my body. Then it passes.

We are, whispers the Other from inside my prefrontal cortex. *I am Eudaimon. We are together.* The venal contentment in its voice drips stickily down the back of my throat.

My body stages a violent rebellion against this ephemeral parasite. Every substance that can be released is released. The surge of epinephrine produces a panic so pure it is like white light in my veins, bursting behind my eyes. My muscles freeze and seize and I cease to breathe, and something hot trickles down my leg.

Don't fight it.

Surrender.

My heart rebels against my effort to slow its wild rhythm, my neurons shock each other blindly in their panic, but the Other checks them like runaway horses. I breathe again, or at least my lungs take in air at his command.

I lie for what seems like an eternity in a paralytic haze as the entity probes and interrogates my internal structures, getting to know the parts never exposed to light. Eventually, it strikes some deep gland and my eyes close into anesthetic sleep. I wake in the morning to a damp ammonia smell and a body that feels shaky and uncoordinated, as if it is not sure it should be taking orders from me. I rise and stand in front of my window, trying to get warm in the feeble light. The entity suggests that I change my bedclothes. I comply vaguely and willingly, glad of some direction.

Now eat something sweet
to replace lost will.

I do not feel hungry. I do not feel. I find my way down to the floor and lie with my head in the sun. The smell of the wood polish is strong and invigorating.

No. Get up. The communication is simultaneously instantaneous and ripples across time, not in sync with breath but rhythmic, subtle, like the slow pulsing of lymphatic fluid. Perhaps the deep resonance of the voice in my cells causes me to assign it the masculine pronoun. Masculine, but far from human.

I discover that I have gotten unsteadily to my feet again, and he propels me down the stairs, peremptorily contracting muscles where I forget to. The morning light has a dissipated quality, as though it were still unwilling to cast off the night. I begin to make eggs and a glass of milk, but this is overly ambitious because my hands make random contractions and I keep crushing the shell into the yolk. The milk does not find the glass very well and the glass does not find my mouth very well, but eventually some of the milk ends up in my stomach.

My parents drift downstairs. "What's this mess?" says my father, surveying the pools of egg yolk on the counter and splashes of milk on the floor.

"Flu," I mutter in a voice that does not seem my own.

"You've been sick so often lately," says my mother. "Should I call the doctor?"

I shake my head too vigorously and a ligament in my neck pops. "I'll just stay. Home from school."

They exchange concerned glances. "Are you sure you're all right?" says my mother. "You look . . ." She tilts her head and seems not to know how to finish the sentence. "Maybe I should call the doctor."

I shake my head, stagger to the couch, and in a spasmodic but successful gesture, grab the remote control and turn on the television. I give my parents a reasonable facsimile of a reassuring smile. They still look at me oddly, but eventually shrug it off and scatter to their respective errands. Soap opera on the television. Zinnia's baby is possessed. I feel like a bomb has gone off in my head. The colors on the screen are aggravatingly bright, the voices shrill and grating. As gaudy music swells, so does something in my mind. A desire. Frail, but mine: *Change the channel.* My arm is like a dead white slab of fish. I wait for him to help, but he demurs.

I pick up the remote and flick the channel twice. Cartoon animals. Slowly, fragments of ego collect at the detonation site, gathering survivors, burying the dead. Emotion seems to be instructed to lie quietly on its back and not move for a while, but I have thought again—volition. I don't know quite what to do with them. It seems likely that I have suffered some kind of cerebral event; a seizure, or even a small stroke. Possibly I am bleeding into my brain.

A seizure of sorts
but you're not hemorrhaging.

Emotion twitches around on its stretcher. Lie still. Please, lie still.

My body feels flabby and cadaverous, a shark-bait of a body, but I wrench it to its feet and stumble to the window. I don't know what I was hoping to see—maybe wrecked cars and people fleeing or falling to their knees as these mind parasites invade humanity—but the actuality is that the world is getting on as it always does. Cars glide at a sedentary pace on the right side of the road, and across the street, a neighbor is doing something arrestingly normal to the gutters on his house.

Whatever this is, I'm facing it alone.

"Who are you?" My voice sounds hoarse and machinelike.

Who are you? Who am I?
Who's to say these questions
mean anything at all?

His consciousness shifts so rapidly, like a bi-colored leaf fluttering in the breeze. A mercurial sigh, from silvery liquid amalgam to fiery planet. And this is absurd, this is out of hand. My mind is so hopelessly agile—how do I know this isn't some game it has invented to torture me? I search blindly for a tolerable explanation, but find none.

You must leave now, I tell the emergent property. You're not wanted here. In my mind, my voice sounds strong and defiant.

You'll do first
and wanting will come.

Stop it, I tell myself. Stop freaking yourself out. Stop playing this stupid game. I am frightened to the point where I need to eat again. I believe I will have a peanut butter and jelly sandwich. A nice, non-apocalyptic sort of thing to eat. I open the refrigerator and survey the condiment shelf. Strawberry jam or apricot?

I can't remember if I like apricots. Are they the little oranges or the little peaches?

My mind feels as fuzzy as the blue-gray mold flourishing in the apricot jam jar. The strawberry looks fine but now I don't want jam of any kind. I put them back and eat bread with peanut butter.

Then, a blinding flash of something I can do next, harmful action against the Other. "These pills will stop the voices," the slightly sinister psychiatrist said. But he wasn't as sinister as this. The bottle is still on my bedside table. Can I do that, traverse the long flight of stairs under my own free will? His cold command is translated simultaneously in every chemical language the body knows: *Don't take the pills.*

Is it that I cannot move, or that I refuse? He pulls in one direction, I pull in the other, and between the two my poor body is torn between loyalty and fear. Don't do this . . . we need one another. Just arise and walk. Dead men have done more. Yes . . .

Like a still heart galvanized for one more try, my body rises to its feet. I puppeteer it up the stairs, hardly feeling the pain as I miss a step and twist my ankle.

With shaking hands, I open the bottle of pills and spill some into my hand. Without pausing to consider the cost-benefit ratio any further I swallow, then choke as the foreign thing's patience snaps like chilled metal.

A flash of staring eye sockets and purple flowers in my mind. A smell like white soap and a little sweaty underneath. The body shakes. What an unfortunate *ménage à trios* we are, and the vessel is the weakest by far, possessing no free will. How it trembles in this prisoner's dilemma. How fast will the drug work? The doctor didn't say. I draw in great gasps of air, but it's not oxygen I need for survival. I don't know what resource I need to draw on now.

You owe me.

The subzero bite in my mind is more terrifying than any kind of hot anger. It's the kind of cold that can take off a finger or a whole hand before you realize anything is missing. And it's still not as frightening as the conviction with which this alien presence uses the first person from inside me.

My ears are filled with the high ringing that remains when something drops from a height and is shattered. Bits of sandwich cling like fungus to the roof of my mouth, they swell and block the passage of air with malicious intent.

You owe me for this . . .

There is a particular horror that occurs when you witness something like a car accident and see its inevitability several moments before the crash and flying glass, powerless to change anything. At these times there is no question that our minds are slaves in a world of objects. With a leaden doom, I see my hand reach into my pocket for my Scout knife and flick it open. I knew that gelatinous sack of water and protein would cave to this mutiny. The tip of the knife traces sensuously along the blue veins of my wrist, across the half-healed scars on the inner arm.

"Please, no . . ."

The knife slashes with sickening power, parting the flesh like butter and exposing things deeper inside than we can bear to see of ourselves. And again, and again, *ad infinitum*. What I have seen in the cracks is that despite my surgeon's hands, I have no desire to be a surgeon, or to see inside anything ever again.

Looking away, my dizzy eyes find an image of the archangel Michael comforting a child. A dusty remnant of my baptism, left hanging above my bed because guilt or some cagey desire to keep my options open prevented me from taking it down when my faith faded. Now I fall upon it, drag it down from the wall and hold it close to my heart. The blood beads on the laminated surface so the angel and the child remain pristine, but soaks greedily into the unfinished back, staining it. I press a corner of the icon to my mouth, and my last awareness is of biting down on it in wordless supplication as my jaw locks and my vision fails and the thing opens its mouth to swallow my consciousness like a godless wolf swallows the sun.

CHAPTER NINE

I first become aware of my breathing—it is deep and regular, under the competent care of my autonomic nervous system. When I try to take over it becomes erratic, desperate, thinking I need more oxygen when really I don't. My eyes open and see too much white. My head is too heavy to lift, but moving my eyes I can see a corner of the room at a time. Monitors in one corner, silent and unlit. My parents in two chairs by the wall, heads bowed and hands limply resting in their laps. My eyes drift closed again.

Someone comes and jabs me with a needle. I swear reflexively and my parents jump up and hover near the bed. "Whitney?" says my mother. Cautiously, as if she is afraid I will not know my own name.

I shift in the bed and a jolt of pain radiates across the back of my hand. I look down and see my arm covered in a pillowy bandage.

"You tried to kill yourself," says the needle-jabber, a nurse in a flowery scrub shirt, in a disapproving tone. How insular to assume it was suicide and not murder. My body feels heavy and adrift, my vision creating blurry haloes around everything. For a moment I wonder if I somehow exorcised the Other, bled him out like snake venom. But with a crushing awareness I feel his consciousness superimposed on mine again, a neutral crimson plane that reveals nothing.

What did you *do* to me. What . . .

His presence is serene and melodic again, like the reading of a haiku.
Nothing at all . . .
it seems even shy soma thinks you're better off dead,
though she could not say it to your face.

"What happened, Whitney?" asks my mother. "Why did you do this?"

"I didn't. It was . . ." But the truth is impossible, and I am too weary to come up with a plausible decoy. "A mistake," I say finally. "Just a mistake."

"We'd like you to stay in the hospital until we feel you're no longer a danger to yourself," says the nurse. "Someone will be here soon to bring you upstairs."

"Upstairs?"

"To our psychiatric facility."

"A psych ward? No, thanks."

"Ah, well," she says delicately, and I realize the insinuation that I have a choice was only politeness. The nurse slides a consent form into my hand. From his comfortable perch in my mind the Other says nothing, but the silence is suffused with a sinister interest as he waits to see what I will make of the situation. I click the pen a few times, indecisively. The nurse's eyes grow apprehensive, and I realize that it's a ballpoint pen and she was probably supposed to give me a felt-tipped pen, and she's worried I'm going to stab myself in the jugular and die or sue the hospital or both. If it weren't for my parents I might have given her a little scare, but they're watching with that rabbit-in-the-headlights look, so I just sign the paper and give her the pen.

Soon, two ER techs come and wheel me down a hall full of people resting doll-like in white beds, then into an elevator. I have heard that psych wards are always on the top floor to minimize the possibility of escape. My parents have gone up by another way and are waiting at the ward door, a steel contraption with a reinforced window that looks like it could survive a bomb. It buzzes and opens to admit me. Someone tells my parents they will have to leave now, but visiting hours are six to eight on weekdays and two to six on weekends. My parents look glazed. They tell me they love me. But I can't say it back. He is listening, and anything I value he will turn into collateral. So I just nod with a sickly smile and hope they see it in my eyes.

The psych ward looks like you'd expect from movies and books, except a little more airport lobby and not quite so Kafka. Droning TV overlooked by a plexiglass-fronted nurse's station, faded people unnaturally still on faded couches. But when I look closer they are not still at all. Limbs twitch, feet tap, fingers shred tissues into a fine confetti. The impression of stillness comes only from the faces, which have a curious blank, oily sheen. Only a black girl with a red scarf over her hair returns my gaze with interest. There is something like a challenge in her face, although I don't know why. We stare at each other from across the room like unfamiliar cats angling for dominance. After a minute she smiles mysteriously and presses a finger to her lips in a silent *shhhh* before turning back to the television.

The ER techs help me into a chair by the nurse's station and wheel the bed out of the ward. Two patients shuffle over with a zombielike gait. "Who're you?" says an old man in a peculiar snuffling voice. He is wearing a hospital gown like an overcoat, the strings knotted over his bare emaciated chest. His teeth are very bad. I do not really want to tell him my name, so I stare vaguely over his shoulder and feign deafness.

"Who're you?" he repeats, stepping closer. "I said who're you?" He breathes a sour chemical smell on me. The other patient, a fat woman with a tangle of unbrushed hair, reaches out and touches my sleeve, rolling the fabric between thumb and forefinger as if testing the quality. The man holds out a sticky plastic cup full of yellow chunks.

"HAVE SOME PINEAPPLE," he says in a terrible, thundering, godlike voice.

I shrink back in my chair. If I keep still maybe he will leave me alone, or maybe he will be angry if I don't take it . . .

What's the matter? Don't you like your new friends? I flinch as the Other erupts into consciousness like an unexpected surge of static from a dead radio station.

A nurse comes out from behind the glass. "Patricia, Anton, stop bothering her." She flicks her hands as if shooing away a couple of stray dogs. They retreat a few paces and watch as the nurse takes my blood pressure, breathing deeply and rhythmically through their mouths like someone sleeping with a head cold.

"This is intramuscular haloperidol," says the nurse, holding a syringe. "I'm going to inject it into your arm, OK?" A sting near my shoulder, and within minutes a foggy paralytic haze has crept over my mind, sealing out every thought regardless of origin. Someone propels me to a room and I stretch out on a hard white bed. To have a drug encamped in one's brain is not so wrong as having another *ego* there. It acts with no malice, no free will. I close my eyes and am not so sad to have lost my mind. If I can't have it, no one should.

CHAPTER TEN

My eyes strain upward in their sockets and my neck snaps back, the cervical vertebrae compressing painfully. At first I am sure this is punishment for my insubordination, but there is no trace, no neural whisper of the Other. The drugs . . . I was wrong that they have no malice. Though my eyes are captive witnesses of the discolored ceiling, I manage to find my way out to the hall. Brisk footsteps approach as I crash against a wall and land on my backside.

"What are you doing on the floor?" says a snappish middle-aged voice.

"I can't see properly . . . my eyes." One side of my face contracts into an involuntary leer.

"You're having a reaction to the medication . . . I'll get you some Cogentin. But get up off the floor, it's dirty."

With a trace of the blind compliance that got me here, I do as she asks. But my perspective is skewed by my straining eyeballs and I quickly topple down again.

"OK," says the nurse, "just stay there." Sensible shoes tap away down the hall, then return with the medication. My brain feels like it has turned to warm applesauce. Gradually, my muscles soften and my eyes relax into their normal orbit. As I crane my neck experimentally in all directions, the nurse reappears.

"The Doctor would like to see you." The way she says it makes it sound capitalized. I get stiffly to my feet and follow her to an office near the entrance to the unit. She knocks, and the door opens.

Dr. Caspian, wearing the same impeccable black suit as before. It seems out of place in the antiseptic dinginess of the ward. He motions me inside. The room is stark and windowless and has a slight air of *interrogation*—the desk and chair are bolted to the floor, and there are no misshapen clay dinosaurs or photographs of dogs.

"Whitney Robinson," he says, gazing down at some paperwork, presumably my File. I'm not sure if he remembers me or is just reading my name from the forms. "You were admitted yesterday. You cut your wrist and were found by your parents in a semi-catatonic state with a message written in your own blood on the wall."

"What?"

"You're not aware of this?"

"What did . . . what was written on the wall?"

"The ER report doesn't say. Why don't you tell me your version of what happened?"

My version of what happened, as if this were a crime. No, I don't trust those probing eyes. The way he has his fingers lightly steepled is too assured for comfort. He seems different here. I wouldn't go so far as to say he looks happy, but he seems more comfortable, like he *belongs*. I would not trust a person for whom this is their natural habitat.

When the silence remains unbroken, he says, "Would this have anything to do with the voice you mentioned when we first met?"

"No. Are you sure you don't know what was written? On the wall."

"I'm afraid not. This voice had been troubling you a great deal, hadn't it? It spoke of the apocalypse, it insulted you. You feared that you were going insane?" His prompts have the airy politeness of someone inducing recall of a chance meeting at some trendy café. *Remember me, in the blue raincoat, chai latte to your double espresso? I quoted Proust and you let me sample your biscotti?*

"Um, I don't really remember."

"You don't remember our conversation?"

"No, I do, it just. It doesn't have anything to do . . . with this."

"Really? And why did you cut your wrist with a razor blade?"

"It was a Swiss Army knife."

The doctor looks nonplussed.

"It's an important distinction," I elaborate. "A razor blade as an implement of self-destruction is a rather egregious cliché, don't you think?"

Dr. Caspian's expression is indecipherable. I can't tell if he's confused or disgusted or masking amusement. I feel like if I could just make him crack a smile, the situation would seem less dire.

"And what caused you to attempt self-destruction in the first place?" he says, dragging the conversation back to vulgar practicalities.

"I don't know. I was probably seeking attention. That's what teenagers do, isn't it? I probably have borderline personality disorder."

"What makes you say that?"

"I was joking. I don't actually think so, but . . . well, I don't know. I was bored, OK? Or no, I'm a whaddayacallit. A masochist. I'm aesthetically attracted to blood and pain. Is that a sufficient explanation? TMI, perhaps?"

The doctor just stares.

"So is there a button in here?" I ask, my voice tinged with hysteria.

"Pardon?"

"A button. If someone tries to kill you, have you got a button to push for help?"

"No, there is no button. Are you having thoughts of wanting to kill me?"

"No, *no*, definitely not. I was just making conversation, as two sane people will do when in a room together. But this is a bad setup, tactically speaking, with the mental patient between you and the door. You've cut off your escape route."

"Do you think about this sort of thing often?"

"No, but isn't it obvious?"

"The patients here aren't dangerous people. You're not dangerous, are you?"

I look at him in wonder. "*Everybody's* dangerous. That's a funny thing for a psychiatrist not to know. How long do I have to be here?"

"We'll see," he says with alarming vagueness. "I've ordered some medications that should control any auditory hallucinations you may be experiencing. Is there anything else you'd like to tell me?"

I shake my head, unable to form the barest bones of an explanation.

"Very well. I'll check back with you tomorrow." His body language tells me that my audience with The Doctor is over.

When I return to the TV room, my parents are waiting on a dingy plaid couch. Apparently it is between six and eight on a weekday or two to six on a weekend, I don't know which. They have spotted me, so I sit reluctantly across from them on a blue vinyl chair which is the exact color of that cartoon train, Thomas or Edward or something. I don't know why this fact captures my attention. I don't know much about my mind, really, it's always done what it's told with cool detachment, perhaps a hint of insolence but nothing like . . .

"Whitney," says my mother. "How—how are you? We brought you some things." She hands me a bag containing my school books, a bottle of shampoo, and enough clothes for about a week. A young nurse in a paisley scrub shirt swoops down on the transaction.

"I'll have to check this," she says, taking the bag. "You're on suicide watch, so you can't have this shampoo—it contains ethanol. Everything else is OK."

She relinquishes the bag, minus the shampoo, into my possession. My mother flinches at the word *suicide*, I notice peripherally.

"Why did you do this?" my father asks quite calmly.

The question again, the unanswerable one.

"I—I don't know, I . . ."

"If there's something we've done, or not done . . ." adds my mother.

"Stop it," I say sharply. "This has nothing to do with you."

"Then why—"

Because the demon that invaded my brain made me do it, but don't worry, it seems to be gone now.

"I just . . . nothing. There is no why. It doesn't matter. It won't happen again. Thank you for bringing my things; perhaps you should go now." I stand up and close my expression to an impenetrable blankness that allows no emotion to be reflected or absorbed. They go. They are leaving me. In a psych ward. The door is locking behind them, they are gone. I am afraid, but only because I feel nothing. The fear is of the void that has formed inside me, not of my circumstances. The circuit for shock and disbelief has been shut off in my brain. A unicorn could walk up to me and recite Latin declensions and this would evoke no surprise. I have merely come to accept, in the span of several hours, that I know nothing of the world or its governing principles. I am a good postmodern child, so this will not destroy me. But I do not like this place regardless—it smells of chemicals, and the air has been re-circulated through too many sick people's lungs. I walk over to the nurse's station and pound on the window until someone comes over.

"I want to leave. Right now. I want to sign myself out."

"I'm sorry, but it doesn't work that way. If you want to be discharged, you'll have to discuss it with Dr. Caspian tomorrow." The nurse hands me a cup of pills and some water. "Here's your medication."

"I'm not taking any more drugs. Just let me out of here."

"Well, we tend to let people out sooner if they take their medication."

Though my first instinct is to struggle and flail and shatter things until I am free, I force myself to remain calm, not give them further proof that I'm part of the natural scenery of this *milieu*. Besides, whatever they've given me has possibly had some kind of toxic effect on the . . . thing. The voice. Don't give it a persona. The disease of mind.

I swallow the pills.

"Good," the nurse says soothingly. "The patients are having their dinner now—why don't you join them?" I glance at the clock on the wall: quarter past five. She leads me to a cafeteria where a dozen people are eating without enthusiasm from plastic trays. The room smells of vegetables cooked to excess and the tabletops are streaked with bits of food and gravy. I take a tray and find a seat with a wide margin of space around it, across from the black girl who was staring at me before. The moment I sit down, she gets up and moves her tray to another table.

I glance at the person next to me, a woman with a purple discoloration running across her neck. From the condyloid process to the gonial angle of the jaw, then disappearing under her throat. I know my *CSI* as well as my anatomy: That's a high ligature mark.

I lower my eyes to my tray. I see now why no one is talking. There is a distinct lack of suitable conversation openers. So, tried to hang yourself, did you?

"FUCK YOU," someone says, suddenly and explosively. "FUCK YOU COMMUNIST PIGS!" A gray grizzled man stands up and hurls a cup of mashed potato across the room. Streaks of gravy slide down the wall like candle drippings and form a puddle on the floor. Most of the patients don't look up. Several staff members surround the man and take his tray, reasoning with him in conciliatory voices. "Is that an appropriate way to behave while eating, Stefan?"

"No, I'm sorry." The man eyes the tray. "Can I have my dessert?" Someone takes the lid off a cup of cheesecake and hands it to him. I wonder if the red sauce will remind him of communism too, if anything red sets him off, but he is docile as he shovels the cake into his mouth, holding his plastic fork in his fist like a child.

A shadow falls across my tray and I look up to see the black girl hovering over me. "I didn't mean to be rude," she says. "But you startled me before. You got a bad aura." She looks about my age, but she's wearing a hospital gown and the flimsy, shapeless fabric makes everyone look simultaneously childlike and old, so I'm not sure. "A real bad aura," the girl repeats, setting her tray down beside mine.

"What do you mean?"

"Auras," she says in a teacherly tone with a faint Southern Baptist twang, "are visible manifestations of your soul. They're like haloes around people, like they show around Jesus and the saints, but all over your body."

A stab of pain radiates down my bandaged arm as I try to squeeze out a packet of ketchup, hoping to improve the taste of what I optimistically assume to be turkey. The girl reaches over and opens the packet for me.

"Thanks."

"My name's Ani."

"So you can see these auras, for real?"

"Sure. They're strongest around your center and they fade once they leave your skin. Some people barely glow and some are lit up like fireflies. But you, you got the darkest aura I've ever seen."

"Really?" I feel oddly flattered. "The darkest ever?"

"Dark as the air after a fire," says Ani, stripping the red sauce from her cheesecake and licking it off her spoon. "Even sitting next to you, I get that smell of burning all over me."

"Oh."

"Well, I saw one darker at a bus station once. Some guy with a suit and a briefcase. He was so dark, it was like his whole self had turned to shadows."

I flash back to the pond as he stood over me, the sun so bright behind him that his silhouette was burned to black.

"What color is Dr. Caspian's aura?" I ask.

"Red," says Ani. "Bright and red."

"Is that good?"

"It's not good or bad, it's just what it is."

"But red how? Like dried blood? An ambulance light? The surface of an apple?"

"All those things," says Ani, "are red."

"But they're different *shades* of red."

"What's it matter so much to you what *shade* of red he is? You hot for him or something?"

"*No.* I just want to know if I should trust him."

"Nah, don't."

"Why? Is his aura sinister?"

"No, but I think he's in the mob. I wouldn't trust any of those people."

"Oh. So can you do other psychic things, like talk to dead people?"

"Sure. When I was a little girl, my pastor said I might be the most gifted medium of my time. One day, I might be so happy that it will rain flowers. And sometimes, angels come to me at night with messages from Beyond." Ani darts a glance around the room and lowers her voice. "But there are bad things, too—evil kinds of angels. They steal into you while you're asleep and if you're not careful, they'll carry your soul away before its time."

I stand abruptly and my Jell-O cup tips and cascades its glistening innards across the table. "I'm going back to my room," I murmur. "I'm not feeling well."

"You didn't take the drugs, did you?"

"Yeah."

"Child, you got a lot to learn."

I wade through the slipping, shimmering air to my room—really, do I want to so freely use the possessive?—and collapse onto the bed, brought half-conscious every few minutes by a nurse opening the door to make sure I haven't contrived some MacGyverish way to do myself in with the bed sheets, my philosophy book, and a bottle of alcohol-free psych ward mouthwash.

Ani comes in later and kneels in front of the window to pray. Apparently she has been assigned the other bed in my room. Or more correctly, I've taken the other bed in hers, since she was here first. I close my eyes, then open them in reaction to a terrible noise. Someone has turned out the lights, and a lump in the other bed is moaning. I sit up, swaying because my head seems to weigh more than usual. "Who's there? What's the matter?"

"The angels," says Ani's voice as a shapeless bulk stirs in the bed. "Can't you hear the angels crying?"

And then it becomes impossible not to think about it. Ani falls back and lies unnaturally still. Maybe she has gone to sleep, but I can't, maybe never again. I do not hear the angels crying, but whatever demon has whispered in my ear will not be silenced forever. There are deep gashes in my arm and a gaping place in my consciousness where something has ripped through, and everything is starting to throb through the analgesia. Nazis and communists and devils and angels and things too dark to be defined . . . everyone seems to have their war here, and soon enough I will have mine.

Chapter Eleven

The next day, I calmly tell Dr. Caspian the truth: that this is a terrible mistake, that being a silly adolescent I was merely experimenting with sharp metal and rebellion and it went too far. Really, there is no need for me to be here. I probably just need Confuse-a-Cat to cure my ennui. But apparently he isn't a Monty Python fan, and in fact, he seems as humorless as this entire situation is starting to become. Worse still I'm a biased narrator here, with a vested interest in sounding rational and far more clever than reductionistic doctors with Mafia-dark eyes and dark suits worth more than my soul. Maybe I'm not quite as smooth and logical as I'm trying to sound, maybe my syntax isn't as crisp as all that and my voice is lost among my words. Maybe I sound like every other frightened mental patient, and this is why he is not convinced.

"The first time we met," says Dr. Caspian, "you had been hearing a disembodied voice and you feared you were going insane. You say this had nothing to do with your suicide attempt, but I have trouble believing that."

"I didn't try to kill myself."

"Then what happened?"

"I don't know."

"That is not an acceptable answer."

"I didn't realize I was being graded."

"What I mean," says The Doctor in his most doctorial voice, yet still laced with a Tony Soprano twang, "Is that is not an answer that will incline me to release you. I can't force you to talk to me—it's your choice—but things will be easier for both of us if you cooperate."

Yeah, and I'll bet Vinny is totally at the bottom of a lake right now.

"Interesting that you say I have a choice," I reply. "Psychiatry assumes, does it not, that mental events correspond to measurable changes in the brain?"

"Yes . . ."

"But if it's all chemical, it's all predetermined, and the illusion of choice is meaningless. Idealism and materialism. If we follow each to their logical endpoints, they both become absurd. Either we can magically create a world to conform to our expectations through volition alone, or we are causally chained to a path dictated by a predestined sequence of chemical reactions, powerless to change anything. They mutually exclude one another, but we need aspects of each to maintain our fragile egos. I suppose the only way around this is to reject even logic. You know, I thought I was going to hate philosophy, but it's starting to grow on me. Is that a bad sign?"

"No, but it crosses my mind that you're using your natural intelligence to escape a more immediate problem."

"Really? Because it crosses my mind that you're getting caught up in petty *qualia* to mask your striking deficit in metaphysical reasoning."

Dr. Caspian looks as though he is not particularly enjoying this phenomenological discouse. "Right now, I'm more concerned with making sure you're not going to slit your wrists again if I release you from the ward."

"Oh, a pragmatist. How dreary. Don't you ever have existential dialogues with your patients? It's much more interesting than keeping them alive."

"I'm sure you can play this game forever, Whitney, but it won't get you anywhere you want to go."

I would continue to plead the Fifth, but the drugs are making me unusually loquacious, lining up punch-drunk words on my tongue that can barely be contained. "Fine, then, if you want the truth so badly, you can have it. The truth is that you look bored when you talk to people. Like you'd rather be somewhere else. A number of your patients think you're trying to kill them, and your demeanor does not make that seem entirely unreasonable. The truth about me is that I'm smarter than you, but I'll die sooner. Except I'm not smarter at all because if I were, I wouldn't need to say it. But I will die sooner—it's basic thermodynamics. Things that burn hot don't last as long."

Dr. Caspian looks at me with the steady silence that makes you regret recent speech. No, I won't be leaving soon.

"Now you tell me something true," I continue, as damned for a penny as a pound or something like that. "*Quid pro quo*, Clarice. What do *you* think is wrong with me? Am I terminally incandescent?"

"I don't know what's wrong with you," he says quietly. "You don't seem to want to tell me."

"OK," I say as my inhibitory neurochemicals fizz garrulously away and break down my lawyerly instincts. "What's troubling me is this: A few nights ago, I felt a foreign entity overtake me. I'd introduce you, but he's not being very social right now. In any case, this demon or alien crossed some membrane that nothing, nothing but a few sugars and mineral ions is supposed to penetrate and it *used* my body to cut my own wrist. So does that on a technicality mean I did or did not try to kill myself? If it had worked, would it have been suicide or murder?"

The silence between us is grim now, almost sad. Maybe he thought I'd just gotten over my head in a mire of teen angst and pop quizzes and a few bad acid trips that I didn't want to cop to. But the wounds of the otherworldly, you don't heal them with Prozac and psychotherapy. Maybe you don't heal them at all.

"So what's the verdict?" I say with a horrible lightness to my voice.

"This has nothing to do with guilt or innocence." The latent ambiance behind this examination was until now something like annoyance or impatience, as if he had better things to do than coax sullen teenagers into telling him why the world is so very bleak. But now his expression has changed from half-masked cynicism to something gentler and almost regretful, and this terrifies me. When he speaks again, his voice is terribly soft and understanding.

"This voice exists through no fault of your own," he says. "It's a disease, do you understand? Nothing more. Now our concern is to find the right medication to control it. We'll try several if we need to, and titrate the dose slowly to minimize side effects."

We find, *we* try, *we* titrate. The plurality is both comforting and unnerving. A part of me wants to surrender to this alliance. But my mind is dangerously alive with flashes of activation that are barely muted before they form meaning, and my baser instincts know the doctor is not the strongest contestant in the war for my sanity or soul or whatever fragile and finite thing is at stake. Whatever it is that the Other wants so badly from the self, and the self isn't sure she wants at all.

———•◆•———

Days pass with aching slowness, as if time too were taking sedatives. Afternoons of endless talkshows and newshows and gameshows and bland meals served with plastic utensils. There are activity groups each afternoon, altering from day to day, in order to help patients mark time when memory would otherwise become a nightmarish soup of bleached halls and sedated clocks and mushy vegetables and people periodically being taken away to the mythic padded room of isolation. We put bean plants in pots and color our emotions on sheets of paper with nontoxic markers. Sometimes a standard poodle comes to visit. I have never liked dogs and am inordinately jealous when, after an hour, it goes trotting out the ward door, tongue lolling and toenails tapping away to freedom.

Each day the patients are summoned before the psychiatric board of inquisition. Usually Dr. Caspian, but sometimes just one of the nurses. Are you feeling safe? Are you hearing voices? Just between us, do you plan to commit suicide or murder? Certainly not, you assure them, might I leave today? We'll see, comes the vague reply, we'll see. Just take your medicine and we'll see about tomorrow.

I try to separate myself from this bleak existence with a protective barrier of Sartre or Kant. Even though my eyes slide helplessly over the words like blackened ice, I'm determined to continue the façade of keeping up with my classes. But whatever else they do, the drugs seal him out. No vicious, viscous, visceral whispers in the hours when the sun is farthest away. Along with everything that matters, he is gone.

One afternoon, a social work intern appears on the scene to lead a "visualization group", which sounds obnoxious enough to avoid. There are two chairs at the very end of the hall, away from the common area, for the more antisocial patients. At the moment one is occupied by me, the other by a wiry woman with a purple knit hat pulled down over her ears. I've gathered that she's "sectioned", meaning involuntarily admitted, and therefore involuntarily medicated. It's good entertainment because the night orderlies include a couple of gym rat black guys who could easily take her down, but want to do the least damage possible, and she won't hesitate to kick them in the balls. During the day, she mostly sits alone and mutters in some language that's either Nordic or made up, I can't tell which. It's usually less obnoxious than whatever's on television, and we and our invisible demons get along just fine. Mine is conspicuously absent, but I think this is only because my inner workings are too frozen to manipulate, tensile as cold molasses and as resistant to penetration. My whole skin itches and my limbs twitch with a restless activation to compensate for the lifeless interior. They say I'll get used to this, but I think I'd rather be insane.

The visualization group is starting and an orderly comes over to the chairs. "Whitney and Jennifer, why don't you join the group?"

"Thanks, but I'm reading," I say, although I'm really just staring at the blur of words on the page. The other woman raises the volume of her muttering by a few decibels.

"You came here to feel better, didn't you? You won't get well if you just sit around isolating all day."

I had thought the use of *isolating* as a psych ward colloquialism was confined to parody, but I keep forgetting there's no such thing as irony here, at least none that anyone else seems to notice.

"Isolate," says the woman in the purple hat. "It's the I that never closes. Sol, the rising sun. Ate, he ate it all. So late. So late."

The orderly continues to pester us until I get up and join a dozen other people draped listlessly across the furniture, a captive audience because the television has been turned off. To my surprise, the woman in the purple hat comes over too. The social worker is parked on a chair in front of the blackened television. She looks young and full of wholesome ambition, with a set of white teeth on permanent display and bushy hair held back in a tortoiseshell barrette that I'm sure could be used as a deadly weapon, given sufficient motivation. I refrain from pointing this out, as such comments seem to be taken the wrong way here.

"I see we have two newcomers," she says, "Would you like to share your names with the group?"

I murmur my name. The woman in the purple hat says something guttural and Germanic that sounds like an expletive.

"I know that everyone here is going through a difficult time right now," says the social worker. "Sometimes when we're feeling sad or afraid, it can be helpful to have a safe place to go inside our heads. We can imagine these places in our minds, or look back to find a memory from our own lives. Whitney?" she says, apparently lacking the instinct to read cooperation or lack thereof in nonverbal signals. "Do you have a safe place you'd like to share with us?"

"Do I look like fucking Marcel Proust or something?"

The woman's smile flickers, making me feel like I've kicked a puppy. Too bad. If she wants to work with psych patients, she'd better get used to hostile subjects. But on the other hand there is no reason to take out my frustration on an innocent young therapist, maybe even a good one, so I sigh and play along.

"OK, so my friends and I used to go to the barn just after dawn, in the summer. That was the best time to ride, before it got too hot. We'd bring the horses in from the pasture and there would be mist rising from the grass. The horses were like mythical creatures surrounded by silver vapor, and the dew looked like scattered diamonds on the ground. Everything smelled clean and alive. Sometimes we'd just stand and watch the horses moving through the mist until the sun burned it away. I guess that's probably the best thing I can remember."

"What a lovely memory, Whitney," says the intern, sounding surprised. "Would anyone else like to share?"

"Sometimes the angels sing me to sleep," says Ani. "They gather around my bed and spread their wings in a shield so the evil ones can't enter."

"Thank you, Ani," says the intern, looking bemused, as though she is not sure how to deal with happy places that contain delusional and/ or religious content. "Anyone else?"

"My stepfather used to rape me when I was little," says the woman in the purple hat, the first syntactically correct English sentence I've heard her speak. She still has an unplaceable accent and I can't figure out if she's from another country or pretending or neurologically damaged somehow.

"Let's keep this discussion focused on positive things," says the intern.

"It *was* a happy memory," says the woman. "I fucking loved it when he'd slide open my door in the middle of the night and push my stuffed animals off the bed so he could lie down and—"

"THIS IS NOT APPROPRIATE MATERIAL TO SHARE WITH THE GROUP, JENNIFER." The intern stands and her folder of guided meditation exercises cascades to the floor. She fumbles to pick up the papers and is saved by the bell as one of the ordlerlies sounds the evening cattle call, ending the group.

"I hear there are a lot of job openings for radiologists these days," I say helpfully as I trail toward the grim, grayish smell of food. "And veterinary technicians."

The intern does not come back, so maybe she took my advice to heart. It's too bad because she seemed nice, but that almost certainly means she'll be happier working with animals or radioactive pictures than with people. And loath as I am to admit it, the Happy Place exercise has reminded me that there are things in the mind which cannot be perverted, that are impervious to decay. The Other can transform stillness to rage or apathy inside me, but memories are stored somewhere beyond his stain. The image of my friends and the horses and the rising sun is a lucid island: unreachable, but inviolate. I'm lost now, everything is colorless around me and blurred with fear, but my inner landscape is full of pure memories that cascade upon memories to remind me what an utterly, stupidly beautiful life I've had, except I didn't realize it at the time.

I close my eyes and I'm a small child inside the massive lilac bush in our garden, playing with cloth dragons that I've sewn. Each dragon family has a cigar-box apartment furnished with doll furniture and tiny toys sculpted from clay. I act out their social dramas: runaway baby dragons, homeless dragons down on their luck, explorer dragons lost in the lilac jungle, dragons in unrequited love. No one else can fit under the boughs, so I'm always alone here. But I like the quiet and the heavy perfume of the lilacs, and I have no trouble filling a dozen toys with consciousness and motivation on my own.

Now I'm older and my father has let me skip my lessons to take a field trip to the gun store and the Russian grocery. No math for a whole day, and I can tell he's proud of me, an eight-year-old demonstrating the Weaver stance with an unloaded Colt .22 revolver, always tracking the muzzle away from bodies because *every gun is always loaded*. At the deli, I'm enthralled by the Russian man and his wife talking in bullets of unknowable language, knives flashing to make paper-fine cuts of salami studded with olives and glistening bits of fat. There are bins of assorted candies with Cyrillic letters on the wrappers. They have things you don't find in American candies, bits of nougat and sour jam. My father says go ahead, get anything you want, and I take one of each kind and eat them in the car on the way home.

Now I'm a teenager trying to memorize the jump course for a mini-medal equitation class. *Outside line, vertical, rollback, diagonal line, serpentine to the liverpool, outside line.* The sun is baking me in my hunt coat and knee-high leather boots, and Apollo's neck is as hot and glossy as a penny in a windowsill. He lays back his ears and flicks his tail as a girl bounces past on a fat pony.

"You're up next," says Alexis, offering Apollo a ketchup-soaked curly fry. He snatches from her fingers, then spits out in disgust. The judge announces my number over the loudspeaker and I gather the reins and give Apollo a squeeze. We enter the arena at a collected trot, but when Apollo sees the first fence, he breaks into a canter. I get to steer, maybe, but there's no checking the ignition now. Three strides, two, one, and takeoff into the first weightless arc . . .

Someone says my name and I blink back to the corrupted moment. It's a nurse asking me to rate my levels of depression, aggression, suicide, and hallucinations on a scale of 1 to 10. They check on us every few hours in this quantitative fashion. I tell her I feel just grand and I'm not hearing voices and I'm not planning to kill anyone, but I'm not going to numerically rate my qualia because it makes no sense. But she's persistent about it. "Can't you try to *imagine* the number that fits best? Just say the first thing that comes to mind," like she won't be able to continue her afternoon, possibly not eat or sleep until she knows whether I'm in a 5 mood or closer to a 6. In the end, I just tell her to put 4 for everything because it seems like a safe number, not high enough to worry them or low enough to seem defensive. She thanks me for my cooperation and says I should sit with with the other patients, that it's not good for me to be alone all day. She doesn't say "isolating," but I guess that's what she means.

My chair in the hall has better *feng shui* if you ask me, but I don't want to gain a reputation as being difficult so I wander over to the common area. The TV is playing *Friends* and the man who threw his potatoes is sitting in the corner with a checkerboard. Three missing pieces have been replaced with pennies. I walk over and ask if he'd like to play. He looks at me in confusion. "Are you my daughter?"

"No, I'm not."

He stares down at the checkerboard. "It's a stupid game for simple minds," he says. His hair is gray and his skin is yellow, but there seem to be patches of the reverse as well. I glance at the shelf next to the table, which contains ancient issues of *Reader's Digest* and a few kids' games. There is a chessboard on the bottom shelf, a velvet bag of pieces. The man follows my gaze.

"You play?" he asks.

"Not for a long time. I remember how the pieces move."

He motions me to the other chair. I take the chessboard and set it up between us. I put the black pieces on my half, but he spins the board around so that I'm playing white. I open with the king's pawn, and the man mirrors and then checkmates me in a dozen moves. He makes a childish crooning noise of delight as I flick over the white king with one finger.

"You fucking pinkos can't play chess for shit," he says, then bites anxiously at a shard of dead skin next to his thumbnail. "I'm sorry. I shouldn't swear in front of a lady."

"I'm not a communist," I tell him as I put my captured pieces back on the board. "And I'm not a lady either."

"You hide behind your queen," he says. "Who taught you to play?"

"Russian monks."

The man looks at me and a slow, gap-toothed grin spreads across his face. "The devil taught *me* to play," he says, and his shoulders shake with a paroxysm of mirth that roughens to a fit of moist coughing.

The nurse's station window opens to dispense evening meds. Many of the patients murmur listless complaints about the drugs, or sometimes yell them, but they always line up obediently at the window to do so. The nurse tells the patients the name of the medications as she dispenses them: my chess partner is on an antipsychotic and an antibiotic. There is a bottle of Purell on the ledge of the window, and I squirt a blob into my hands before I take my pills. After meds, everyone watches *American Idol* and makes the kind of comments people always make about the show—So-and-So is only getting by because of his cute hair, what a travesty to let these kids cover the Beatles, and what kind of drugs is Paula on, anyway? No one sounds like a psych patient during that hour; we could just be a group of people watching TV. I don't even like the show, but I stay because it's a link to the world. The daytime programs are so surreal that they make me feel worse. I think only people who have been defeated by life watch television before 8 p.m.

The kitchen opens at nine so the patients can have a snack before bed. Today is Styrofoam cups of pink ice cream and shortbread cookies in foil packets. I ask an orderly for a tea bag and a cup of hot water, which he gives me only after checking my chart (no, I am not going to throw boiling water on myself or someone else). Anyway, it hardly matters, because the water is lukewarm and only a few brown tendrils emerge from the teabag and gradually diffuse to turn the water faintly golden.

I open the package of cookies and dip my improvised madeleines in the tepid liquid—bittersweet memory, in search of lost time—reflecting that there is a certain joy in manipulating a humorless circumstance to create a small joke that no one but yourself and some urbane universal audience understands. Actually, it's not that awesome, but you take what you can get here. It's better than wondering when I'm going to get out of this place or what will happen to me when I do. I have a feeling that this bleak stasis is preferable to what's still to come.

CHAPTER TWELVE

A week later, during one of our ritual guarded conversations, Dr. Caspian slides some forms across his desk for me to sign. Release forms.

"So, that's it? I'm going home?"

"Yes. Your parents will be here soon to pick you up. But that's not it. I believe you have schizophrenia, a disorder characterized by delusions, hallucinations, and distorted thinking. It often manifests in late adolescence, possibly because of the academic and social pressures placed on young people during this time."

"Oh."

"There is no cure, but symptoms can be managed with medications like those I've prescribed. But you have to keep taking them. Every day. Probably for the rest of your life."

"I'm not psychotic."

"No, not right now, which is why I'm releasing you. You've been on medication for two weeks now, and I think you've stabilized nicely. What you'd feel if you stopped your treatment, when invariably you began to decompensate, would be frightened and terribly alone. This entity of yours might convince you that you were chosen or special in some way, the only one who sees things as they really are. But it would be a delusion, a trick of your brain."

"Is no one ever chosen, then? Are none of us ever illuminated?"

"My advice to you is this, Whitney: Take the medication. Go back to school if you can. Live your life. It can be quite seductive, especially for someone of your abilities, to think you've been shown something that others can't see. But believe me, the aberration is chemical and it is destructive."

"All right. But Dr. Caspian?"

"Yes?"

"Imagine you'd spent your life chained up in a cave. Imagine that one day the bonds are broken and you are able to step out into the world and see the sun for the first time. It would be like seeing the face of God, wouldn't it? But when you go back into the cave, the ones you left behind will have no idea what you're talking about. They'll think you're insane. They'll probably kill you in the end. The blinding light was there before your very eyes, but to the ones who never left the cave, it's an impossible fantasy, a delusion. Do you deny the sun because they tell you it can't exist?"

"Is that really fair, making me argue with Plato?"

"Probably not."

"Then be a pragmatist. A dreary pragmatist. Go home, see your friends. Do whatever it is teenage girls do. Go roller-skating or something."

"Um, we don't go roller-skating."

"Well, whatever it is you do."

"I have a horse. Named Apollo."

"That's even better. Go see Apollo, then."

"OK."

I had thought my release would be momentous, the free world rushing back to greet me as the vault doors open like the hold of a submarine. But once I'm outside, the return of normal context makes me realize how abnormal I still feel inside. I had hoped this might be solved with clove cigarettes, poetry, and strolls in a peaceful garden. A civilized nineteenth century rest cure. Not with horse tranquilizers and unspeakable labels that start with *schizo*.

When we are in the car, my father clears his throat and says, "So, are you, ah, feeling better?"

"I suppose."

We drive the rest of the way in silence. I want very badly to know what was written on the wall, but I will never ask. At home, I collapse into bed and remain comatose until early the next afternoon. Such bliss to sleep without the subliminal psych ward soundtrack in the background. When I get up and go into the bathroom, I am startled by my reflection in the mirror. There were no mirrors on the unit, presumably because they shatter into sharp pieces. Windows, spoons, and other reflective surfaces distort the image, and my self-concept had begun to take on a carnival fun house quality. It's reassuring to see how normal I look, the mundane geometry of my features and the familiarity of my own eyes, resting uneasily as they always do between blue and gray. I look sleep-deprived and in desperate need of some exfoliating facial scrub, but there is no tangible evidence of sickness, no horror film blackness gathering in my eyes.

The phone rings and my mother calls me to answer it. I go into the hall and pick up the extension.

"Hello?"

"Whitney, you're back! It's Alexis. Evie's here too. We've been calling for weeks. Your mom just said you were in the hospital, but she wouldn't say why, and my mom said that she met your mom at the hairdresser and she told her you were in a *psych* ward. What's up with *that?*"

"It's a long story."

"Well, fuck, come meet us at the Crystal."

I agree and put down the phone. When I enter the kitchen, my parents are sitting at the table with cups of coffee chilling in the silence between them.

"I'm going to meet Evie and Alexis downtown," I tell them.

"You're walking?" says my mother, sounding doubtful or maybe fearful, as if I've announced my intentions to search for Atlantis on the back of my invisible rainbow alpaca. "I'm not sure that's . . . why don't I give you a ride?"

"I'm not an invalid, you know." I step past them out the door.

Evie and Alexis are waiting outside the Crystal Springs Dairy Bar on Main Street, shivering under the gray November sky.

"Hi," I say, walking up to them. Evie returns my greeting coolly; she doesn't like it when people outshine her in the personal drama department. She's dyed her hair since I've seen her last—it's platinum blond now with orange streaks, and for some reason she has wound strips of black velvet around the legs of her jeans.

"Oh my god, girl," says Alexis, bouncing impatiently in her zebra flip-flops. "What the fuck?"

I shrug, words being too much effort and an actual explanation being impossible. Alexis searches me up and down, impatient to fill in for herself the gaps in my communication skills. "Is that a bandage on your arm? Did you slit your wrist?"

"No. I just cut it a little bit, you know how it is."

"Yeah."

"And they freaked out."

"Oh, is that all? And they kept you in the loony bin for two weeks? What was it like? Were the people scary? Were there guys? Were any of them hot?"

"I wasn't really trolling for a date, Alexis." I glance away from them into the restaurant, although the glass is reflective so I am only seeing light refracted to again form the images of the people I do not want to confront directly. "So, are we going to get something to eat or what?"

"Whatever you want, Whitney," says Alexis solicitously. I grit my teeth and motion them into the restaurant. It's not like I think they're going to stiletto me from behind, but I have always preferred stepping in people's shadows to yielding my blind spot. In horses this is a sign of dominance, but I don't know what it signifies for me. As we enter the restaurant, Evie stops in her tracks so that Alexis and I bump into her. "Check it out," she says. "They have a new flavor."

It's true. Beneath the staple list of flavors that has remained unchanged since I can remember, there is a hand-lettered sign containing the word *Mango!* and a blobby orange and green sphere that is probably supposed to be a mango. We settle into our regular booth. "The usual?" calls the waitress from the register, because nine times out of ten, Alexis orders marshmallow on coffee ice cream, Evie gets chocolate smothered in chocolate and sprinkled with more chocolate, and I get butterscotch with strawberry syrup and gummi bears.

"Yeah," I say, "the usual."

"I think I'll try the mango," says Evie.

"Me, too," says Alexis.

We sit and pinch our drinking straw wrappers into origami horses while we wait. It feels like there's a weight pressing on the delicate sphenoid bone in the center of my head. They're shaped like butterflies. I wish I had just stayed home to sleep. Finally, the waitress brings our order. I take a bite and reflect that butterscotch ice cream doused in strawberry goo and littered with gummi bears, while visually arresting, is a rather nauseating combination, and I wonder why I've never noticed this before.

"How's the mango?" I ask.

"What?" says Alexis, looking up at me with startled eyes.

"How is your ice cream?"

"Oh, fine."

Better than fine, apparently. Evie and Alexis have polished off their dishes in record time. Their eyes dart nervously toward the door.

"I should really go," says Evie. "I put my brother in front of Sponge-Bob, but my mom gets pissy if I leave him alone. The other day, he cut up one of the sofa cushions to see if it had bones." She flutters some money onto the table to pay for her ice cream.

"We'll call you later, Whitney," says Alexis, standing too. "And if you want to, you know, talk or anything . . ." They exchange another uneasy glance.

"Yeah. See you later."

I stay in the booth after they have gone, watching strawberry sauce ooze down the sides of my dish while gummi bears float in the pool of pastel foam like drowning victims. The image causes a glimmer of pleasure, but I'm not sure if I can rightly call it mine. He's not quite there and not quite gone inside me, the Other. I think he would say something if it weren't for the drugs, which seem to stop him from using innocuous environmental noises to catalyze his facsimile of speech. They make my own inner words too slow and stupid to be manipulated with such finesse. Anything I feel, though, could just as easily belong to him.

"Can I get you anything else?" says the waitress. I look up and see that the light has changed. I've been sitting here nearly an hour.

"No, thanks." I put some money on the table and leave the restaurant.

My parents are still sitting at the table with their coffee when I get back to the house. In my room, I face the surrounding walls with the intensity of an FBI agent sizing up a group of murder suspects. But the one will not confess its secret, and the others will not capitulate and give up the fourth wall. There is a charge in the air now that tells me he could say something if he wanted to. This, perhaps, should signal me to take another pill, diffuse the potential. But maybe it's better to have a mind and an adversary than to be empty and alone. It seems to be a question of Which is Worse from those girly magazines Alexis is so fond of. Hair in your food or food in your hair? To burn alive or suffocate in silence? I don't remember that one in *Seventeen*.

Just tell me this, I ask the waiting quiet. I know I am crossing some line, engaging him directly. Some red line drawn across ivory skin. Tell me this. What did you write?

You . . .

not I

or we,

but why?

The reply is an immediate shimmering echo of the question, though distinct in content from the words half-formed on my lips. Something glimmers red in the corner of my eye. Under the dresser. I get on my knees to look and fish my Scout knife out of the shadows. When I pick it up, there are rusty flakes on the blade. I wipe them away on my jeans and return the knife to its rightful place in my pocket, then fall back into bed and drift off into a fog of dirty gray half-nothing that covers his sharp bright consciousness and inserts static between my own frail thoughts. Yet something is nagging at the edge of my awareness, something about the room itself: the knife, streaks of red syrup running down the sides of the silver ice cream dish . . .

The phone rings. I don't answer it. I turn onto my side: There it is. The walls . . . they are immaculate. Something made that happen, the transformation from crime scene to safe haven. My parents, scrubbing my blood from the walls.

My mother's voice calls from downstairs. "Whitney? There's some boy on the phone. He says he's in one of your classes."

"I'm sleeping."

One of my horse posters is missing, I realize. The mare and foal in the field of marigolds. Perhaps there was arterial spray.

"Should I tell him to call back?"

"I don't know." My voice barely penetrates the surrounding air.

"Whitney? Did you hear me?"

"YES. TELL HIM TO CALL BACK."

"And don't . . . don't forget to take your medication tonight?"

"OK."

"Whitney?"

"I WON'T."

The house lapses back into silence, soon broken by the *pop* of an airtight bottle opening. A faint gagging as someone swallows pills and pride without water. The half-life of straitjacket sanity is a good ten, twelve hours. At least this night to rest before sabers at dawn. At least this dark night to figure out how you destroy what doesn't exist.

———◆———

"Where the hell have you been?" says Scott as I enter lab ten minutes late. "You never answer your cell phone, and you haven't been to class in weeks. I thought you might have dropped out."

"No. I've been . . . sick."

"Oh, are you OK?" The concern in Scott's voice makes me uncomfortable. He'll be listening. He'll use it.

"Fine," I say, snapping on a pair of gloves. My parents didn't want me to go back to school but I begged them, please don't take this last facade of normalcy away. Maybe I can still be saved. So my mother drove me here in worried silence because I told her to turn off the *god damn radio* before I could stop myself. I didn't mean to say it so violently, but there is too much seething in the quiet static between chords of Beethoven broadcasted eerily to half the world.

Dr. Caspian continues to see me twice a week as an outpatient, and they have added reinforcements. Now there's a clinical psychologist and a social worker who has the exact accent of the Geico gecko. I keep inadvertently snickering and/or snorting when I talk to him, and he probably thinks I'm quite rude, but I keep thinking he's about to tell me I can save a bunch of money on my car insurance. On Tuesdays I just see Dr. Caspian for half an hour, and on Thursdays there's an awkward roundtable meeting with the three clinicians, my parents, and myself. Now that they've decided I'm schizophrenic, there's no stopping them. They blather on about negative symptoms (alogia, anhedonia, avolition: no speech, no pleasure, no will) and positive symptoms (hallucinations, delusions, disorganized speech). They expound on prodromal phases, first episode psychosis, and a cornucopia of medications with names that sound like the product of overcaffeinated focus groups—seriously, *Abilify*? My parents, the traitors, just nod and swallow it all and occasionally produce gems like "She did have odd mannerisms as a child," or "She's never been good at connecting socially with her peers," and generally act like they were expecting this all along. *Then why didn't you do something sooner?* I seethe at them internally. *Why didn't you have someone fix me while I was still nice and plastic?*

But I uphold a stoic silence while my parents accede all too eagerly to the conclusion that my brain is broken, that it's probably been this way since I was born. No guilt, no insinuations of emotional refrigeration. I have not been inadvertently placed on a shelf to chill next to the pickles and mustard; I was simply a scrambled egg to begin with. And it's true, they're good parents and I have many childhood memories that border on idyllic cliché: painting blobby watercolors on a tiny easel next to my mother's, hiking on misty New England mountains with my father, splitting a package of old-fashioned lemon drops or root beer barrels when we reached the summit. It's just that there was always a larger than average radius of space between us. We perched on separate branches like a parliament of owls instead of chattering and wrestling like otters or other social mammals. I do not hate my quiet *Strigidae* family, but it isn't nice of them to break ranks and start calling me the little stranger whom they never felt they knew. But at least everyone agrees that it's best for me to go back to class as long as I don't flip out again, or "decompensate," in their sterile clinical jargon.

Now Scott is hovering nervously over a sheep's brain laid out on a tray, but he does not appear to have made any surgical headway. The meninges still cover the hemispheres like the tough white fiber surrounding an orange, shielding the actual brain matter decorously from view.

"Holy shit, what happened to your arm?" says Scott.

Without thinking I have pushed up my sleeves, revealing the half-healed knife wounds that have begun to itch too much to leave bandaged. They look ghastly under the fluorescent lights, congealed scabs the color of jam in the center of a tartlet cookie. The surrounding skin is shockingly pale. I stare mesmerized at the ravaged strawberry-vanilla surface until I remember Scott.

"Nothing," I say, rolling down my sleeve. "An accident."

"It looks like you cut yourself."

"I didn't."

Scott seems too distracted to press the issue. He is wearing gloves for the first time I can remember in the course. "So, um, are you up for dissecting Dr. Einstein here?"

"What?"

"Oh, haha, I named the brain Dr. Einstein. Like we named the pig Wilbur? And you know how they preserved Einstein's brain after he died? I don't know, I was trying to get friendly with the brain, but I really think you're better at this sort of thing. So, you're perfectly welcome to take over the slice and dice of Dr. Einstein. Or we don't have to call it Dr. Einstein. Whatever." Scott is beginning to babble and make vague, nervous motions with the scalpel. I take it from him but trace the point over the ridges of gyri without penetrating. Sheep brains look not so different from human brains, and I am suddenly empathic. The study guide tells me to disarticulate the frontal lobes to reach the deeper structures, but I can only imagine dead-eyed mental patients with bruised orbital rims and disarticulated souls.

"You look kind of pale," says Scott. "I can handle this if you want."

"No, I'm fine."

The brain is so much chilled *pâté* now, and it was only ever a sheep to begin with. Cut. I try to send the order directly to my arm, but it doesn't obey language.

"Your eyes are all glassy . . ."

I perforate the meninges, and I can feel it, I can feel my own head splitting open...

"Seriously, you look like you're about to pass out. Let me take over."

I let Scott prize the scalpel out of my grip. He shoots me a concerned glance as I collapse onto one of the stools and clench the seat to stop my hands from shaking.

"Are you sure you're going to be OK?"

I can't bear to answer that, so I just direct his attention to preserving the corpus callosum as he separates the brain's temporal lobes.

"Don't worry," says Scott. "I'll totally take care of everything. You just relax. There's some warm, slightly flat ginger ale in my backpack if you want it."

All around me are metal surfaces that reflect students probing and prying and cutting into delicate cerebral tissues. All that's safe is the floor, with only blobs of nameless goo on white linoleum to contemplate.

"So I just have one tiny question," says Scott. "Is that the corpus callosum or the hippocampus?" He gestures with the scalpel, but I can't bring myself to look.

"Um, which do you think it is?"

"Well, the lab manual said the hippocampus is shaped like a sea horse, and this thing here looks nothing like a seahorse, so I think it must be the corpus callosum. Is that right?"

"Yeah," I say without looking, choosing the optimistic probability. "Good."

Scott looks pleased. "You're so awesome—you're actually making me learn this stuff. Hey, do you want to catch a movie after class?"

"I'm not living in town anymore. I'm, uh, commuting. My parents dropped me off today."

"I can give you a ride home."

"I live like an hour away though."

"Another hour to spend with you, then." I had never realized until now, because I've never had sappy romantic clichés directed at me, that they take on a whole new effervescence when you're the object, when they cease to be trite universals and are delivered with a twitch of a smile and alchemical eyes that turn reflected light to gold. I look at Scott's face, beaded with perspiration as he jabs unsteadily at the brain, and I can't admit defeat just yet.

"Give me the scalpel," I say. "I'll finish this."

The brain lies impassive before me, and maybe I'd be a decent surgeon after all because my hands stop shaking as soon as the blade touches gray matter. I am able to find utter concentration in the separation of tissues, and even the professor who thinks I am a lying sack of slime sees fit to compliment my technique. Scott does not break my concentration to question me further about our social future as I work, and the lobotomy goes smoothly despite everything.

———◆———

"I used to think gummi bears were analogous to high school students," says Scott as we wait in the tiny art house theatre for the movie to start. My knee is jammed against his in the narrow row of seats. Around us people are coughing and muttering and nibbling treats with rodent-like sounds that make me think of being buried in a mass grave.

My parents were reluctant to leave me in the company of a stranger, and a boy nonetheless. But like me they cling to the hope that this might all pass like some capricious storm and leave the ground still fertile.

And it almost seems like it could be true. This day has been unbearably idyllic, just existence the way it should be: writing up flashcards for the bio final and discovering that the geese on the campus green will eat Starburst but it makes their beaks stick together, and then the other geese get pissed off because they're not getting fed, and their beaks aren't stuck together so then there's a lot of running and general enjoyment of being young and alive, but not self-conscious about it or thinking too desperately about how this is all we have, this once, and we never know when or how it will be taken away.

"You know, the red ones were the jock bears," Scott continues, nibbling the toes off one of the aforementioned. "The clear ones were the lab geek bears, and the green ones were the sexy cheerleader—uh, never mind."

"Mm."

"What about you? Did you play when you were a kid, or did you make naturalistic observations of the other children while reading Greek philosophy?"

I try to come up with a witty reply. It ought to be easy since he thinks I'm some kind of wunderkind polymath when really I'm just ferrety-eyed and facile with words, which creates the same impression. Someone who is only articulate when it doesn't matter, like when angling with friends for the last Hot Pocket and you craft an argument so compelling it would make John Locke cry. But now? Now I'm forcibly mute.

Anyway, the movie is starting so I don't have to answer. Unfortunately, it turns out to be a devastatingly sad, excruciatingly long subtitled film about a paralyzed man who wants to be euthanized, and Scott and I both end up uncomfortably gulping down gummi bears for three and a half hours while people sniffle into tissues around us.

"I'm sorry the movie was so sad," says Scott as we stand on the chilly street corner outside. "Next time we'll just go to a regular theater and watch a movie about animated penguins. Are you still having a good time?"

"Oh, um, yeah . . . er, good. I mean lots."

"Good," says Scott, smiling slightly, making my palms go slick and my heart turn arrhythmic. Good heavens, this isn't even love; it's mild infatuation at best. How do people survive it, much less the damage of the real thing?

A streak of some bloodshot emotion crosses my field of vision. Jealousy.

No. Not now.

He changes his scent to clean white soap, a little sweaty underneath, and I unconsciously move away from Scott so his smell doesn't conflate with this perversion.

"Hey, did you hear me?" says Scott.

"Um, what?"

"I said did you want to get some dinner?"

At the word *dinner*, my mind flashes to an image of maggots writhing in the viscera of some dead animal with white fur. A cat. It opens its blue eyes and they are windows to worlds never imagined. A radiant white shape glows in the center, incandescent ivory, cold enough to vaporize on contact. It offers me its hand. The cat's eyes close and the light fades, and I turn to Scott and suddenly he is so ugly I have to look away. I catch my reflection in a shop window and I feel as though I have been torn in two, that I must destroy this grotesque protein facsimile and liberate the pure soul contained within. The world around me is a lumpy Play-Doh model of a world, a fallen image of the perfection I have just witnessed.

"Um, I think I should just go home. I'm not feeling very well. Too many gummi bears..." I avoid his eyes, his meaty face.

"No problem," says Scott, visibly disappointed. He drives me home, and perhaps my pallid face smeared against the passenger seat window lends credence to my lie. It's not even much of a lie. Only the tenuous internal silence saves me from actually vomiting in his car, and I manage to dredge up an occasional remark about the movie or the impending bio final. A fresh surge of stomach fluids overtakes me as the car slides to a stop. I look up blearily and see we have reached my house. I close my eyes as Scott leans forward to kiss me, but it's all salivary and tangled and I pull away as his hands slide beneath my shirt and glide upwards toward my bra. Apparently I can only deal with bodies that mean nothing to me.

"Good night, Scott. Thanks for the nice evening." I step out of the car and flee to the house before I have to observe his disgust. *Thanks for the nice evening*, I parrot sarcastically in my head. That has got to be the stupidest phrase ever uttered and I deserve to die alone, maybe after being publicly mocked or hit with things.

Never alone, never again, says the Other.

The house is dark except for a faint glow under my parents' door. They call out to ask if I'm home, as though it were possible my footfalls were those of a ghost. I answer affirmatively and flee to my room. I don't bother to change my clothes, just collapse into bed and let him think his oily silver thoughts that collide with my own until they are melted into each other and chemically indistinct.

Thanks for the nice evening, he says insipidly. As if it's not bad enough to have this mind parasite take such liberties with your person, it then uses your words to ridicule you from within, playing them back with a humiliating distortion that amplifies your dorkiness and uncertainty by exponential sums, which it then sneers at you for not understanding. I want him never to do it again.

Thanks for the nice evening.

Thanks for the nice evening.

In mocking me, we have achieved a sickly unity. I could hardly say who is mirroring whom. And despite everything I feel like I'm about to fall asleep, the inside of my mouth still sour with decomposing gummi bears. I guess people who survive an apocalypse don't walk around forever in a daze, saying "Wow, that was some apocalypse. Very unexpected." Maybe for a while, but then they build shelter and gather medicine and plant crops. I assume. Likewise for me, it's just another awkward date post-Awakening, somewhere in the second month of the first year CE, which we'll let stand for the Common Ego, because that sounds so much more important and historic than the Calamitous Entity or the Changed Eternity or the Childhood's End or the Collapse of Everything.

CHAPTER THIRTEEN

Victorious, his pleasure is like skin scraping on graffittied cement. But in this case it's the graffiti that's radiantly alive while the skin cells are mostly dead. They have shed their telomeres, they are close to the end, pray for them. Pleasure to the object and pain to the subject, except imagine these are one creature with no boundaries between them. I stand at my window and glare at the moon, as though somehow it's to blame for my troubles.

Come out to the rose garden,
we'll start a revolution by starlight.
Off with their heads, the whites and the reds.

He shatters every silence like a disobedient child throws a glass down on the floor. Even in his absence the air is tainted with the words he might have spoken. But I hardly recoil. My body is borrowed and limp, my only volition is to listen. Visionaries starve in the desert for enlightenment, offer themselves freely to the mirage. Sometimes you hear of a person who goes to Alaska to see the Northern Lights and never returns. Maybe they're found in the spring, frozen and torn apart by wild animals because they could not stop looking at the prismatic messages rippling across the sky. Because they had to find meaning in them and there was no meaning to be found, but they were so beautiful the wanderer could not look away.

My room is redolent with the stuffy sweetness of a long illness, of old books and poster paper and innocence gone past its expiration date. Outside, the sun glitters on patches of melting snow. Apollo . . . the world and the horse are the same color, dappled white on rich brown. You should ride in the woods and smell the damp leaves and the cold pines. Listen to icicles dripping off rock formations and hooves crunching on frozen earth and you will need to listen to nothing else. You wanted a horse so badly, you love him more than anything in the world. You are afraid you might hurt him, destroy every center with mass, annihilate everything in this world that you love so you are free to move beyond, to . . .

Kill kill kill.

It could be a lullaby in another language.

The words have no meaning, only the meaning we give them.

Only because you are sick do they make you sick.

Kill kill kill.

Let's kill Scott, I don't like him.

With a violent motion I grab the bottle of antipsychotic and gulp down some pills, the only defiant action I can take. I start to read up on Camus and existentialism for my next class, but I can't make the words form into meaning on the page.

They say that mental problems plague philosophers. John Stuart Mill had a nervous breakdown around my age, and Nietzsche spent most of his twilight in an institution. But maybe this isn't permanent, just an object lesson of a breakdown. Maybe I can still go to one of those old-fashioned asylums where you write in a journal in a walled garden until you are well enough to join the world. And then I'll become a thinker, a writer, something of value. I'll justify my existence somehow.

Is your wave-function collapsing,

or are you just collapsing?

Hail Mary . . .

Or is it Mary quite contrary, shall we see how the garden grows.

The end did not lilt up; it was not phrased as a question. Small invisible roots are coiling upward, sliding snakelike through my viscera. I am to see how the garden grows. Don't be ridiculous, I tell myself. But if I want to breathe again, I will. I slip out of my bedroom with the soft steps of one who is used to sneaking. I still unconsciously walk with the weight on the balls of my feet, settling them so gently that no surface can creak and raise alarm.

The night is cool as the fingertips of a sick person pressed against a healthy cheek. Beads of condensation have gathered on the grass, and I feel the nervy cold like an ice cream headache in my feet. The brush of each blade is like a hookworm burrowing into my flesh, wanting to become a part of me. I hurry to the garden where there is safe, dead mulch to stand on. I find myself under the rose trellis, and this appears to be the destination because the imperious internal vegetation melts away like dry organic matter before a flame, dissipates to carbon dioxide and is exhaled to nothing. I look up through the lattice and find the moon, a sharp crescent of Cheshire smile. Is this the purpose of my nighttime constitutional, to encounter the ghost of an old nightmare that wasn't a dream at all? No, don't be ridiculous. Frightened children imagine impossible things, see faces in random shapes and monsters in shadows. But you are not a child any longer.

I look up coldly at the moon, the observer gazing and the object gazed upon, allowing no deeper connection between us. Human beings are aggregates of particles drifting into law-abiding structures for brief incarnations, and everything else is an unnecessary complication. I don't know if I believe this, but there is nothing I believe more.

I return to my room as silently as I came and exchange my philosophy book for my lab manual. At least the governing rules of dividing cells are unequivocal, not open to interpretation. Between my mind and the page, hot flashes like embers cast off from Fourth of July firecrackers obscure my vision. He is pleased because he has moved me, a physical object, through the world by the mere power of suggestion. I feel his happiness, I *am* his happiness, because he uses my chemicals to manufacture it. But I am not happy. How could I be? I haven't memorized a single stage of mitosis. He playfully rips X chromosomes in half behind my eyelids when I close them, and they sparkle also.

When I finally lapse into an uneasy sleep, I dream of a walled sanitarium where Victorian-era young people cavort on a grassy hillside, elegant and urbane until they laugh. Their peals of merriment are a hyena keen that goes on for too long to be comfortable. A high wall surrounds the place with no visible entrance or exit. Rose bushes spill over the wall in riotous reds and whites, and I am the only one in the merry crowd who notices how quickly they are growing, how they have already swallowed a stone table and a journal filled with someone's mad thoughts.

—◆—

At a certain point it becomes necessary to cease to have an emotional life, an internal environment beyond rudimentary stimulus-response. Unfortunately this isn't possible, because evolution doesn't give refunds. We can't unlearn language, even though without it there could be none of this torture. Would god but I could have been a lemur.

So when Dr. Caspian asks, "How are you feeling today?" after more insomniac nights of gunpoint banter, broken images of places for which I have no cognitive map, I deflect the spasm of some dire emotion with a breezy "I'm not sure if 'am I' has been resolved thoroughly enough to beg the question 'how.'"

"I see. How's school?"

"I'm sure it's fine. I'll ask it next time I'm there. I need more Ativan, by the way."

"I just wrote that prescription last week."

"Yes, but I've used all the pills."

"For *what*?"

"Well, the other day there was an incident that troubled me. While I was sitting in my philosophy lecture, I was overwhelmed by the certainty that I would truly be able to see if and only if I cut out my eyes. Except don't worry, I'm not quite that far gone. But he likes vivid images and desires to make them actual. It's an aesthetic thing, he's hopeless that way. Yet I'm not sure if it was he or my body itself that willed this action so deeply. It felt obligatory, like I *had* to do it, as opposed to supererogatory, which is just like a nice thing to do. But it wasn't so much a matter of deciding what's morally right, but an overwhelming knowledge of what I needed to do next, combined with the physical sensation of being choked by some sinister plant. It reminded me of the categorical imperative, which, um, Immanuel Kant developed as a formula to determine right action. Like, you create a maxim for your action—"

"Yes, I'm familiar with it. What happened?"

"Really? You've taken philosophy?"

"A long time ago."

"Yeah, I bet. Who was your favorite philosopher? Democritus? Hobbes?"

"Actually, I was partial to Aristotle. But returning to the categorical imperative and the rapidly disappearing Ativan . . ."

"Well, I thought I'd take an extra dose to mitigate the understandable anxiety these events caused. And then it started to wear off, and before I knew it the bottle was empty, then empty again. I guess that's how addictions get started. But you *gave* me the drug, so it's not like it can be *bad* for me, right?"

"Maybe you need something stronger."

"Like Valium? Oxy? Sweet, I knew you were holding out on me."

"Not that kind of drug. An antipsychotic, similar to the one you're taking now. It's effective in refractory cases."

"I'm a refractory case?"

"I think this medication could help you."

"Then why didn't you try it sooner?"

"It has a more concerning side-effect profile. You'd need to go back to the hospital so we could monitor your condition."

"Don't be stupid. Don't be *absurd.*"

"You just said you felt you had no choice but to *cut out your eyes.* How can you possibly focus on your studies in such a state, particularly if you are already failing?"

Already failing. I want to say something cruel, and I watch him appraisingly. Some people are easy to hurt; you just think of them, everything you know about them, drop the thoughts like eggs into a pot of water and watch bubbles stream from their microscopic fault lines. It's a trick I've learned all too well from *him.* But Dr. Caspian looks at me impassively with his guarded eyes, and I can draw nothing from him.

Finally I settle for "I'm pretty sure you have no fucking idea what you're talking about." It comes out more emotionally than I intended, which makes me angry enough to want to throw something at him. Years of practice have apparently equipped him to anticipate this, and he reaches across the desk to move a plastic snow globe out of range. It has a happy reindeer in it. He must hate seeing patients in this office.

"I have only your best interests in mind," he says.

"Right, you're bound by the sterling morality of the Hippocratic Oath. Which in its original form promotes nepotism and prevents doctors from performing surgery, abortion, and euthanasia."

"And you said you were failing your classes?"

"I only know things when it doesn't matter. Hippocrates was also fond of leeches, incidentally."

"We've come a long way since then."

"Have you? I've seen people in the ward on the drug you're talking about. Asleep on the sofas because they're too tired to make it back to their rooms after *Jeopardy.* So fat and slow they can't open a fucking pudding cup because their fucking hands shake too much, and I would rather die than have that happen to me."

"Whitney, I don't think that could ever happen to you," says Dr. Caspian, and in that moment I would take cyanide if he asked. "But you can't continue like this, and you know it. Under such pressure something will break."

"Like my spine, maybe?" I pause, bite my lip, fall silent because I do not want him to know that I am close to crying. He sees it anyway.

"Just give this drug a chance," he says. "And I promise that one day you will have a normal life again, with boys and parties and horses. But it won't happen unless you work with me. So, do we have a deal?"

Dr. Caspian offers his hand, an elegant academic gesture too civilized for the situation. I look into his eyes and know that if I do not agree, I will end up between the locked doors regardless. I take his hand. The mass of it is terribly dense and real, and I hold on to it for perhaps a few seconds longer than etiquette finds necessary.

The inpatient unit is across a grassy lawn at the edge of the hospital complex. There is a brochure in the waiting room that says the grounds are home to the nation's oldest ginseng tree, and we pass under its bare winter shadow on the way to the ward. I look up at it pleadingly, but it only holds up its twisted arms in an eternal shrug as if to say, "What can a tree do?"

The bracing smells of winter landscape and free city disappear in a swish of sliding glass doors, replaced by a lukewarm blast of hospital air. I notice a sign outside the unit I had not seen before: *Caution: high bolt risk. Check hallway for patients before entering and exiting.*

I have only seen the term before in conjunction with horses. Not just running away, bolting implies violence of motion. Bolting horses don't take care to preserve themselves, they just run.

"Got you again, did they?"

I look over at the TV area. Ani is sitting on the same worn couch by the television, her eyes reflecting the flashing lights of some game show. I wonder if she is here again, or if she never left. The other people on the couches look the same also, or indistinguishable in type from those who occupied their places before. Blank-faced and glossy-eyed, lips moving faintly to music from Walkmans or MP3 players or their own deliriums.

Soon my parents come, wanting to see me. They have brought a bag of my things, but they have to hand them over at the door because the staff can't let them in without my permission, and I don't have the energy to be their child now. The nurse on this shift is less strict than the one before, and she lets me keep everything—clothes, CD player, little bags of cheese popcorn, and my Nietzsche compendium, which is heavy enough to be used as a weapon if the right circumstances arise. But most objects can.

"What are you reading?" asks the nurse, glancing down at the book after I've emptied my pockets and relinquished my Swiss Army knife, which I'd forgotten was there.

"*Twilight of the Idols*," I tell her.

"My girlfriend said those books are good, but I'm not really into vampires."

"Neither was Nietzsche, so far as I know."

The nurse shuffles through my chart. "Are you hallucinating now, Whitney?"

"Um, no . . ." These admittance conversations are always uncomfortably direct, and one never manages to answer poetically.

"Do you feel like hurting yourself or someone else?"

"No."

"What's that written on your shoes?"

"Wisdom to live by."

"I'm afraid I need to take them. The laces."

"What about them?"

"They could be dangerous."

"Because they're long enough to choke someone?"

The nurse doesn't answer, just waits while I take off my shoes and hand them over. She brings me a cup of pills, an Ativan and a yellow one that tastes like oranges and fizzes in my mouth, dissolving so I cannot save it to discard later. The nurse shows me to a room where a girl with limp brown hair is sitting cross-legged on one of the beds. Her jaw bulges rhythmically as though she is chewing gum.

"Hi," she says. "My name's Zoë."

I make a relatively polite facial expression and set my bag down on the other bed.

"What are you in for?"

"Excuse me?"

"Your diagnosis," says the girl. "I have anorexia nervosa. At one point I weighed 74 pounds. That's a body mass index of 13; 18.5 to 24 is normal. My heart swelled up and I nearly died. That was last year, when I was eighteen."

Now that I look at her, she does appear to be on the brink of starvation. She spits something into her hand. It wasn't gum . . . she was chewing on a hair elastic.

"Is that a Walkman?" she asks as I sort through the items in my bag. "Yeah."

"My iPod's dead and I can't sleep without music. Could I maybe borrow it, just for a little while?"

I shrug and hand it to her with whatever CD is in it. She curls up on her bed like a fetus to lose herself to the music. I lie down and fall into some kind of gray space, trying not to think or move or feel. When it's time for a meal, Zoë gets up and follows behind me, close enough that it must be said we are in one another's company. In the cafeteria she sits across from me, eating Rice Krispies one by one out of a fun-sized box.

"You could be ana you know," she says. "You have the bone structure for it."

Personally, I would rather have dessert than show off my fine bone structure. But not the dessert here, the ubiquitous square of cheesecake dribbled with blood-red sauce.

Zoë sets down her cereal box and looks warily at her tray. "Do you think they used real cheese for the macaroni or the spray kind without any calories?"

"Does that matter to you, Zoë?" says Ani from across the table in what I can only assume is a mock psychiatrist voice. "Do you think about that sort of thing a lot?"

"Shut up, Ani." Zoë stabs a few pieces of macaroni from her plate but leaves them impaled on her fork instead of eating them. "By the way, you can have your CD back," she says. "I hate Nine Inch Nails. The stupid lead singer sounds like he's slitting his wrists while he's singing."

"Trent Reznor's not just the lead singer, he's the whole band. He writes everything, produces everything . . ."

"Whatever." Zoë harpoons another piece of macaroni. The plastic fork is so full that the tines are splayed out of place. "He needs a fucking Prozac. No wonder you're depressed. I heard someone listening to Shakira in the hall—I'll see if I can borrow that." She yanks her tray from the table and heads for the door.

"Zoë," Ani calls out languidly. "Aren't you going to eat your macaroni?"

Zoë looks down at the loaded fork, dropped furtively behind the untouched soup dish on her tray, and something in her face trembles. "Fuck off, Ani," she says. "I ate the entire box of cereal, and you have no idea what you're talking about so just shut the fuck up." She drops her tray onto the trolley by the door and flounces out of the room. Ani smiles with cat-like satisfaction.

"Why are you so mean to her?" I ask. Ani's eyes are hard as flint as she opens her container of cheesecake and scrapes up the cherry sauce.

"She believes the lie," says Ani. She smiles, suddenly and incongruously, her teeth and lips sticky and red. "Not like us, we see everything. We're chosen."

"Chosen for what?"

"I don't know, but we listen, don't we? So, we'll know it when it's time." She picks up an orange from her tray. I feel suddenly dizzy, as though my perspective has shifted. When she digs her fingers into the rind, I flinch as though her nails were piercing my own skin. I can't look away, but sometimes the destruction of objects is more than I can bear. Ani is peeling apart the orange sections. As she picks off bits of white fiber, my nail beds ache as though the cuticles were being ripped away. She is not destroying the orange, only making it part of her, I remind myself. She stretches a crescent of fruit until the skin splits and I feel juice sacs rupturing inside me, taste the acrid sweetness of hemorrhage in my mouth. Ani drops the orange piece onto her tray and says, "You're always reading those fancy-ass college books. What's a real bookish bad name to call somebody?"

I tear my eyes away from the orange slice bleeding on the placemat. "Whom, specifically, do you want to insult?"

"Shrinks."

"Oh. Call him an autocratic slave to materialist reductivism."

"OK."

"And tell him he's a fucktard."

I return to my room before she can start mauling the orange again. Zoë is in the hall bartering some sugar-free gum for loan of the Shakira CD, and my only companion is a small brown spider suspended from a thread of silk above the windowsill. I feel like time has completed a weary full circle as I gaze through the glass at the floodlit grounds below. An ambulance pulls up in front of the building, a night nurse hurries to her car, and the nation's oldest ginseng tree stands unmoved by it all. The moon shines coldly above, rarefied points of starlight beyond.

Truth used to be that our destinies were written in the stars, but now truth finds our futures trapped in delicate strands of double helix inside us. The stars are only dead things glittering in the sky. To assert this is barely the incipience of our power. We can look through warped glass into the very past and see how the world was born. We can paint probability pictures in the finest shades of quantum gray to predict how it will end. I can feel the weight of the progress in my bones, and the change feels like decay.

I want to tear it away like cobwebs and bow down to the stars as rational spirits, entreat them to help me through this trial of faith and reason. Send me a poet, a guide.

Yet hard as I try, I can see the stars only as spent photons creating the illusion of brightness on my retina. The hope in light is reduced away to nothing, and the trials in darkness must thereby be denounced as madness. Maybe I should be relieved to relinquish my chosenness, but the universe only seems to get heavier around me, and the physicists bear me out on this point. It will get heavier and heavier until a time past imagining, when it collapses back in on itself once more.

Chapter Fourteen

More days pass in the dreary psych ward routine. Breakfast, medications, sit in a chair. Lunch, obnoxious therapy group/craft project/poodle visit, sit in a chair. Dinner, medications, lie in a bed and try not to listen to the suffocated sleep sounds and night terrors from the rooms beyond. Repeat *ad lib*, except you're not at liberty at all. My parents come every few days and bring me chocolate bars and other thoughtful gifts—last time it was a Neil Gaiman book on CD because I complained that the drugs make it difficult to read. The stories are mythic, demigods and demons and other fragile things that are only supposed to exist in fiction. I listen to them while perched on the windowsill in my room, looking out at the city beyond the hospital gates.

Zoë follows me around like an underfed puppy, complimenting my delicate wrists and high cheekbones. She says we should start a modeling agency when we get out of this place, rent a loft in New York City together. Ani gives me dark looks whenever she sees her in my company, even though I didn't exactly ask for it.

One morning I'm awakened from a drugged, dreamless sleep as someone opens the curtains beside my bed. I'm on my feet by the time the person turns to me, clutching the pocket where my Swiss Army knife normally resides.

"I'm glad you're up," says the nurse, as though blissfully unaware she is the causal factor in my awakening. "I need to get a blood sample."

"You took one yesterday."

"We need another one."

Zoë stirs in the other bed, sunlight shining on the gaunt angles of her face. I can't seem to focus my eyes properly, and a ghostly echo of the scene lies a few degrees off-center of the original. There is a dull ache in my kidney area and a sharp ache in my head.

"If you've got the needle, I can tell you where to stick it."

The nurse marches off to appeal to some higher authority, and I trail after her, ready to argue my case. Put your drugs in me, fine, but my blood is all I have left that's *mine.*

We meet Dr. Caspian entering the unit, avoiding eye contact with patients as he heads for the sanctuary of his office.

"This patient is refusing a blood draw," says the nurse in the same tone one might use to report the theft of a juice box or a teddy bear. "She's being very hostile and uncooperative."

Dr. Caspian does not seem surprised by this news. "Just move on to your next patient, Gloria," he says. "I'll take care of it."

The nurse looks faintly disappointed that my behavior doesn't warrant a nice humiliating shot of Haldol in the ass. Or maybe I'm just projecting. Dr Caspian walks over to the blood draw chair and taps the arm. "Sit down, Whitney. We need to take a blood sample to determine how your body is reacting to the medication."

I focus my eyes in a wintry stare. "Shake, Whitney. Lie down, Whitney. Roll over, Whitney, or you'll get the shock collar."

"There are serious complications that can arise from this medication, so we need to monitor your white cell counts carefully."

"You certainly glossed over that when you were telling me about this wonder drug."

"The condition is rare, and I believe the risks of the medication are outweighed by its benefits."

"Oh, my god, you're a utilitarian. I should have known."

"Please don't make this harder than it needs to be."

"Would you hold me down and take it if you had to?"

"Whitney . . ."

The air around me seems to have turned to shimmering gelatin, through which I plod lackadaisically to reach the chair. The tissue they use to cover the surface looks like butcher paper. It's strange to see Dr. Caspian handling a syringe, like a general stepping into the front lines of the infantry.

"Are you sure you know how to do this?" I ask.

"I vaguely remember a lecture or two on the subject at medical school." Dr. Caspian slides the needle from its plastic sheath with the careless precision of countless repetitions. He infiltrates the vein so painlessly that I can't even complain. In fact, he manages to do everything without touching me at all. With both our gazes held by my blood flowing darkly into the plastic tube, the only point of contact between us is the needle.

———•◦•———

I have become one of the others. Sitting with donut-glazed eyes on the horrible chairs, shredding mountains of tissue between restless fingertips. This ceaseless motor activation is a byproduct of the drug, which anesthetizes everything in the middle but forces the limbs into compensatory motion. My vision is hazy and abstract; at times there are two televisions, two Oprah Winfreys speaking earnestly about a new chocolate-flavored dietary drink mix.

"I can't see. I think I'm going blind."

Ani, sitting on the far end of the same grimy couch, glances languidly in my direction. "Everything's all swimmy and your eyes don't focus?"

"Yes. What's wrong with me?"

"What do you think? Rule Number One: Spit, don't swallow."

"The medication? But it's the only way."

"The only way to what? Deny your destiny?"

"What destiny? I'm no Joan of Arc, Ani, and it's not angels I'm hearing."

"Whitney, Whitney." Ani turns to face me, leans forward and takes my hands lightly in hers. The catty arch of her eyebrows suggests someone who *knows things*. "You think you gain anything staying here, listening to these doctors in their fancy suits who think they know everything about the world? Maybe you go to their little *dialectical* behavior therapy groups, maybe you watch some TV and take your pills, and meanwhile your entire destiny slips away. Our destiny is all we have. People who deny it don't turn black, they turn *gray*."

And suddenly, horribly, I see it. Everyone is gray. The color on the surface is only a formality. Beneath it, they are as fuzzy and colorless as mold on the surface of rotting jam.

"You been a good girl so far," continues Ani, "So they don't check your mouth. Just flick the pills up with your tongue into the space between your teeth and your cheek. Right above the dogtooth, the sharpest one. *Don't* put it under your tongue. The medicine gets into your blood real fast that way. Then go back to your room and spit it in the sink."

"I don't know."

"Trust me. And another thing, they won't let you take soda cans out of the dining room, but sometimes they're real stupid and don't check if the tab is missing. Just like a razor blade if you break off the top part. I always put one in my sleeve just in case."

"In case of what?"

"In case of needing it."

"Thanks Ani, you're a real Virgil."

"I keep body pure because it's the only way to see them, the angels. The spirit gates open only for those who burn for their Lord and Savior, Jesus Christ alone."

"They open for other people too," I tell her, and go to the window to remind myself there is still a world outside this place. The next time medications are given, I push the pills into the fold between my lip and my gum. Usually they make you wait in sight after they give medications, but sometimes they forget if they're busy or someone is freaking out, like the guy in the hall talking about giant spiders on the ceiling, and doesn't anyone see the giant spiders, and why doesn't someone kill the giant spiders. Nobody stops me as I walk back to my room.

The door is shut, even though they usually drift open as soon as you stop touching them. Dead weight resists as I push it open, but I shoulder through and see that someone has shoved one of the beds against the door. The lights are on in the bathroom and I hear running water.

"Zoë? Are you there?"

No reply. With a sense of foreboding, I step into the bathroom. The pills are melting in my mouth, bitter liquid streaming down my throat, but I hardly notice.

Zoë is jammed in the narrow space between the toilet and the wall, the way a child tries to hide behind something far too small. Foamy yellow vomit streaked on the toilet seat. Vivid spatters of blood on the floor. Something silver stuck in the soft flesh of her inner arm. Shards of CD gouged into her skin with enough force that they stand upright.

Zoë looks up at me. Conscious, not dead. It doesn't matter. Her eyes are devoid, a curtain drawn back to reveal an empty room.

"Checks," says a nurse outside the door. "What's going on . . . why is this bed here?" The nurse steps into the room and stands gaping for a moment, as though Zoë were a rare sea creature brought to light.

"I didn't do it," I say. "I found her like this."

The nurse has already gone for reinforcements. Two orderlies come in with a stretcher. They pull Zoë away from the wall, limp as a ragdoll. Her eyelids flutter protectively over sightless white crescents. Could I have imagined those empty seconds of empty stare? Her arm falls open at a sickening angle as they pull her out of the corner. The curve and paleness and the bright rivulets of blood make me think of a gutted fish. And the jarring silver shards, for which no analogy will be attempted. Maybe I make a noise, because one of the orderlies looks up and pushes me back out of the room.

"Go watch TV, sweetheart. We'll take care of this."

I go and sit in front of the television, obedient mammal. It was my CD, probably. Or maybe she borrowed someone else's. Maybe it was the Shakira CD. Does it even matter? Yes, it matters more than anything. I ask them, What CD was it? Was it Shakira or Nine Inch Nails? Please, I know it sounds crazy, but I need to know—

It's OK, they tell me, it's going to be OK, and do not answer my question. If it was my CD, I started the causal chain that led to that horrible picture. Maybe the lyrics told her everything she was afraid to tell herself, but she couldn't stop listening because then she would have to hear the sounds of a psych ward in darkness, the tranquilized breathing and apneic gasps for air, sometimes people screaming about Nazis or evil angels or purple dots under the bed. So she kept the music on, and somewhere in the night she lost hope, and it wouldn't have happened with Shakira, it just wouldn't.

Zoë is taken out of the ward on a stretcher. Several orderlies stand guard to make sure no one tries to make a break for it when the door opens. When they let me back into the room, the air smells of lemon bleach and the floor gleams. The bed is made with tight hospital corners and there is no trace another person was ever here. I spend the rest of the day in the quiet hall with Nietzsche. Information is water and my mind is oil and the two try hard not to mix, but Nietzsche is worth struggling for, so I trickle the words in a phoneme at a time until they form a perfect, shattering whole.

What if some day or night, a demon were to steal after you in your loneli-
est loneliness, and say to you, "This life, as you now live it and have lived it,
you will have to live once more, and innumerable times more, and there will
be nothing new in it, but every pain and every joy, every thought and sigh,
and everything unutterably small or great in your life will return to you, all
in the same succession and sequence—even this spider, and this moonlight
between the trees; even this moment, and I myself. The eternal hourglass of
existence is turned over again and again, and you with it, speck of dust."
Would you not throw yourself down, gnash your teeth and curse the demon
who spoke thus? Or have you once experienced that tremendous moment when
you would have answered him—

A shadow falls over me. I look up and see Dr. Caspian.

"How are you today? I meant to check on you earlier, but I've
been . . . busy."

"How's Zoë?"

Dr. Caspian's expression turns wary.

"Is she dead?"

"I can't discuss my other patients, Whitney. But I'm sure it must
have been a shock, finding her there. Would you like to talk about it? I
can arrange for one of the counselors to meet with you."

"How thoughtful of you. No, I'm fine."

"What about the medication? Any side effects?"

"Nausea, terror, dry mouth and trembling. Status quo."

"We still haven't reached therapeutic levels, so I'd like to increase
the dose again today." His voice is so perfunctory that I wonder how
many times he's said the same words this week, this afternoon. Some
regulatory mechanism inside me snaps with a stinging recoil.

"As a matter of fact, I'm not finding your drugs to be therapeutic at
any levels, and I've had enough of your arrogant presumption that you
know exactly how my brain functions. You've never seen inside it, so
you're really just guessing like the rest of us."

"Whitney, it hasn't even been a week. If you'll just give the medication a chance . . ."

"Don't you get it? You *can't* fix what's wrong with me. We're so
stupid, all of us, searching for answers, for anything beyond ourselves.
And then something finds us in the dark and for as long as we live we
are *never . . . alone . . . again.*"

I am shouting now, and I seem to have risen to my feet. My Nietzsche compendium goes sailing out of my hands and crashes against the wall near Dr. Caspian's head. Two nurses hurry over, drawn by the noise. One is uncapping a syringe. Dr. Caspian holds up a hand, almost sharply. "Leave her, I'll handle it."

They shrug, doubtful, but retreat.

"It was probably my CD that killed her," I say, sinking to the floor with my back against the wall. "Not everyone can handle Nine Inch Nails."

"She's not dead," says Dr. Caspian. I notice suddenly how deep the creases in his forehead are, how tired and absent he always looks, and how he always has to deal with it. Every time someone creates violent art out of their forearms or sees giant spiders on the ceiling or just can't take it anymore, he has to stop the damage, try to set the world right.

"I know you feel sick," says Dr. Caspian, "but your body will adjust to the medication, and the side effects will diminish in time."

"Will they really? Because I hear the other patients, the ones who've been like this since they were my age, complaining about the exact same things. Maybe I could take it if it were a week or a month until I were cured. But it's a lifetime of *this*. Of holding a pillow over his face, but he doesn't breathe so it doesn't matter, and there is no fucking cure."

"No, there isn't a cure. I wish I could offer you one. But these drugs are the best treatment we have, and . . ." Dr. Caspian seems to run out of kinetic energy midsentence. He looks at me and the black centers of our eyes align for one brief measure of time in which all my rage and helpless terror seethe directly into him, and he takes it without flinching. And I see enough of him in the gap to know that he means everything he says, that he is not in the Mafia and he is only tired and distant because he has so many futures to keep from ending, and he has lost ones before, and he sees how close he is to losing one now, maybe a favorite if he could have favorites, if we were kittens instead of patients.

"Once upon a time," I say, reciting from the book I have just thrown at my psychiatrist's head, "poured out and glittering among innumerable solar systems, there existed a star on which some clever animals invented knowledge. That was the highest and most mendacious minute of world history—but only a minute. After nature had drawn a few breaths, the star grew cold, and so the clever animals had to die."

Dr. Caspian looks at me for a long time without speaking. I sense that he would touch my shoulder or my hand if it was allowed. "I'm sorry this is happening to you, Whitney," he says finally, and in one true moment does not reassure me that it will be OK. He rests a hand briefly on the arm of my chair, then continues down the hall to his next patient, to talk another defeated soul away from the abyss.

I think maybe I have been doing this for eternity and the cycle of birth and decay is having some kind of additive effect on my cells, wearing out the matter, the very elements themselves. I don't retrieve my book from where it has landed on the floor. Nietzsche's demon is too familiar to look in the eye, and I am already so close to collapsing under the weight of this moment alone.

CHAPTER FIFTEEN

That night I awaken to hard iron breathing. A fever seeping dragonlike inside me, heat blazing through my mouth. I stagger down the hall to the nurse's station and ask for pineapple juice, which my mother always gave me when I was sick. Sure, they say, we'll get you pineapple juice, then bring me some kind of juice, but not pineapple. Yellow does not a pineapple make. This situation must be rectified. I inform the nurses that I was promised pineapple juice.

"What did they give you?"

"Swill." Sweat prickles on my skin and chills me as it evaporates. Everything seems blurred and indistinct, an impressionist painting of a psych ward. The nurses close the window through which medications are dispensed.

"She does look a little delirious."

"She's psychotic, what do you expect? Send her back to bed."

"Yeah, *Guiding Light* comes on at eleven."

"I wonder if we'll find out who's the father of Dinah's baby."

Actually, I made that conversation up. They say something I can't hear through the glass.

I tap the window. "Excuse me, I think I'm dying."

The window slides open. "You're not dying. Your body is getting used to the higher dose of medicine. Now go back to bed before—"

"I'm pretty sure I know a fucking pineapple when I see one." I step away from the desk and collapse on the floor. My head strikes linoleum with a surprising visual starburst, but I feel no pain from the impact. Staccato footsteps and a cold hand on my wrist.

"Christ, she's hot. Get a read on her."

Something penetrates my ear and a blood pressure cuff tightens around my arm, then relaxes. "One-oh-four point five, and her blood pressure isn't even registering."

"I'll page the on-call."

After that, some twilight moments at the edge of consciousness. I awaken from time to time with people standing over me, prodding me with needles and instruments, but I take little interest in their coming and going. When my mind finally clears, it's daylight and I'm in a bed with an IV catheter taped to the back of my hand. A nurse comes in and takes my vital signs.

"Your temperature is down, and your blood pressure has stabilized," she says. She opens a plastic container resting on the bedside table. "Drink this. If you can keep it down, we'll take the IV out."

I sip the juice, yellow and acidic.

"Is that what you wanted?"

"It's fine, thanks."

"Just fine? After all that fuss about pineapple juice, we had to hijack some from pediatrics."

"It's good. Thank you." My hand shakes and sloshes juice down my shirt. I'm about to ask what happened when someone knocks perfunctorily on the door, then enters the room. The Doctor has come to pay a house call, and the nurse slips out with a deferential smile.

"Nice job, Dr. Doom," I say. "Apparently your utilitarian calculus got a little fucked up somewhere. The drug is supposed to make me less dead than I otherwise would be, right?"

"This medication can occasionally trigger adverse events," says Dr. Caspian, his gaze trained on a faint stain on the wall behind me. Like a Rorschach blot . . . I wonder what he sees. "It's a rare reaction, especially at moderate doses," he says. "It figures you'd be the one—" He stops himself short, covers it up by saying, "We'll give you a few days to get the drug out of your system. Then we'll try a low dose of—of something else." He seems at a loss, close to apologizing for something he clearly is not going to take blame for.

But I'm not willing to let it go that easily. "You know the difference between you and *him*? When *he* wants his way, he doesn't pretend to share the power. And I want one of those forms, to leave against medical advice. Seventy-two hours . . . that's how long you can keep me once I sign it."

"And what happens when you leave, and this entity of yours comes back and tells you to . . . do something harmful?" Clearly, he does not want to give me specific suggestions.

"I don't know. I don't know anything except that being here and taking your drugs hasn't fixed anything. I'm done with this place."

Dr. Caspian regards me for a moment, then nods curtly and exits the room. Part of me wants to call after him and say *wait*, how can you give up so easily? But the rest of me is ready to stop this horrible dialectic also. One way or another, the situation will be played out to the end.

———◆———

The next afternoon I sit hunched over a scrap of Sudoku puzzle in the TV room, and suddenly my breath is taken away. I see the deep equilibrium, the same crystalline logic as the unknowable writing on the physics blackboard. Maybe an algorithm for the rhythm of hearts and the transcription of proteins and the expansion of galaxies, all locked into a little Japanese number game because the universe is whimsical like that. I imagine walking up to Dr. Caspian and saying, "It's funny, did you know that in every one of these puzzles, an exponent of the sum of the rows raised to the fourth power adds up to the square of the difference of the columns, and if you take this number and multiply it by itself, it divides perfectly into *pi*?" or something like that. Doctors have to be pretty good at math, so he'll see the underlying truth, even though he never would have thought to manipulate the numbers that way, and he'll show it to someone else, maybe a polymath colleague, and my proof will be published in one of those journals that publishes math, and eventually someone will give me a Nobel Prize and all the pains and insults and sleepless nights will be atoned for, and this will mean something after all.

I scribble furiously on scraps of anything I can find—torn bits of magazine, meal menus that no one bothered to fill out because the choices are all equally depressing. But after two hours I have nothing but a jumble of grade-school ciphers, and I seem to have added 28 and 7 wrong in my calculations. John Nash I am not. I fall back into my cotton wool apathy, allowing myself to be mesmerized by the spinning Wheel of Fortune without trying to figure out where the wheel will fall, or how I can use this to save the world or destroy it or even just understand.

"Whitney," calls a nurse from the medication window, "Come get your meds."

I stuff my dead-ended equations beneath the chair cushion and walk over to the window. "I'd really rather not," I say. "In fact, I'm pretty sure that your drugs are merely obfuscating truth and allowing you to deny uncomfortable contingencies. You don't even know how they work, but you offer them with such assurance. Doesn't that bother you at all?"

"Dr. Caspian ordered this medication for you. He's a very smart man . . . he went to Harvard, you know." Evidently, she has been observing me and knows me better than I realized. Still, I am not swayed, and I continue to stand in bleary nonviolent protest.

Patients drift around me. A woman with a Down syndrome face steps up to the window, a stuffed rabbit clutched to her chest.

"Here's your medication, Karen," says the nurse, handing her a paper cup.

"She's ahead of me," says the woman, jabbing a finger in my direction.

I step out of line. "No, I'm not."

"I'm not taking it either," the woman says slowly. "I think that girl's right. You don't know as much as you say."

"You need to take your medication, Karen," says the nurse with steely authority in her voice.

"No."

"I know," says the nurse. "Why don't we give some medicine to your bunny? Then you'll see that it won't hurt you."

A shabby suicide attempt, bloated and sour-faced, snorts derisively behind her. "God almighty fucking loons." He is a CEO by daylight. He shouts this aloud when pretty nurses try to tell him to do something. But stripped of his suit and tie and trapped between the locked doors, he is only one of us. He wears a hospital johnny over a white undershirt because his wife has not yet come to bring him clothes. Possibly his wife has left him, which is why he swallowed a bottle of Valium and a bottle of Scotch in rapid succession. He's on an antidepressant but not an antipsychotic, so he probably really is a CEO. There is no privacy here.

"Here's some medicine for your bunny." The nurse presses a paper cup against the rabbit's snout.

"His name is Hector."

"Sorry, Hector." The rabbit's nose is made of pink velvet. Its button eyes are so black and bright that one can almost imagine life in them.

"See, now you can take—"

The woman shrieks, a piercing cry that causes the necks of even the most catatonic patients to snap around.

"YOU KILLED HIM!"

"Oh *Christ.*" mutters the nurse. The CEO snickers.

"YOU KILLED HIM HE'S NOT BREATHING OH MY GOD MY GOD YOU KILLED HIM. HECTOR . . . HECTOR . . ."

The woman has sunk to her knees with her body shielding the rabbit. Her cries thin out to a whimper. No one is laughing now. All the staff on the unit have gathered, and even Dr. Caspian has been drawn from his office by the noise. The psych techs immobilize the woman and stick her with a syringe. They surround her and bear her away to the isolation room where her lamentations echo unheard from the padded walls. Within a few minutes, the evening nurse has returned to her station.

"You can come and get your medications now," she says, addressing the room as though nothing out of the ordinary has happened. Perhaps it's all in a day's work to her, this business of poisoning innocent stuffed animals, but we the insane are not so similarly jaded. No one moves.

"Did everyone hear me?" she says with an edge to her voice. *"Medications* are *ready."*

"Fuck you," says the CEO.

"Fucking Nazi," says the old man who played chess with me, or one who looks a lot like him. "Fucking rabbit-killing Nazi."

"Autocratic slave to material reductivism," says Ani, looking pleased.

The nurse slams the window and calls the other staff for a conference. Dr. Caspian has gone home, and they are paging the on-call psychiatrist from another unit. I go back to my room and notice something under the bed. A sparkly hair elastic. Suddenly, I am sure they have lied to me and Zoë is dead. And the woman with the rabbit, she'll never come back either. I have reached the point of no return, fatalistic enough to be a character in a Russian novel, to merely shrug at some universal audience and say, "These things will happen. Such is the way of the world." But following Zoë's advice, I slip a metal soda tab into my sleeve at the next mealtime. These things will not happen to me.

"You have a revolutionary's gift," Dr. Caspian says, taking the seat across from mine in the hall. The orange vinyl clashes with the fine material of his suit. "I spent most of this morning coaxing people back onto their meds."

Another of those qualities that sounds so good on paper. A revolutionary's gift and a surgeon's hands. Yet all I've managed to do with them is stir psychiatric patients to revolt and slice up various parts of my own anatomy.

"I wasn't trying to proselytize. I don't care what they do. They shouldn't listen to me."

"But they did. Some of them were very upset."

"Yes." I wonder if she still has the rabbit, if she clutches it now as a lifeless corpse. If it has regenerated into a new Hector, or she has asked for it to be burned or buried or embalmed.

"How are you feeling today?" says Dr. Caspian. The cuff of his sleeve edges into a pool of milk someone has spilt on the chair. He recoils at the dampness and brushes at the spot, looking annoyed. "Any recurrence of auditory hallucinations?" The milk spot is definitely preoccupying him. He seems to be mentally tabulating the dry cleaning bill.

"It insults him when you call him that."

Dr. Caspian stares at me.

"No. No recurrence."

"You'll be discharged from the unit this afternoon, as you requested. I don't think you're an imminent danger to yourself or others, and legally, I cannot compel you to stay. But I'm worried about you nonetheless."

"I appreciate your concern for my welfare."

"You didn't seem this angry when I met you, Whitney."

"I'm not angry, I'm cynical. There's a difference. I'm not sure what, but it sounds more clever. It's really all I've got at this point. Knowing words to place me above the situation. I think if my own brain were lying on the ground, I'd step on it and squash it like a slug. I wonder if I'd see him in it, like a parasite engorged among the tissue. But don't worry, it's only my words that are alarming. Like most mental patients I'm really quite docile, so I'm sure there's no need to be afraid."

Dr. Caspian clears his throat. "Do you have any plans for when you're released from the unit?"

"I want to go back to school. I'm *already failing*, of course, but I've become attached to my fetal pig. I'd like to say goodbye to him before the semester ends."

Hours later, the vault-like doors open for me once more. My parents are grim and silent, maybe wondering if this will become a habit. I jump in my skin as something clinks to the ground beside me in the elevator. Only the soda can tab fallen from my sleeve. At the reception desk, I claim my Swiss Army knife and the other things that were taken from me when I was admitted. On the ride home, the world passing by the window looks like an alien planet. People walking dogs, chasing taxis, striding along with briefcases and self-important airs. Through a tunnel I see my face reflected in the glass, pale as a cave-dwelling frog with eerily reflective eyes, unreadable even to myself.

What have I done, what can I say? Unless I'm deceived, the girl's gone gray.
Tell me you do not speak in rhyme now.

No no only when I'm happy. Veryvery happy. Proudly preening on my pretty perch. Prediction is matching up beautifully with the collapse sequence. Barely a trickblur when laid across one another. You're destined for great things, softsoftsoft as butter.

My head spins with his bright bursts of repetition, helium pitched and unlike anything I have heard from him. Isn't he angry?

Angry? Certainly not. His voice regains its knife-edge composure.
You came back to me.

CHAPTER SIXTEEN

*Y*ou *are cutting that potato very badly.*
You have no sense of potato geometry. Destroy yourself at once.

I continue to chop vegetables with more aggression than necessary. I am making minestrone soup to show that I am a fully functioning human being, not an empty shell, not one of those people who will eventually procure a shopping cart and fill it with trash that cries out to be saved, and converse with this trash and enjoy its company better than that of the people around me.

Unfortunately, the bell pepper I cut into next is moldy. Rotting vegetable matter fills me with unspeakable horror, and my stomach lurches as the knife collapses into the cancerous interior. Trying not to gag, I sweep everything into the trash and lean against the counter. The knife on the cutting board flashes oddly in my field of vision. It *smiles*, wickedly.

Don't be stupid, I tell him. But my hand takes hold of the knife and it moves toward my eye, the point digging into the soft crease beneath my orbital bone, creating a black circle ringed with light in my field of vision. How often do you get to see inside yourself? I want . . .

But soma is not so easily seduced as psyche. My hand jerks and the knife falls to the floor with a clatter. In the meantime, the soup has burnt on the stove. By the time I serve dinner, skimmed from the top of the pot, I've plotted out an affectedly normal conversation about the new season of *American Idol*, which I was subjected to somewhat involuntarily on the psych ward but now makes for excellent sane-person conversation. That Chris Daughtry, how cute is *he*? Possibly this comes off as trying too hard, but this sort of thing doesn't come naturally to me. Or if it once did, not anymore.

———◆———

Night is worst. In darkness, formless things can too easily be given shape in the mind's eye. I sleep a little in the warm glow of my bedside lamp, but invariably awaken in the deepest part of the night when the light seems to be consumed greedily by the darkness, the circle of illumination smaller than mere physics should dictate.

I was dreaming something delicate and wonderful: castles made of nothing, or hunting Easter eggs that are also souls. Something utterly separate from all this, suffused with a wonder and calm that makes me ache to stay forever. But it's not to be. The world vanishes and the light seems to tremble as I open my eyes, as if it knows what burden it bears, how desperately I need it not to falter. Still reactive from losing the dream, I feel a deep affection for the burning bulb and its weak halo. Since sleep would create the possibility of dreaming and I could not bear to dream again, I turn to my books for distraction. There is a vague comfort in the dry descriptions of the fetal pig alimentary canal.

". . . The proximal two-fifths of the small intestine is known as the jejunum, and the remainder is the ileum. A double-layered fold of peritoneal membrane called the mesentery suspends these areas from the posterior portion of the abdominal wall . . ."

Science won't save you, little seeker
this idol offers no eternity.

I'd wondered at the now unheard of combination of nighttime and peace. Where can he possibly have been?

Having my dinner.

". . . The colon from the cecum to the splenic flexure is known as the right colon. The remainder is known as the left colon . . ."

Slivered heartache, he replies unasked.
Balsamic reduction of broken will,
slurry of innocence.

With a creeping unease, I notice how his voice sounds more real in my head than my own, his tones richer and more varied. He is so comfortable with my neurons, they *want* to obey him. There is some

Cartesian split, some isolated piece of soul that rebels utterly, but it is small and feeble, a little girl's voice in a warehouse filled with great machines. Which of us is the hallucination, which of us owns this body?

I am your mirror, your mask, your master.

I am your divinity in darkness.

You do not exist. Entities should not be multiplied beyond necessity. Occam's razor.

He does not answer, and does not need to, because he knows as I know that in my heart of hearts, I could not say which of us needs to be negated.

Realizing the futility of studying for my quiz at the rate of six words per minute with frequent interruptions, I abandon my textbook and head for the kitchen. I pass my father's study in the hall, the door cracked open to reveal shelves of dusty books on law and poetry and communication with the dead, bottles of rare alcohol and amusing packets of foreign foods: Mushy Peas from England, Mr. Squid Snacks from Thailand. There used to be a large assortment of firearms as well, but these have been transferred to a locked safe in the basement.

From within the room, I can hear the rise and fall of my father's voice chanting *"Om Namah Shivaya."* It's still disconcerting to realize that parents are seekers, like everyone else, that they do not know some unequivocal truth against which you may or may not choose to rebel. Sometimes I wonder if my father ever truly embraced the doctrines of Christianity or if he only wanted to raise his child with unambiguous morals, since I did not seem to come equipped with a set of my own. But it was characteristic that he would live rigidly by the conventions of a jealous faith for more than a decade and compel his family to do the same, only to cast them aside for some reason only he would ever know. *A foolish consistency is the hobgoblin of little minds,* he used to say. For my whole life people have told me how much I am like him, and I've never known whether to take it as a compliment.

I continue down the hall and pause again at the doorway to my mother's studio, where she is painting at her easel. The house is filled with her illustrations—lifelike, dreamlike oils of worlds that never were. A taxidermy fox wearing a plaid scarf crouches in the shadows atop a bookshelf, poised to pounce. My mother turns to dip her brush in a jar of cloudy water and startles as she sees me standing motionless in the doorway.

"Whitney—I didn't know you were there." She presses a hand to her chest, almost theatrically, as though she is accentuating surprise to mask actual fear. I stare at the painting, a herd of unicorns running through the outskirts of a bleak industrial city. It's for a book she's illustrating, a children's poem, *Where Have the Unicorns Gone?* It looks real. Everything my mother paints looks real. It's funny how all things symbolic seem to contain more life than the objects around us that exist so mundanely, so vulgar in the certainty of their own truth.

"Is something the matter?" asks my mother, her hand still pressed against her heart. I shake my head, but the sorrow has grown too cold and heavy inside me to continue on in silence. It's like a piece of spoiled food that must be ejected from my body before the sickness can pass.

"I'm sorry," I say finally, my eyes still trained on the unicorn fleeing the urban wreckage. *Silken and swift and silver they streak, they have galloped through yesterday into next week . . .*

"Sorry for what?" My mother's eyes search my body for new signs of damage.

I close my eyes. "Everything."

They have all disappeared to the back of beyond and into the flowering moment of dawn . . .

"Do you want me to call Dr. Caspian?" says my mother, alarmed because I have probably never apologized for anything before. "Do you need to go back to the hospital?"

"No," I say, taking a few steps back. "I'm fine."

Buddhists say that certain souls are incarnated together into families to force each person to confront lessons unlearned in previous lives. I hope my purpose here is not to teach my parents about the pain of attachment, how all things leave us before we are ready to let them go. I start to turn away, then pause. "The painting," I say haltingly. "Is very pretty."

I go downstairs and take a jar of peanut butter from the refrigerator, dissolving it by the spoonful in my mouth until the jar is empty but I am no less so than I was before. I used to play games with food when I was young, like imagining that I was an ogre and my soup was a teeming ocean that fed an island of tiny people. One by one I would consume each ingredient, the carrot fish and the noodle eels and the chicken whales until the imaginary people were left to starve on a pillaged planet. But now I lack the whimsy to do anything but mechanically integrate the fats and proteins into my body. My psychology professor told us that all kinds of happy neurochemicals are released when we eat, that all the deep and ancient parts of our brains really want is to be fed. This is where the Other has taken up residence, these reptilian structures, and his latest interest is vicariously sampling, through me, the contents of the refrigerator.

I am furious because the pasty bulge around my midsection is swelling by the day, but there are compensations. Nearly as much as words the Other likes to play with chemicals, to make them form brain states that amuse him and leave their host enraged, aroused, or nauseated in turn. I can still think my own thoughts during these times, but it hardly matters because they only declare *And so much for free will* before abandoning themselves to each moment of hostage emotion. I have always been so coldly rational by nature that passions melt on contact to a lukewarm twinge with all the appeal of a watered-down Coke. It is enthralling to *feel things* with such clarity and force. I drown in them like an Epicurean lost in a mouthful of century-old wine, bittersweet and subtle, beyond my natural means. This is the true meaning of intoxication: being not the consumer but the consumed.

Tonight is just a night of quiet melancholy, a hunger that cannot be satisfied with food but will compel me to consume vast amounts of it regardless.

Give me a cookie, says the Other. *The nice ones with the shortbread and jam.*

In the milky ghost light of just past midnight, my patchwork cat Sasha pads into the kitchen toward his bowl of dry food, belly slung low to the ground. He merps an affectionate greeting when he sees me and searches my face with troubled eyes. He worries about me.

Oh, delicious, says the Other with glee. *Meat to feed the starving orphans for a week.*

"Shut up," I mumble aloud, my words lacking conviction even to my own ears, so often have they been repeated and ignored. Sasha looks at me anxiously, unsure if my words are directed toward him.

"It's OK," I say in the most comforting tone I can manage. He gives me a last doubtful glance and waddles to his dish. A moment later, a deafening *crunch, crunch, crunch* fills the room. There is no noise quite so loud as a cat eating cat food in a quiet room at night.

I consume the requested cookie and then another for good measure. This pleases the Other so much that he makes the ooze of strawberry jam between my teeth feel something like sexual release. The night's performance ends when the box is empty, leaving me numb until the encore. The black curtain falls and the audience of one sits in stony silence. Sometimes I wonder where the Other goes when he leaves me. Sometimes I wish he would take me with him and never bring me back.

My mother has left her studio when I go back upstairs, and my father's study is dark. I'm glad they are getting some sleep. But a moment later, I hear the scuff of slippers in the hall. My door cracks open and I hear my father's voice say a few words I can't make out—they could be a Sanskrit mantra or a line from a Christian prayer. The door starts to close, but I must have made some kind of noise or otherwise betrayed my awakeness, because it opens again and my father stands in the doorway. I meant to feign sleep, but instead I sit up and we look at one another across my chaotic sea of a child's outgrown room. Horse posters everywhere, *Black Stallion* and *Saddle Club* books on the shelves, rocks with sedimentary stripes or chips of quartz that seemed so beautiful sparkling in riverbeds or parking lots that I had to put them in my pocket and take them home, where they remained in my room and faded into ordinary things that I nonetheless refused to return to nature.

"I'm tired," I finally say, which is stupid because I'm already in bed, I'm resting, all I ever do now is rest in borrowed silence, but I never sleep. My father enters the room and sits at the edge of the bed.

"When I was a child," he says, and this seems even more like a dream because my father doesn't tell stories about his life, not unless they contain moral lessons in disguise. For example, he was so poor in college that he once had nothing to eat for an entire month but popcorn coated with wheat germ. I know that his father collected antiques and raised peacocks—we have a vase full of their feathers in the dining room—and that his sister accidentally spin-dried his pet cat to death, but little else.

There is one story about his mother that he tells only after a glass or two of spirits, on occasion: Once upon a time, she returned from grocery shopping to find that one of her lamps had been broken. My father had three sisters, and his mother made all the children sit at the table in the normally forbidden parlor, and returned with four glasses of soda. This was a treat, because they were only allowed soda when they had company. And she said, "One of these glasses is poisoned. You will either drink your sodas one by one and lose a sister or brother today, or someone will tell me who broke my lamp."

My father always has a good laugh when he tells this anecdote, as if it were one of the more amusing incidents in his early years. And for all I know, it was. My parents have saturated me with so many stories and words, marinated me in them since I was born, yet there is a silence between us in which whole litanies could be swallowed, epic poems consumed.

"When I was a child," says my father, "younger than you, I became sick with a fever that wouldn't go away. I was confined to my room for weeks, and one night I awoke to find a demon sitting at the foot of my bed. I was paralyzed, unable to fight it off, and the demon offered me a deal. It would let me live, but only if I acknowledged that it was real. I knew if I agreed, the demon would follow me for as long as I lived. I had to defeat it before my fever would break, but it seemed impossible. In fact, there was only one way. I had to let it inside me, let it crawl right in and trick it into thinking it could stay. That's the only way to deal with them . . . when they become a part of you, you've won. For the rest of your life, you won't be shadowed by demons—you will say, 'I am a demon, but I choose to be good.'"

My father looks at me with eyes I hardly know, although I've never seemed to escape their scrutiny.

"I'm afraid," he says, "that you were born here from a darker place, dear one." It's moments before this makes sense to me, as though it first had to be translated from another language. Although the books and bronze idols have inhabited my father's study for years, this is the first I've heard him speak of reincarnation.

"I've been hard on you, and I'm sorry," he says. "You're here to learn different lessons than the ones I tried to teach you." He reaches up and briefly rests his hand on the crown of my head. From my clandestine perusals of his bookshelves, I know that this is the *Sahasrara* chakra, the body's connection to the divine. This is where the Other curls to rest, where he blocks the way.

My father lets his hand drop and leaves my room. As the door closes behind him, some far-flung shard of grace seems to pierce my heart. In the middle of the longest night I have ever known, I am filled with a stillness that no demon can simulate or take away, that is not a product of chemicals or their absence. Come morning I will be called again to fight my own war, but for this night I rest in the silence of a sacred protection.

CHAPTER SEVENTEEN

"Can I go to church with you?" I ask my mother on Sunday morning. For a moment, she looks so surprised that I wonder if I've spoken in long-lost Latin unearthed in the constant raking of my brain and its contents. I haven't gone willingly to church since I was a child, and even then I was mostly there for the coffee-hour doughnuts, gathering as many as I dared onto a paper plate to sustain me while I doodled dinosaur-centric illustrations for the Bible stories in my Sunday school book, anticipating the Internet meme by a solid decade.

Yet even though the system is riddled with inconsistencies and forbids the most interesting activities, I could never share the contempt that most of my peers have for organized religion, or any notion of a guiding purpose in their lives. As my capacity for nuanced thought began to develop along with all those tantalizing and inconvenient secondary sexual characteristics, I began to understand why some people would want to relinquish their souls to a higher power. Otherwise, we must rely on some tenuous notion of social contracts to keep our desires in check, and the image of good and evil battling it out on some universal stage is appealing in this world of mundane tragedies. The rituals alone are so beautiful that I can see why some would place them on a higher pedestal than freedom.

And now, in the year of the demon, who is there to turn to but God? There are many from which I could choose, but this is the god of my bittersweet childhood memories, the god of stained glass. My mother and I drive in silence for a while, then she puts on NPR. I writhe in my seat until she takes the hint and turns it off again. I know it's not rational, but I just can't tolerate words without bodies, even if they are only speaking of bee farmers or the war.

My mother is in the choir, but I'd sooner independently solve the first law of thermodynamics than sing on key, so I sit in the congregation below. The familiar hymns are like a balm, even if their content is shadowed by doubt. As people line up for communion, I notice an unfamiliar icon in a glass case near the altar. The parishioners prostrate themselves before it. Father Gregory reads from the list of souls who are in particular need of divine intervention. I am startled when I hear my own name alongside the pious old ladies who are now dying of cancer.

When the service is over, people come up to me and ask how I'm doing. Kindly and without specifics—clearly my mother has been talking. She is still upstairs with the choir, practicing for the Christmas service. I can hear strains of "Silent Night" drifting down from above. As people file downstairs for coffee hour, I go up to the altar to take a closer look at the icon. The image is of Mary and the child Jesus, framed in metallic, almost garish gold-plated haloes. But the icon is damaged, wet—liquid is streaming from Mary's eyes and the strip of cotton wool that lines the case is saturated with an oily amber fluid. The air around me is scented with an almost painful sweetness.

"Incredible, isn't it?" says someone behind me. I turn and see Father Gregory standing behind me in his gold robes. He is a kind man—he speaks of God with joy, not threats of damnation, and I've always liked him.

"Why does it do that?" I ask stupidly, even though I think I mean to say how.

"It was an ordinary icon once, until the priest of a small parish in Pennsylvania found the Theotokos weeping, and the stand on which she rested dripping with her tears."

My first impulse is to ask whether they've done any tests to see if it's a fake, if the icon was somehow hollowed out and filled with oil.

"Your mother has told me of your recent struggles," says Father Gregory. "She's asked me to pray for you."

"I don't really believe in God anymore," I say. "If I did, it would only be to restore a sense of equilibrium. Some white chess pieces to balance out the black ones. He doesn't speak to me."

"Nor to me, although I have spent much of my life in his service."

"Camus called it the unreasonable silence of the universe."

"Camus? That's right, you're in college now. I still remember you as a little girl. You always stared out the window during the service."

"I was staring *at* the window, actually. Whenever I imagined souls, that's what I thought of—stained glass. But I don't know if I ever really believed in God. It's just what I was told. Except now I think maybe it's the most convincing proof of his goodness, if not his existence, that he doesn't condescend to words. They're like snakes weaving lies to tempt us. They make us into gods, or else they turn us into demons."

"Is that what you think you are? A demon?" Father Gregory speaks lightly but not with reassurance, no amused connotations of absurdity.

"No, that was wrong. I misspoke. We don't become demons, we have them. They possess us. Isn't that true?"

Father Gregory stares at me with a peculiar intensity, and I squirm beneath his gaze like a cockroach under a magnifying glass. "Yes," he says finally. "All beings on this earth are children of God."

"And the demons, are there rituals to make them leave?" I ask.

"The Orthodox Church has prayers of exorcism. But it's not like the movie—there is no tying you down, no spewing of fluids. Most of our demons leave us quietly, ashamed before God, when we ask for his light to penetrate the darkest corners of our hearts."

I am fairly certain my demon will not leave quietly, but I don't know what to say in warning. "Can you do them now?" I ask.

Father Gregory brings me to a small room beside the altar. He takes a red book of prayers from a cabinet and tells me to kneel. I dig my palms into the bristles of the carpet, hoping to pierce the skin. I do not see how this can be done without blood. Father Gregory rests an embroidered cloth on my head and begins with some preliminary Lord Have Mercies before he changes to a sterner voice.

"Be rebuked and depart, all unclean spirits residing in this host. Come forth and depart from this His created image!" It sounds impressive in the small room, but he is really thundering no more than a professor driving the finality of a due date home.

"O Satan, through us His unworthy servants command thee and all the power which worketh with thee to remove thyself from him who hath been sealed in the Name of our Lord Jesus Christ, our True God."

My eyes move restlessly over the faded carpet. This is little more than a civil request; where is the fire, the brimstone, the threat? I had hoped the Other would cry out in agony from within me, singed and cauterized by the light of the Holy Spirit. I wouldn't have minded cracking my head against the wall a few times if he would have felt it too.

"Banish from your servant every evil and unclean spirit hidden and lurking in her heart, the spirit of error, the spirit of evil, the spirit of idolatry and all covetousness. May the Lord rebuke thee, O Satan."

Father Gregory continues for a while in a similar vein, then says some bland, sweet prayers about forgiveness and virtue, like a sorbet to cleanse the spiritual palate, before he closes the book and removes the cloth from my head. My hands are mottled from the rough carpet, but not bleeding. Father Gregory dips a palm spear into a vial of holy water and brushes a cross onto my forehead. I don't feel a sting of some psychic wound being disinfected, or hear the leathery flap of departing wingbeats. Yet doesn't the sun shining through the window seem more radiant than before? Surely there is some revelation in this silence.

When we go out into the main part of the church, Father Gregory opens the case that covers the weeping icon. He tears away a tuft of the soaked cotton wool and offers it to me. "Peace be with you, Whitney Anna," he says, using my baptismal name. He gives me a beeswax candle to light by the altar, then goes downstairs to join his flock for coffee and doughnuts.

I light my candle and dig it into the sand with a dozen others burning down in staggered lengths. Some have already gone out. The stained glass saints are clear and bright with the morning light streaming through their bodies. John the Baptist walking on water, Saint Nicholas surrounded by children, Agnes with her lamb. Most of them gaze gravely into some middle distance, but Agnes the virgin martyr wears a knowing smile. My footsteps make a hollow sound as I walk the perimeter of the church. When I reach the door I feel a crawling desire to look back and see if my candle is still lit, but I don't indulge it.

Downstairs, the children are having Sunday school. Small feet kick restlessly under the table as a girl stands up to read from the Bible. She has butterfly clips in her long blonde hair. "Now, the serpent was more crafty than any beast of the field which the Lord God had made," she recites in the precise reading voice of a precocious child. "And he said to the woman, 'Indeed, has God said you shall not eat from any tree of the garden?'"

On a table in the corner, there is coffee and homemade Albanian pastries. I pile my plate high and listlessly pick the walnuts from a piece of baklava. The pervasive scent of incense, sweet as golden raisins, is beginning to nauseate me. Maybe it's a side effect of exorcism. Maybe I will literally vomit him up, some black and vile fluid that will ooze into the sewers of its own accord. Or perhaps I'm only allergic to church.

The girl reads on. "And the woman said to the serpent, 'From the fruit of the trees of the garden we may eat. But from the fruit of the tree which is in the middle of the garden, God has said, "You shall not eat from it or touch it, or you will die."'"

She has apparently reached the end of the page, and sits down to let another child take a turn, but I mumble the rest of the passage from memory. "And the serpent said to the woman, 'Surely you will not die, for God knows that when you eat from it, your eyes will be opened, and you will be like God, knowing good and evil.'"

Of all the stories in the Bible, the temptation and fall of Eve. Can that possibly be an accident? My senses vibrate in anticipation of that cold sardonic voice, but there is only the drone of conversation punctuated by a burst of decorous church laugher.

With a clatter of scraping chairs and thumping books, the children are dismissed from Sunday school. Most of them race shrieking to the pastries and descend on them like proverbial locusts, but the girl with the butterfly clips walks sedately behind the others and takes just one cookie from the tray. She walks off nibbling it delicately with one hand cupped beneath her chin to catch the crumbs. With an odd sense of hostility, I cram a sugared pinwheel cookie whole into my mouth, then find myself in a tactical bind because it is full of hard-baked edges that collapse violently when my teeth clench against them. I crunch it up gracelessly and am forced to hold a napkin in front of my face and regurgitate small amounts of half-chewed cookie into it to avoid choking.

Out of the corner of my eye I see that the girl has taken a seat alone in the corner, licking the palm of her hand like a cat to finish the crumbs. The other children have gone somewhere else to play. I take my pastries and step outside the church, blinking in the weak winter light. Rainwater from last night's shower runs down the street, carrying a sheen of oil scum. Looking out at the dripping, ordinary gray world, I allow myself to hope.

Do you feel absolved? he flashes from inside me with sickly sweetness, my cockroach mate scuttling through the fragments of a powdered cookie explosion. I put a hand to my face and dig my fingers behind my eyes until dark circles eclipse my vision. I'm in a black box with no exit and no God above and only an abyss below. I have always thought of churches as powerful, elemental forces, sparking brutal inquisitions and the downfall of civilizations. Maybe once, but they have fallen before an inquisition of their own. It started with the Enlightenment, with candles, and the light just kept getting stronger. Lightbulbs that keep burning, burning into the night. Floodlights, lab lights, light microscopes so powerful they can see the souls of atoms. There is no shadow left, no place for things that remain unexplained.

But they are here, oh, they are here. I finger my wad of cotton wool—the Mother's tears have dried to a pale golden stain. Someone's miracle, but not mine. Who then do I turn to, to take away the horrible pressure that is building behind my eyes?

Go home
Take your pills
and again
and again
and again . . .

The silence of the universe, the lack of everything but *him* is like the writhing of insects over my skin, like awakening in a small airless place and hearing dirt falling from above. If all the world were his, every coffin would have a window to the outside. I stand stupefied before the stained glass saints, not even pleading. Agnes, holding her lamb, is serene. In my mind, there are lights shining down on a metallic surface and my scalpel is touching a spongy wad of tissue, trembling because I could not separate it from myself in my mind.

Mary had a little lamb,
Its fleece was white as snow, he burbles as I relive the perforation again and innumerable times again.

And everywhere that Mary went,
The lamb was sure to go.

I never paid enough attention in Sunday school to know whether it's faith or grace I lack, but I end my stint as a born-again Christian by throwing a piece of baklava against the side of the church. It hits Saint Agnes between the eyes.

CHAPTER EIGHTEEN

Morning classes should be illegal. Professors who teach morning classes should be tortured and burned at the stake, denounced as heretics, insurgents, saboteurs of wisdom and truth. No learning can take place when students are wrenched from warm sleep into painfully bright lecture halls, windowless and lit by interrogation-style lights from above. It was overcast when I came in, and probably the sky beneath the clouds is still dark. I look at my watch: 2:32 p.m.

We could go somewhere else. We could get an ice cream.

I twitch in my seat, causing students to glance in my direction. Nervously, I take an emergency packet of strawberry Pocky from my backpack and cram several sticks into my mouth. Brief oblivion, dryly comforting carbohydrates with their liquefied My Little Pony glaze, and another near-choking experience. I really need to learn to chew my food. The box is nearly empty and I feel a fleeting twinge of panic. Could I be developing some kind of binge eating disorder? No, you're just a growing child—must you pathologize everything? Oh, but you aren't a child anymore. Not for weeks and weeks now.

He followed her to school one day, that was against the rule;
It made the children laugh and play, to see a lamb at school.

I make another violent and unintentional motion and my textbook clatters to the floor. I stay crouched for as long as possible while I retrieve it, then realize this is only drawing attention to me rather than removing me from the situation. I settle back into my seat. Oddly enough, I want a fucking ice cream now, something with chocolate and coffee and caffeine and stimulation of the autonomic nervous system. Mocha and hot fudge and sugary rainbow things, lots of them, and seriously now.

"OK, let's get started," says the professor, sounding disgustingly awake, unfathomably almost cheerful. She is wearing a turquoise blouse with an Indian print skirt, a violation of colorful intersecting lines. She can't wear gray or black like a normal person? Everyone should just wear shapeless gray jumpsuits, and *masks* so I don't have to look at their stupid faces.

And so the teacher turned it out, but still it lingered near
And waited patiently about, 'til Mary did appear.

"The topic of today's lecture is schizophrenia."

Of course. I wait for some acerbic comment like drops of acid flicked from his fingertips, but find myself disoriented when he says nothing.

"The disorder was first described by Swiss psychiatrist Eugen Bleuler in 1908. The word *schizophrenia*, derived from Greek, means 'shattered mind.'"

Maybe if I chewed off several of my fingers, that would create enough of a diversion to make her stop talking. The laps of students on either side of me create an impassable visual cliff. The slides for the lecture are set against a background of Vincent Van Gogh's *Starry Night*. He also went insane, if I recall. But he had an excuse, ingesting all that lead-based paint. What have I ingested lately? Is strawberry Pocky pathogenic for psychosis, delirium, bouts of fear and trembling, shattering of the mind and spirit?

"The disorder affects one percent of the population worldwide," says the professor. "This may not seem like a large number to you, but consider that the capacity of this classroom is over one hundred students. Indeed, schizophrenia often strikes in the early adult years. About half the people with the disorder will attempt suicide. Ten percent will ultimately kill themselves."

How dismal. What if someone, say, recently diagnosed with such an illness were to hear that and become so despondent about their future that they stopped trying altogether? Surely, a psychologist should know better than to enact that kind of self-fulfilling prophecy.

"Thanks to antipsychotic medications developed in the 1950s, many people with schizophrenia are able to maintain relatively normal lives, even find steady employment."

If they hit the right drug cocktail, they might be promoted to junior manager at Burger King, she all but adds.

I raise my hand. "But some people with, um, that disorder are highly successful, right?" I say. "Like John Nash, the Nobel Prize winner?"

The problem with speaking up in class is that people turn to *look* at you. A curiously intense gaze, like they can't believe someone was listening closely enough to the lecture to question its content. Like you are some rare animal that is not supposed to exist in nature, a unicorn or a two-headed calf.

"John Nash was extraordinarily gifted to begin with," says the professor. "His intelligence probably started out so much higher than yours or mine that he could lose a significant portion of his rational skills to disease and still produce notable work. And really, the proof for which he won the Nobel Prize was completed before he developed psychotic symptoms."

I do not take notes on this key point, but sit rigidly clutching the pen. Aren't you going to *say* anything? Silence in my mind as he abandons me to the situation, casting not a ripple on the mercurial lake between us.

"Turning to symptomatology," says the professor, "schizophrenia is characterized by delusions, which are false beliefs, and hallucinations, which are false perceptions, particularly of an auditory nature. People with the disorder tend to find this symptom the most distressing of all. Imagine, an unseen voice commenting on your actions or commanding you to do terrible things."

Something cracks in my hand and a flood of ink seeps across my lap. I have bent the flimsy Bic into a parabola and the casing has snapped. The ink has the viscous texture of blue-black blood, sinking deep into my epidermis.

"To illustrate the distortion of reality experienced by people with schizophrenia," the teacher edifies relentlessly on, "I've compiled some images by Louis Wain, a prolific artist in the early twentieth century, known best for his drawings of cats. As his career progressed, Wain suffered from paranoia and delusions that became increasingly severe, and his artwork provides a rare glimpse into the destructive processes of psychosis."

She clicks to a slide containing four images of cats. The first is a well-rendered tabby staring primly from the painting with innocuous blue eyes. The second cat and the third are increasingly stylized, and the final painting consists of fiery crystalline shapes that radiate outward like a mandala, their pattern forming a sensuous feline figure. Once again, I raise my ink-splattered hand—stigma, stigmata, stained hands, internal blood is blue, I never oxidize for anyone, maybe even a Jesus parallel—god I should have taken comparative literature—and yet he fails to point this out in his cutting manner. Why does he let another opportunity pass him by?

"Actually," I say acidly when the teacher nods in my direction, "the last painting is by far the most interesting. See how he incorporates the crystalline figures into the underlying image? Maybe he got bored with 'cat as such' and wanted to move beyond the perceptive experience into the ontological core of what it means to be a cat. So, actually, the less simpleminded and reductionistic you are, the more you appreciate the deconstructivism of his later work."

The teacher is beginning to look slightly annoyed with my class participation. "The artist drew the picture that way because his world had become so fragmented by disease that when he looked at his cats, the animals he loved best, he saw terrifying demonic creatures," she says. "He was eventually committed to a mental asylum, where he remained for nearly two decades until his death. By all accounts, he lived in a constant state of paranoia and his illness destroyed his life."

Once more, I wait for the professor to acknowledge my raised hand before speaking.

"I'm pretty sure you have no fucking idea what you're talking about."

In the silence that follows, I think of trying to cover it up with something that sounds sort of like what I just said, like, *You incompetent retard*. What did you say to me? *Uh, you sure try hard*, but I can't think of anything remotely similar, and I think it's too late.

"Excuse me," I mutter, flailing across an ocean of knees, knocking notebooks aside in my bid to reach the aisle. In a final lurch across someone's hastily retracted legs, I manage to tip the contents of my backpack onto the floor. Sticks of strawberry Pocky and wadded-up balls of assignments roll gently toward the podium. I don't linger to retrieve them.

A blast of icy wind greets me as I step outside, and I turn toward it in welcome. I collapse onto a bench and rip off my jacket, then my sweatshirt, and just stop myself from disrobing to the point of indecency. I feel like my skin is suffocating. I want every inch of it exposed to the wind's driving needles—I want to be frozen to cryogenic absolute zero and then force-fed a few popsicles. Anything to quell the fever.

"Hi, Whitney," someone says.

Not Scott, please not Scott. My eyelids are covered in a film of sweat. The folds feel sticky as I open my eyes.

"Scott. What are you doing here?"

"I have a free period before Poli Sci. What are *you* doing here? I thought you had a class now."

"It got out early."

"Why aren't you wearing a jacket? It's freezing out here."

"Is it?"

"Come on, let's go inside. I can't let you catch pneumonia before the bio final."

"I've missed two weeks of class. You're probably better acquainted with Wilbur than I am by now." I fumble with my jacket until it's back on me, inside-out but I don't have the energy to undergo the process again. And Scott is not leaving, he's still standing there smiling like it's made his day to find me collapsed, sweat-soaked and verbally incommunicative, on a windswept plaza bench.

"I still don't want you to die," he persists. "Let's get something to eat. The Thai place at the student center is pretty good."

"Yeah, um, alright." Simultaneously, as I stand on trembling legs, the Other surges into consciousness and my knees buckle. Scott catches me by the elbow, leaving his hand there when I am steady.

"Are you OK? You look sick or something. Uh, I mean you look pretty, too . . . but, like, pallid. In a pretty way. Maybe you've got mono. My cousin had that and she always looked like she was about to faint."

We have things to do. Endpoints are encroaching. Get rid of him.

Right. I'm going to tell him I need to go play with my imaginary friend. Fuck off.

Tell him you have more important things to do.

No,

Tell him you're taken.

I like him. I will not give him up for *you.* I force a breath, but it does little to ease the searing pain in my chest, a feeling like when you are ready to cry but also very angry, and this volatile mixture turns to pure heat in your internal cavities. Actually, it's not like that; it is that.

My body seems caught between fight and flight, realizing the futility of both. The Other is on the brink of ecstasy, his pleasure flashing not-quite-white like the inherent hostility in humor, incisors shown in laughter (they are for cutting meat), like the pearly streaks in off-color jokes or milk.

I jump as Scott lays his jacket across my shoulders. "You were shaking."

I swallow hard but something will not go down. A fibrous lump, a coarse pit. A seed sprouting, a delicate tendril unfolding, choking, flourishing in the heaving contents of my digestive system. I realize, then, that I'm done. With school, with my friends, with the nice boy I'd like to know better. The insidious roots unfurl upward to lightly crush my larynx, and I have about thirty seconds before I lose consciousness.

I straighten with effort and shrug out of Scott's jacket. "I just remembered, I have to go. To study. For a physics test." I say this without breathing before or after, because I will not be permitted the luxury of respiration until I have cut another of the ties that bind me to this world.

"And you have to leave right now? You can't even eat lunch? I had no idea physics professors were so sadistic."

"Well I have to study, or I'm going to fail." My voice cracks. I have never been able to hold my breath long underwater. My muscles burn and turn to jelly in seconds, sending me gasping to the surface in panic.

No, I will not. I will not give in to you. I will grab his hands and kiss him here in the middle of everything. I will fall into his arms as I lose consciousness, and when I wake up, you will be gone.

His eyes are pretty, aren't they?
They'd look nice in a bottle of formaldehyde.
You could have them to look at whenever
forever
You're good with a scalpel.

Scott stares at me in alarm as I stumble and claw ineffectually at the base of my throat. I am sure a tentacle of vine is going to burst through my trachea at any moment, like in that movie.

"Are you choking? Should I call an ambulance?"

Other students are beginning to drift over, attracted by my imminent death. Scott's eyes are wide and frightened. He just wanted lunch, just some pad thai and light conversation to move us incrementally closer to having sex, but now I am gasping and wheezing and falling to the ground. Girls, he must be thinking, you just never know with girls.

And now it's all ending. Hypoxia. Neurons are dying, part of me gone forever with every undrawn breath. Neurons don't regenerate, don't reproduce. They have no sons and daughters, no afterlife. In grainy class movies, they look like frail alien life-forms as they extend delicate tendrils of dendrite to foreign axon, communicating by brief chemical waves across synapses. Hebb's principle: Neurons that fire together, wire together. How fatuous, how facile. How do we know they do not love one another, do not grieve for the dead? How do we know that dopamine is not a love letter from one neuron to another in the synaptic dark?

Dimly, I hear Scott's voice and am aware that my center of gravity is lower. Will the lesson be taught when the black creeps to the center and my surroundings fade? Is he bound to soma or psyche? What an interesting experiment this could be. If I come to consciousness, hazy and tense in the anticipation of pain, he is a disease and a function of my brain. If I never awaken, he is something else. Other.

How stupid. That doesn't follow the scientific method at all. There needs to be two of you, one for each experimental condition. One of you to die and one to live. And a third that does neither for a control group. A self that exists in the vacuum between alive and dead, like Schrödinger's cat. A perfect world in which there are no variables to vex and confound. What hubris to think you are anything but that, a variable. You are a smear of *h. sapiens* on a chocolate agar slide teeming with life, too small to see the observing eye behind the great domed lens of the sky. It's cloudless blue now, smoother than glass and bluer than eternity.

"Whitney . . ." Scott rests his hand on my arm. I can see through his skin, nearly translucent in the cold air, like an anatomic model. I can see through to the bones and know where each one ends and the next begins, where easiest each could break. Only observation, not intent, but still. Who notices that first when seeing the hand of their beloved, when returning to consciousness or leaving it?

"Is she all right?" Through my staticky vision, I see half a dozen students gathered around me. One seems to be taking a video on their cell phone in case I am dying. But I'm not, I'm breathing somehow through the symbolic choke. You cannot choose to suffocate.

"I'm fine." I smile in sickly reassurance and stagger to my feet. "I choked on a piece of gum. I'm fine now."

The students drift away, disappointed that they have no excuse to miss their classes, that they are unable to say they have watched someone die today. Scott remains beside me. I don't quite look at him but I can feel his uncertain shifting.

"Are you sure you're all right?" he says.

"Fine."

"You, um, weren't chewing gum."

"Yes, I was."

"OK," he says hesitantly. And still he doesn't give up. His idiocy and poor taste is appalling, and his eyes get more beautiful every time I look at them. The emotion twists to perversion, and briefly I desire them more in a jar than in his head. This inability to maintain any thought pure and whole inside me compels me more than the threat of suffocation to cut deep enough to sever.

"I have to go. I'm sorry, but my physics test is the most important thing right now." I say this firmly, coolly, hoping he will get the impression that I do not like him, do not desire him, do not want to be near him.

"Need any help? I'm a crack shot at holding up flash cards."

"If your skills in lab are any indication, I'm better off without your help." I cauterize my words with a frosty little smirk and walk away before I have to watch his expression change. Before he can take a good look at mine. He might not be so hot at biology, but he'd know lachrimal secretions when he saw them.

Simultaneously with my obeisance, the roots dissolve and elasticity returns to my chest wall. Something of myself is rotting away with them. When I step through the library doors, the wind and cold stop abruptly, replaced by light classical music and the powdery smell of old books.

Say something. You've destroyed everything, so say something. You have my attention.

Externally, someone asks for back issues of *Nature.*

Internally, silence.

Thoughtlessly, in the state of absence where environmental cues take over, I grab a random book from a random shelf and sink into an empty chair. Other students are gathered nearby in pairs or small groups, feverishly mumbling summaries of Shakespeare's plays or the formula for change in velocity on a circular trajectory. Two students behind me, sleepy disembodied voices, discuss the key metaphors of *Death of a Salesman*.

"So Linda's stockings foreshadow Willy's suicide?"

"No, Linda's stockings represent betrayal."

"What's symbol 3 on the study guide, *the paradoxical symbol that represents both death for Willy and life for his family?*"

"The gas hose, obviously."

"And diamonds—what do diamonds represent?"

Opening my book, I look down at a crowded, earnest page of diagrams and footnotes. What am I even reading? *The Agronomist's Guide to Soil Denudation.* I toss it aside and it falls in the crevice between chair and wall, never to be missed. The students around me are bleary-eyed and apathetic; calculus and Shakespeare have nearly got the better of them, but they are holding on. Desultorily tipping back drinks in plastic bottles, letting gravity run the liquid into their mouths rather than actively sucking to create a vacuum and speed the process.

"So we agree that diamonds are The Impossible Dream?"

"This is stupid. Do you really think the author sat around wondering, *What can I use to represent the dichotomy between Willy's desire for tangible wealth and stability, and his inability as a blue-collar wage slave to ever obtain that scintillating dream? Oh, I know: diamonds!*"

"Yeah, probably not."

"I should just write that on the test. Diamonds mean diamonds, gas hoses mean gas hoses, death means death."

"Don't do it, man. My girlfriend took this class last semester and she tried the same thing. She got a C-."

"Fuck that."

"Yeah."

"Wait, what did you say a minute ago?"

"About what?"

"The dichotomy between . . . something and something?"

"Um, Willy's desire for wealth and stability, and his inability as a blue-collar wage slave to obtain that dream."

"Scintillating dream, wasn't it?"

"Maybe. Wait, are you writing that down?"

"Hey man, it's pretty good."

"Fuck you."

Scott could come after me. He must have seen that I went into the library. He could come after me and say, I do not accept that you will not eat Thai food in the student center with me, messily with chopsticks because someone has taken all the plastic forks for their hideous modern art project. I reject that premise, he will say, and the world will right itself again.

"I'm so fucking tired. I haven't slept in days. Weeks. My girlfriend's cat . . . I'm going to poison it when she's not home."

"She'll get another. She'll get a pair of kittens."

"Christ, god, no. Maybe I could cut its vocal cords. Jesus fuck, I'm so tired."

"Here, have some of these."

"What are they?"

"Chocolate-covered espresso beans."

"What do they taste like?"

"Like fucking espresso beans covered in chocolate."

Without bothering to consult me, my body rises to its feet. Perhaps it thinks *chocolate* is a good idea, because seems to be heading for the vending machines. It comforts itself with empty calories because I have failed it. I wish it wouldn't, I will be fat soon. Oh, the elevators are the destination. Maybe in the face of this puzzling danger, some instinct has risen to the surface, unneeded for the past few generations but not yet antiquated enough to work itself out of the genetic material: Seek the higher ground.

It's rumored that the weight of the library is such that bricks occasionally fly out and strike passing students on the head. The physics of that don't make much sense to me, but I'm not doing so hot in physics lately. In the elevator, I light up the button for the twenty-sixth floor. As close as this structure can take me to the sun or oxygen deprivation or God. Not very close at all.

When the doors swish open, the smell of poorly ventilated books and new drywall assails me. The library is being remodeled and the corridor is taped off. I duck under the tape and explore the forbidden hall, hoping to feel a breath of wind seeping in from outside. But the construction crews have been safe and conscientious. The doors are locked, there is no exit. The only way down is the elevators, which move stubbornly back to earth by prescribed degrees, forcing physics to be civil with the weary students even when they have absorbed so much meaning that they desire brutality.

But the drive has awakened like a recombinant virus inside me, vectoring relentlessly until the host is consumed. Even to a mere psychology student, it's so obvious what the endpoint is, what is needed to complete this metaphor. They're all we have, metaphors. In the enclosed silver space of the elevator, sublimated desire incubates into words, for once my own:

Find a place. Find a place and fall.

Chapter Nineteen

My socks ooze water into my sneakers with every step, and my numb hands scrabble to find a hold on the rock. There is a breathless peace in the act of climbing. But you can't climb forever. Soon I have reached the summit and there is only sky above me.

Below, an open vista falling steeply away to a river, a gray city beyond.

Life prevails in the strangest places. There is a tree growing through a gash in the solid granite. Or growing, perhaps, is the wrong word. Subsisting. I don't pause to commune with it as I walk to the cliff's edge and observe, without emotion, the vertical drop to a ghostly pine forest, sharp points of evergreen rising from the mist. I have been hiking here many times with my family, but now I am alone. Small rocks crumble beneath my feet and cast themselves into the abyss.

He has driven me to this place with words, but now his silence keeps my feet bound to the earth. Since awakening in darkness, I have begged for silence and been filled with speech, craved emptiness and been violated with meaning. Now I search for words, but I am empty, and the world is empty around me. Dark arrows move across the sky; the geese are leaving for the winter. Is this symbolic too? Suddenly, I am sure it doesn't mean anything, that all of language is the embers of insanity, smoldering words that ignite a chosen few and consume them. All suffering comes from thinking nothing means something, from taking the random activations of a broken mind and forcing them to signify. The words hold me away from everything, and I note dispassionately how the wind whips my unwashed hair from my face, how the dull sky bathes me in dissipated light. My palms are turned up in supplication, in submission. Who could look upon this and not be shaken?

Yet I feel nothing. I am watching these events unfold, detached and drained of compassion for this weak, trembling sack of water and proteins that leaks salty fluids from its face and utters pathetic noises. And I can't stay here. I can't live like one of Seligman's dogs in their electric pen, never knowing when the next sudden shock of speech will rip through me and tear me in two again. I can imagine a world of drugged solitude, where thoughts must be coaxed in gently and each is utterly my own, but I cannot rationally will such a world to come about.

I search every catch in the wind, every cry from the birds above and the city beyond for a trace of his voice. Nothing. This moment is as barren as suicide note. I don't even have one, no trite *I love you, forgive me*. I don't recall ever saying those things. Possibly I did long ago, but now I don't remember. We forget so many things. Little islands in the dark, these are all we keep.

But I know love. Maybe not the warm gush of emotion that enamors poets and inspires greeting cards, but if someone I loved was being hurt, I would try to stop it. I would take the place of my parents or my friends as some malevolent stranger cut demon symbols into their arms and did things with broken glass, with wires, with butane lighters. If that is not love, nothing can be love, and I would do it, I would do it, I would die, I will die to save them from what I could become.

I am ready to surrender to gravity, but my body will not end this. 4.6 billion years of evolution have created this humble case of meat and bone, and it will not yield so easily to that indulgent epiphenomenon, the mind, still in its teenage rebellion. My neurons, individually, are schizoid and alone. Not enough of them will rally around me to make a jump, a lunge, a feeble twitch of muscle fiber. It is possible I will remain here forever, a frozen statue gradually turning to bone because everything within me hates the thing next to it too much to cooperate and create motion.

Here we are at the end of everything, he says, and the world is choked with meaning again. The Other's voice is a sickly adhesive, a nauseous glue of boiled dead animals that binds my lost self together again. By now, whatever courage or anticourage that led me to this place has failed. I am suddenly terrified I will fall accidentally. I can't make my body move, so I relinquish it to him and feel a stab of electroshock *jouissance* as he jolts my cells into cooperation so that I turn and walk stiffly from the ledge.

Safely away from the precipice, I sink down beneath the lonely tree so that as much of my body as possible is in contact with the ground. I just want to dissolve to carbon, essential to the universe and utterly without consciousness. Restful carbon, the pains and insults of the world dissipate with the collapse of synapses. The brilliant minds, the tortured ones, and the ones who lived in thoughtless waste will ultimately break down to a homogenous, indifferent element. Chemistry doesn't care. Catabolism will set us free.

But you don't want to be free.

It doesn't matter what I want; the breakdown has begun. My muscles are liquefying and nourishing the soil. I suppose eventually someone will find what is left of me, maybe take me somewhere warm. It's getting nippy out—I can't feel my anything.

But it doesn't end. It won't, it can't. I can't surrender this ceaseless slow burn of breath and desire and empty words.

Take it. I don't want it, so take it, it's yours.

His being circles me like a black star, drawing all that I am into its void. Everything I reflect vanishes into the abyss. It's the darkest peace I have ever known.

Are you ready to become a Perfect Being?

Yes.

You have no idea what that means.

Anything it means. I am yours. I belong to you. If I am ever happy again, I will direct that happiness toward you. You will be the object of my happiness. If.

Then you have already begun to know.
There was bird feces on the rock
and your bleeding hands touched them.
Go home now
and wash your hands.

I fail to take this cue.

Get up.

I can't.

You will.

I stagger to my feet, go home, and wash my hands with gobs of oily pink antibacterial soap. My palms look like ground meat where they scraped the rock. Mostly he does it for me, patting the towel on my skin with surprising gentleness. He tells me to gather my things and go to class, to be still and rest. I feel he wants a chocolate bar from the vending machines outside the classroom—he enjoys sweet things even more than I do, and the wretched body could use the energy—but I do not have a dollar. The psychology teacher speaks of conversion disorders and I have no idea what the hell the physics teacher is talking about.

I am drained, gray, probably quite ill to the casual observer, but he is vibrant, manic, bouncing. He is so happy, he finishes his poem for me in his most expressive explosive way, someone's viscera bursting like fireworks in my mind—our mind—in his triumph. The content of his will would splatter into a smiley face if a receptive surface were held up to meet it; he is feeling just that whimsical.

"Why does the lamb love Mary so?" the eager children cry;
"Why, Mary loves the lamb, you know," the teacher did reply.

CHAPTER TWENTY

I have little patience for people who coat their childhood memories in a syrup of nostalgia, but my recollections of Christmases past are of unadulterated joy. My family always gathered at my grandmother's on Christmas morning, the house filled with relatives and the scent of Polish cooking. The presents formed a beribboned mountain vista surrounding the tree, and I was usually reduced to a state of twitching consumer overload before I had finished opening my gifts. For the rest of the afternoon, I tumbled around with cousins I only saw at holidays or funerals, ignoring the expensive new toys to play hide-and-seek among the cobwebbed nooks and cupboards before collapsing among the gift-wrap entrails and sucking multicolored candy canes in dizzy, psychedelic silence.

Now I just wish it would all go away, the lights and the cheery music and the bright-eyed acquisitive children. What do you want for Christmas, sweetheart? A pony? No, I've got a pony; how about a soul? My grandmother died several years ago, so my parents are hosting Christmas this year. Relatives I vaguely recognize come, and I give them gifts I have never seen before, gifts my mother has bought and wrapped and signed my name on. Great shoals of aunts and uncles part to avoid me with understanding smiles; they have been warned about me. I eat a great deal because this gives me something to do with my mouth that isn't talking. One cousin has remembered that I like Pocky, and her gift to me is a dozen packets of novelty flavors: green tea, custard, umu, and Giant Tsubu Tsubu Strawberry.

"I saw them at a corner grocery when I was in Japan," she explains.

"Japan?"

"I did a foreign exchange there. It was so educational to be immersed in such a different culture. Did you have an interesting semester?" A look of consternation crosses her face as she realizes her gaffe. I feel kindly toward her in light of the Pocky and quickly reply, "I think I'll try the green tea kind—would you like one?" instead of saying, "I flunked out of school and went insane and the statistics say there's a good chance I won't make it to next year's annual holiday gathering," which would just make her feel worse. I won't deny that I am envious of the people around me whom brutally kaleidoscopic and needlessly verbose internal demons never saw fit to torment, but there is a saying that, while simplistic, has always managed to comfort me: "Play the hand you've been dealt."

The green tea Pocky are rather disgusting, but it was nice of my cousin to bring them back from Japan for me.

— ◆ —

"I think I had a peak experience recently," I say, staring at a poster on the wall of Dr. Caspian's makeshift office. A rainbow-spotted Dalmatian puppy in a sea of Dalmatian puppies proclaims: *Dare To Be Different.* "And you have no idea what a loathsome pun that is. I hate word play, but it makes him positively *sparkle.* It doubles the meaning of things, you see? Until we burst with it. Everything dissolves into chaos when we first confront things outside our narrow conception of reality, but maybe our minds are just too small to see the system, given how fond we are of microscopes."

"And you've come to see things differently?"

"Not while I still have eyes, I'm sure. It hurts to open ourselves to truth, to *expand* inside. It always hurts at first. But events are being set in motion, teleologies. Which is just a fancy way of saying destiny. I am a pretentious little twit, aren't I? He brings it all to the surface. Nothing hides in the light of the examined mind."

I can't help but notice that while a number of childlike, nondenominational holiday adornments have been added to the general kitsch of the office—candy cane animals, dyed macaroni pasta wreaths—the reindeer snow globe is gone.

"This destiny isn't, by any chance, that you continue to take your medication, graduate from college, and live a fulfilling life?" says Dr. Caspian.

"No, I don't suppose it is."

"I don't see things turning out that way either, the way you're talking now. Unmedicated schizophrenics tend to meet bad ends."

"Whoa, was that like a threat?"

"No, Whitney, it wasn't." Dr. Caspian sounds weary.

"Sometimes, I wonder if it's jealousy that makes people refuse to see these things. Maybe it is brain configuration, maybe it does reduce materially, but maybe there's also an otherworldly realm, and only one time in a million do the nucleotides combine to express the right receptors to communicate."

"One time in a hundred."

"What?"

"One per hundred is the rate of schizophrenia in the population. So maybe you're not quite as exceptional as you'd like to think."

"Yeah, I've read Occam too, except you probably haven't. And to be perfectly confessional, neither have I, but that's beside the point. I get what he was trying to say: Why posit a demon when some faulty wiring will do the trick? But did you ever notice how fond the great minds are of hypothesizing demons? Nietzsche, Descartes, all those physicists. Supposedly they're just to illustrate, but with so many diverse sightings, might it not be more parsimonious to make them real? All the hypothetical demons existing in some realm of universal truth, drinking their blood-laced wine and playing dice with the universe?"

"And what exactly is this *teleology* that you and your non-hypothetical demon need to attend to?"

"I don't know yet, but you seem to become more sarcastic every time we meet, have you noticed that? I suspect the endpoint will involve a suspension of the ethical to reach the sublime. He saved me once, many years ago, before he ever existed. There was this cat, you see, and I think he *was* the cat, or maybe he became it later if time is a circle. And I don't know why, but he saved me from becoming . . . an object lesson of human nature, to phrase it decorously. A dead child decomposing in shallow water, to be less so. But there's always a price, right, always a balance? And he's no vegetarian. He's not steaming brown rice and broccoli for supper, you can bet, so I know what he'll eventually want. Protein, you know, it's the catalyst for everything. But do you understand—do you understand he's the only idol I can find in the dark? I cannot be my own center."

"You sound disorganized and distressed right now, Whitney. Dangerous, even."

"You psychiatrists are very perceptive, aren't you? Pleasantly alliterative and syntactically correct, but yet your category errors seem a shade melodramatic. Does synthesis then make you syncategorematic?"

"Another stay in the hospital might allow us to try a different combination of medications and—"

"You just keep trying to send me back to that place, don't you? I'm glad you moved the reindeer globe; I think I really would throw it at you today. It was so *spherical*, I just don't think I could have resisted. Maybe you can tell me if Nietzsche's eternal return has something to do with Kierkegaard's spheres. They're both circular in shape, like shimmering soap bubbles that dissipate to nothing with every wistful touch. First we seek beauty, and then we seek truth, and then we seek God. But if the only deity who will speak to us demands that we do unspeakable things, must we learn to worship beautiful images instead of what is good? And yet with every moment, we carry the burden of knowing that our choices may return to us countless times more, so really all we can do is try to be graceful when we destroy . . ."

I pause to breathe, freely but shallowly and more quickly than usual. "Does that make sense?" I ask with a catnip smile that is not my own.

"No, but please remember that I'm only a psychiatrist." Dr. Caspian flushes and coughs. "However, I strongly recommend that you return to the inpatient unit while we stabilize you on a new medication."

"*We* do not take my medication. *I* take it when *you* tell me to, and our experiences cross in no other way. As such, I wonder how much more we really have to say to one another."

"But you're still here, because you know it's not right. You know this entity, this demon, is an illusion created by—"

"By my own mind? If I had *that* much power, I'd be saving the world, or ending it, or at least changing it to make it less like hell. I only have my freedom, such as it is. The rat may choose to press the button or not press it as he desires, but can we really call him free? You continually refuse to engage me on this topic of personal relevance, so I can only assume you haven't got half the answers you claim."

"Whitney, I am sick of this! Why do you assume that because I can't satisfactorily answer your philosophical paradoxes I know nothing about you, nothing about the world, and that none of my predictions could possibly be true? Do you really think I'm such an intractable reductionist that I've learned nothing from my experience? You think you're an exemption, an aberration, an exception to which the rules do not apply? You're not. All of them think that, and they're wrong. You are clever to the point of making reasonable people question themselves when you yourself have lost all reason, and that is a dangerous thing. You could make people believe you. You could find people who would listen. But behind your intelligence, you are sick in the same way as hundreds of other patients I have treated, and the only way I can help you is if you *listen to me.*"

The last few words increase in volume so he is almost yelling. A droplet of his saliva lands on my cheek. I start to wipe my face, then drop my hand. Doctors get all kinds of fluids on them every day, worse things than saliva. Getting spat on a little probably doesn't even enter their radar. I wonder if Dr. Caspian ever did an autopsy in medical school. He must have, but I can't imagine it. It would have totally ruined his suit.

"You struck me as a nice girl when we met, Whitney. You seem different now."

"I'll strike you in any way I want. Any way you want. You have no idea what kind of nice girl I'm not. Just pick a mask, pick one and I'll put it on instead. How about the kind that doesn't let you breathe, except through a straw, except when someone decides. That's always a hot one. It's starting to become one of my favorites."

"Do you think you're wearing a mask right now?"

"Aren't we all? It seems to be the fundamental activity with which we concern ourselves as a species, putting on masks and trying to take them off again. Fucking Mardi Gras is what it is. Perpetual *carnivale.* You show me your demon, I'll show you mine. It's all in good fun until someone gets *stuck,* until the mask gets ideas about *ownership* and civil *rights,* until it wants to be *enfranchised.*"

"You need to be in the hospital right now, Whitney. If I have to, I can—"

"*Section* me? Or like, vivi-section me, since I suppose in all technicality I'm still alive. Good luck. Did you hear me threaten anything? I believe I spoke in careful generalities. I wish you could help me, but I don't think you perform abortions or lobotomies. You could, though, since you've broken with Hippocrates—maybe if I'd had the former, I wouldn't need the latter. I did a lobotomy on a dead sheep once. It didn't seem to mind, but I don't know if its mental health improved."

"Listen to yourself. Do you hear the creature of supreme reason and enlightenment you claim to be?"

"I'm far from enlightened, and miles beyond reason. He came to me in darkness, so I suppose that's where it will end. Metaphorically speaking. Thank you for trying, Dr. Caspian, but ultimately we face our demons alone."

I stand up and walk out the door with the cast-off doctor's cast-off prognostication fading behind me: "Whitney, this isn't going to end well."

❖

I feel better, I think. But then, I have arbitrarily chosen first-person narration, where the pronoun *I* refers to the thing that I am, but might as well be *it* or an empty *the*, with nothing trailing after. Substitute any morpheme you like, and we shall just say that what is left of me is the smallest unit that contains meaning. But the joke is on me because there is no meaning inherent in things. The comfort, however, the solace, lies in the fact that I am beginning to Know. The projective membranes of my inner eyes are alive with light and color, the arithmetic of the universe turned into flashes of wordless understanding. Now every question has an answer, every enzyme is fused with its catalyst. The best of my words are mere fallen images, but even his most fleeting ideas are violent perfection: cancer cells multiplying kaleidoscopically, neurons firing like flashbulbs at a rock concert in *grand mal* seizure, burning themselves out as they go. The release of sugars in my bloodstream makes me love these things, want to feel them in my own body. Sink the ship, we only need the frostbit sky.

How do I unify it all? I don't know. Maybe I missed that lecture in my philosophy class. Perhaps because God is dead, we collapse our own wave functions and live forever in whatever universe we imagine for ourselves. Whatever we believe comes after death comes after death, whatever demons we make real are real.

Your metaphysics are appalling. Destroy yourself at once.

Metaphysicists are fucktards.

His laughter is all broken bits of icicle raining down, a surprisingly melodic sensation that sets my teeth on edge. Tripping along the streets in the cold gray light of what promises to be one hell of a new year, my cramping calves propel me past another existential traffic sign, another dog pissing on the sidewalk. With every step, I'm able to leave another schema behind and take up something for which there is not yet words.

Lesson the first, Perfect Beings are utilitarians and hedonists
We contradict ourselves/we do not contradict ourselves
We seek poetry above all else
To purify our sins . . .

This accompanied by a sensation like fingernails scraping the scales off butterfly wings. No, something external—

I look up and see that I have wandered into the street and am about to be hit by a car.

Tires shriek, the car skids sideways and bounces off a telephone pole. Tail lights shattered, the hood popped into an arc and emitting a column of dirty smoke. A man gets out of the car.

"JESUS FUCKING CHRIST," he screams, "ARE YOU INSANE?"

"It's quite likely," I say, and leave him fuming behind me. Another step and a little more self becomes a little more Other, to the point where separate pronouns are hardly needed. Our conversations are almost wholly rhetorical now, hollow ironic banter because the truth in it can only be translated electrically, arrogant suns bursting into darkness behind my eyes. And my head hurts, and I am cold, and I don't know how to interpret what I'm being shown.

This? (One of those surges that can't be put on paper. For our purposes, vitreous humor leaking out of a pierced eyeball, something eating it and living forever. Deer, I think, eating it, and crystal being tapped lightly and harder and harder until it shatters . . . but really, synesthesia is hopeless to describe.)

This means the world is ready
to listen through their drugphones and flatbelly diets
to make me the god of everything.
But you were my beginning
and I would cast it all aside to make you and only you eternal at your end.

His restlessness, his desire, is like a mouth trying to swallow itself alive. I gulp at the dry ache in my throat and realize it hurts because I have been contracting the muscles in time with his speech. We are becoming, losing ourselves in the sublime strangeness of knowing biblically everything that is *not-me*. Sacrificing this distinction for the greater good, the shuddering wholeness lost in the sum of parts.

Yet each revelation is so transitory, and we're running out of time. Now the world external is thrown into vivid relief: A crow's shadow passes its negative image over me, and the street is dripping and cracking in comfortable winter entropy, all frost heaves and peeling paint, muted except for some primary colored children's toys scattered on a lifeless lawn. The crow lands on an electrical wire and looks into me with shining, knowing eyes. The world is crushingly real between our gazes. And this is the illusion. There is *nothing* with inherent truth, and I myself will decay most quickly of all. I look down at my arm and see that already the molecules are beginning to lose cohesion. The spongy white flesh of my inner arm has all the integrity of marshmallow. I hope it doesn't rain.

For the second time, he says in pure language, supplying no image to guide me,

> *are you ready to become a Perfect Being?*
> How?
> *You don't love me enough.*
> Why don't you make me?
> *Because you are free,*
> *unwilling as you are.*
> *Enjoy Nirvana.*

Though the orderly dissolution of elements is a comforting image on the surface, my ego clings so tightly to itself that it will not submit to the parsimonious end. Faithless, but European to the core, I could not bear surrendering my capital *I* entirely, extinguishing into the silence I tell myself I crave. Yet somewhere in this negation delirium is an answer, something mathematical, but with only ones and zeros so even I should be able to figure it out. I do begin to wish I had paid more attention to unit conversions in physics class, to the nuances of Newton's first principles. But my will is good, my objective clear amid the shadowed ambiguity of existence. He feels it too, pleasure spreading like frost across a pane of glass along with the formation of crystalline intent in my eyes. Whatever currency needs to be slipped under the table for the universe to condone this nauseating synthesis will be paid in full. Whatever needs to be negated for this delirium to never end.

CHAPTER TWENTY-ONE

We find ourselves at the playground one day, alone except for a teenage girl and a child of ambiguous gender. It has one of those china-doll faces and lots of glossy brown hair in a pudding-bowl cut. The girl is twisting the chain of her swing into a tight coil as she talks on a cell phone.

"Fucker doesn't even play basketball, but he needs 300-dollar shoes, and he won't buy a video game for his goddam son . . ."

I can smell her perfume from here, cheap and fruity, like liquefied drugstore candy. The child is crouched behind her, following a beetle that has managed to evade the early frosts as it scurries through the grass.

Good morning. What's your name?

The child looks up, stares through me and into me and beyond me. He can hear you. That's not possible. You belong to me.

He's like you, empty in all the right places.

But his sin will be action, not words . . .

Don't be stupid. He's a little boy.

His eyes, they shine,

I want them.

That's a pretty bug . . . what's your name?

The child looks at me with his head tilted like a puzzled bird. He says his name. A current runs through me from groin to crown chakra. The child turns its attention back to the beetle. He picks it up between thumb and forefinger and squeezes until the shell crunches and the internal workings ooze like melted chocolate from a crushed M&M. A shiver of some high emotion runs down my core, a static blue shock in the dark. *Thanatos.* We who have crashed into bodies are ripe to rotting with potentials that, for the most part, we just barely manage to suppress. This must be the forbidden truth of the garden, that in every moment lies the infinite possibility to create or destroy. Things fall apart—this is the natural tendency of the world, the way in which it keeps itself beautiful despite our vulgar efforts to explain and taxonomize, to become more civilized and ugly with every rising generation.

But I will not. I will never.

You can, you will, and furthermore you have always wanted to.

I can't breathe, but it doesn't matter. My body no longer deals in oxygen; it wants something else. No, that is unacceptably sociopathic. I fish in my pocket for an Ativan and swallow one dry, then walk sightlessly through the woods to the only possible endpoint in a world so fond of circles. The pond is the color of dull iron, reflecting the poker-faced sky. I think the anxiolytic is kicking in, but even so, the emotional valence is wrong here. This doesn't feel as cataclysmic as it should. Sure, I'm filled with angst, but aren't I always? It's probably above the mean, a peak experience of angst for most people, but I'm an angst outlier. I've felt this much angst over CD selection, over a plain chocolate bar or the kind with almonds. What makes people like me so dangerous is that we react with equal intensity to everything, so a light shining too strongly in our eyes can be a little shattering to the nerves, and utter depravity can shatter us only a little.

There is a noise in the woods behind me, and I turn.

The child has followed me here and is stepping on some dry leaves or something—there is a crushing or crackling sound emanating from his body. A sound of burning without fire. And I can't help but notice that the world has turned to weapons. Sticks and stones and knives and deep pools of water with hungry fish. Heat radiates from my body, and the sharp scent of sweat rises from the collar of my jacket.

Are you ready to become a Perfect Being?

The boy looks at me with a sudden increase in intensity, a new dilation of the eyes. He hears, and yet he doesn't seem afraid.

Don't you want to be everlasting,
my morning star, my eternal?
Just seal it with a promise,
for you can't with a kiss . . .
seal it with a flash of silver to symbolize my very bright eyes.

This vicious burst of language is hardly catalyzed by any external source, and when it is over, I find I have fallen to my knees and am shaking as though a small earthquake has formed in the epicenter of my frontal cortex. With hands that are only incidentally mine, irrelevant meat claws, I fumble my Scout knife from my pocket and flick open the blade, which sticks on the taffy from many years before. After this one moment of contemplation I mean to throw it into the water, but I can't seem to separate it from myself.

The boy is staring at me and I wonder what he sees, a demon or a girl. The endgame is upon us now, for no longer can the black and white pieces exist simultaneously on the board. I step forward, and my hand touches his face. His skin is impossibly soft and unblemished. He watches me with eyes that absorb but do not mirror. I cannot see what I am, nor what this child will become.

He'll shatter the world
with a beautiful sound . . .

The blade of the knife in my hand forms a linear contrast against the soft curve of his cheekbone. A voice calls out from the woods behind us. My fingernail catches on his cheek as the child turns toward the sound. Now here is a tiny smear of blood on his face that wasn't there before. My blood on him? His blood on me? Did they ever mix? That's forensically bad. It doesn't matter. The world is constructs, symbols, ideas. There is no self, no soul, no blood, no right and wrong. A stranger to myself, I do not know what is going to happen now, or by what criterion action will be decided.

Perfect Beings are utilitarians.

But what do I care of the greater good, or the needs of the many in some possible future?

Perfect beings are hedonists.

No. This would not give me pleasure. And even so, we can't just destroy things—we can't hurt them because we are numb and burning inside and this is the only kind of lust we can . . .

All is one, says the Other. *There is only desire.*

The energy coursing through my body could detonate a bomb. It could destroy the world if it were liberated into action. Destruction or creation, it doesn't matter, it's all just energy changing from one form to another. Hero, antihero. I contradict myself, I do not . . .

Stop it. This is not a thought experiment, this is not a work of literary fiction. The voice calls from the woods again and I am touching cold metal with ambivalent intent. We are wicked, perfect, golden utilitarians. If I take this action, meaning will throw herself from her ivory tower and destroy herself for the greater good. Self and Other will be indistinguishable, and the human wreckage will break down to the same elements of origin. My demon offers me the world and in return asks only for my soul, that gemlike point of light we imagine lodged in our meat-based hearts, the only thing that's ever really ours to give. And when I offer this, I will be pure, because what is done for love is always done beyond good and evil.

His mother calls again, and she is close now. Here I have a choice: to hold or release. The child slips through my trembling fingers, turns and runs toward the sound of his name. Now, on this windswept stage between earth and sky, there is only a girl standing alone with an open knife in her hands, and she is leaking a substance more precious and ephemeral than blood. The world, if it has shattered, makes no sound at all.

PART III

A Danger to Self and Others

We travel in a vast sphere, always drifting in the uncertain, pulled from one side to another. Whenever we find a fixed point to attach to, it shifts and leaves us; and if we follow it, it eludes our grasp, slips past us, and vanishes forever. Nothing stays for us . . . We burn with desire to find solid ground, an ultimate foundation for building a tower to reach the Infinite. But always these bases crack and the earth crumbles obstinately into the abyss.

—

Blaise Pascal

Chapter Twenty-Two

"I must admit I'm surprised to see you, Whitney. I thought you had a destiny to attend to."

I say nothing, and after a moment Dr. Caspian motions me into his not-office. Still unable to formulate a reply, I stare at the carpet. This morning, my eyes meeting my eyes in the mirror were that same color: blank and calm and gray, like water far out over a dirty lake. If I were a designer, I'd call that color "floater gray," the color I imagine when bodies turn up in the harbor after everyone stopped looking a long time ago.

"You were right, you know, that this wouldn't end well."

"What do you mean?" Dr. Caspian looks as if he has not been sleeping well. His right hand massages his temple, and I notice the glint of a wedding band. I realize suddenly that I have no idea whether he has children, or anything about him outside our endless stalemate of word and will.

"There was a boy at the playground. He looked up when the Other spoke. He's a proven universal now, or at least not only my insanity."

"A boy? What are you talking about? What happened?"

"I don't know. I think everything falls now. But when I saw that bit of blood on his face, it was like the world became entirely hypothetical."

"Blood?" A current of tension runs through Dr. Caspian's voice. "What do you mean?" His eyes stray to the rust-colored particles staining my nail beds.

"I don't know." My fingers begin to fray the hem of my shirt. I always need to destroy something when my mind is in turmoil. "His eyes, I couldn't see myself in them. Maybe they were like mine, they were never supposed to open. No, I didn't hurt him, I didn't …"

Dr. Caspian stands up with an absence of expression masking some strong reaction. For a wild second, I think he is going to hit me, but no, he is reaching for his phone. Stepping into the hall and telling the hospital there will be a new admission. Only as my fingernails dig into my palm do I realize that I instinctively reached for my knife when he blocked the door. But I dropped it in the woods at the end of everything, so it isn't there. Would I have used it, instinctively, if it had been?

Dr. Caspian motions me outside, and I'm disconcerted to discover that it's a beautiful day. Frost glitters on the ground and the mottled bark of the ginseng tree. Somewhere, echoing high and bright across the city, children scream in delighted, murderous play. As we get closer to the unit, I begin to walk a little more sideways with each step, as though there were some invisible force field surrounding the building. I just can't handle the dead air in that place now.

A hand grabs my upper arm and propels me through the door. He doesn't leave it there for comfort once I am inside.

"Sit down," says Dr. Caspian when we get upstairs, breezing past me into his office. "They need to take your vital signs."

Vital signs. A moment of confusion in which the words are in the same unknowable category as *cell phone*. Vital signs? I'm sure I don't have any of those. Behind my eyes are all possible configurations of light and color, with special attention to purple, like an afterimage of the sun when the sun is all you have ever looked upon and finally you look away. The sun's antithesis, when I close my eyes. A nurse comes and wraps a blood pressure cuff around my arm.

Suddenly and nonsensically, I remember something. *Eudaimon.* You said we are *eudaimon.* In the dark, you were *eudaimon.* I remember the word from somewhere, a philosophy text skimmed but never quite comprehended. I try to dredge the page into photographic memory, but the exposure must have been too fleeting to potentiate. No answer comes from the murky intracellular space, and I imagine him sullenly bouncing sodium ions away from my axon terminals. Like a petulant chi—no, something else. But Latin, the dreadful subject that sucks the joy from any childhood, tends to be obnoxiously useful later on. *Eu,* good, *daimon,* demon. No, not by any convolution . . .

"It just means happiness."

"What?"

Dr. Caspian has come out of his office. "From Aristotle. *Eudaimonia* is a state of perfect happiness and virtue."

"They're not the same thing."

"What?"

"Happiness and virtue."

Dr. Caspian begins to walk away toward one of the rooms. Sometimes he visits his patients personally when they will not leave their beds, or when he has nearly killed them.

I am eudaimon. We are together. That's what he said. Shutupshutupshutup. None of it matters. Nothing was real. *Eudaimon.*

I stand swiftly, dragging the blood pressure cuff out of the startled nurse's hands, and catch Dr. Caspian by the sleeve.

"You never answered me, the first time I was here. The problem of mind. You said it didn't matter, but it's really all we have. So, tell me, are we bound to a predetermined sequence of chemical reactions? If we're free, we're also guilty. Is this the final revelation, when we realize that we are, and this knowledge paralyzes us forever? Or is it the other, that we're causal prisoners, and we dissolve into apathy once the denial fades?"

Dr. Caspian casts an irritated glance at the nurse for not restraining me properly, and extricates his arm from my grip.

"You're a doctor—tell me, which is it? Are we responsible for everything or nothing? *Tell me!*" My voice has taken on a shattering pitch.

"Yes, we are accountable for our actions," Dr. Caspian says finally, running a hand down the sleeve of his jacket as if to remove some invisible residue.

"Then *reductio ad absurdum*, Doctor. Your profession is based on providing excuses to the weak and evil."

"Sit down, Whitney," says Dr. Caspian wearily. "They need to take your blood pressure." He turns and continues down the hall to his patient's room.

I return to my seat and wait serenely while the nurses make sure I'm suitably alive. I don't fight the needle's sting when it comes. A pleasant sense of unreality has drifted over me. Who collapses the wave function? Not me. One of the nurses checks my pockets for sharp things and administers the Mini Mental Status Exam: My date of birth, please, and today's date and the name of the place I am now and to please remember a brown chair with the number three.

I contemplate that I could answer wrongly and say a brown chair with the number two or a brown chair with the number four or a red chair or I don't remember what you said, or I could take the chair I am sitting in and throw it at her. I could break her spine above or below any of twenty-four vertebrae, in doing so diminishing her quality of life incrementally as the fracture moves higher up the spinal column. I then remember that there are any number of songs, both religious and secular, patriotic and non-patriotic, that I could hum to myself or sing aloud while doing so. The power to split the universe into endless tributaries is not the shining culmination of evolution; consciousness is an -*itis* of soul, freedom is only a demon.

It becomes my mantra, my response to any situation in which I might create horrible new realities for other Is and thous to suffer in. If my response is constant, the world cannot break apart. *Whitney, will you eat these peaches? Dr. Caspian would like you to take this medicine. Whitney, your parents are here to see you. Whitney, can you hear me?* Never have I heard my name so many times before. The utterance begins to lose all meaning, but still they speak it like a talisman to draw me back to the world.

"Free will is a demon." I say it in monotone, afraid to even modulate the tone of my voice in case the deviation shows up in staff notes. A particularly vehement rendition of my universal truth might prompt them to record, "Patient spoke only in aggressive echolalia," whereas a subdued mutter might be documented as speaking in a depressed manner. That, in turn, might alter their choice of medications and, by some billionth degree of convolution, raise the price of mangoes in Somalia, causing economic collapse and the death of millions.

I'd surrender myself entirely to this sickness, but minds don't want to be lost—they cling to their hosts despite everything. Like sad children they cannot die just by holding their breath, however much they want to.

"Whitney, can you hear us? Will you eat something?"

My parents. How hard they have tried not to make the same mistakes with me that their parents made with them, but it doesn't matter because I ended up a thousand times worse.

"Free will is a demon."

The tears running down my face are two divergent streams, but it's not as bad as it sounds because eventually they join, pooling beneath my chin before dripping onto my shirt. This comforts me, but not enough.

"We brought you some of those Japanese cookies. Aren't they your . . ." The word *favorite* dies before it reaches open air. Maybe it seems like a frivolous word choice. The packet of Pocky is pressed into my hand.

"Free will . . . is . . . a . . . demon." The words are choked past understanding, but I don't need to worry that this will alter the staff notes. They aren't listening; most of the nurses have gone to a meeting, and the one left behind is trying to catch the last few minutes of *Dr. Phil* under the guise of watering the limp potted plant in the corner. She has forgotten about photosynthesis and the plant has no light—it will die soon. I feel amused, I think, or despairing. When language fails, all emotion is fundamentally just energy moving through us. Creation and destruction are the same. It's so beautiful, I don't really care.

CHAPTER TWENTY-THREE

The next afternoon, I find myself in a conference room opposed by Dr. Caspian and pair of clinical psychologists. Featureless mannequins in pinstriped suits, their eyes concerned reflective pools in their blank concerned faces.

"We're concerned, very concerned, about your recent episode," one of them says, and the other agrees. I stare at them in silence. It annoys them when you don't reply, so they will try to play your game and stare right back, hoping to make you uncomfortable enough to talk first. But they have busy lives and practical minds, and do not last more than thirty seconds.

"Since you don't seem to be responding to your current medication, we'd like to try something different. It would involve placing some circular pieces of plastic on your head and delivering a series of pulses to your brain. We do this a lot for patients who don't get better from taking medicine, and they often say it helps with sad or angry feelings and voices in their heads."

Dr. Caspian says nothing, his stare fixed on the polished grain of the tabletop. Electroconvulsive therapy. Does their innocuous terminology ever fool anyone? Collateral damage, friendly fire, extraordinary rendition. Seizures induced by electrical shock, however you frame it. And yet, this may be the solution I've been searching for. Maybe the problem is not that I have lost my mind, but that higher thought and reason are intact. Perhaps the answer is not to get the integrating structures back, but to lose everything. An electrical cleansing, an obliteration of damaged tissues, a cauterization of infected thoughts. Maybe this is what I need, or what I owe.

One of the psychologists slides a consent form across the table. With a hand gone limp and icy, I scrawl something that could pass for a signature. The lawyer's daughter signs another document without reading it. For all I know, I have given them permission to perform unanesthetized vivisection. Maybe there is a clause stating that if I die, they get to divide my possessions and cast lots for my clothing.

They bring me to another part of the hospital, and I am told to trade my clothing for a hospital gown. I'll be asleep for the whole procedure, a nurse reassures me. It won't hurt at all. Her shadow lurks outside the door while I change in the bathroom. I wonder if when I awaken, I'll remember none of this, if it will be like reincarnation and the weight will be gone with the soul.

No, it isn't like that. It's not a lobotomy, for god's sake. It doesn't destroy anything, sever anything. But I can only think of Hemingway. "It was a brilliant cure, but we lost the patient."

"*No.*" If I were to stop to think now, whether the fear is of forever losing the self or forever losing the Other, I could not say. "I changed my mind. I don't want to do this."

"It's really not so bad, hon," says the nurse. "We do this every day. I promise it won't hurt at all."

"Pain is not the issue. I revoke my consent. *I revoke my consent!* Let me go."

For a moment of terror, I am sure that I don't have a choice, that a whole flock or pride or murder of nurses in their shuffling soft-soled shoes will surround me, that a needle will sting from behind and then nothing, and when I wake up, the world will be a passive experience that travels through my eyes without leaving any impression behind. I will view it with the dull gaze of an animal, an operant being who is patient and safe and fond of crossword puzzles, who will eat the tapioca pudding cups without sarcasm, who will never be herself again because we are bound to this body for as long as we live. Beyond that I will not speculate, but if the structures are damaged, something could be lost forever and only enough of me will be left to know it is gone.

Oh, god, I signed the form—are they going to pin me down and tell me to relax, that I won't feel a thing? But the nurse just gives me a look of half pity and half exasperation, as though I were a shivering goose-fleshed child refusing to enter the deep end of a swimming pool, and brings me back to the ward. I go to my room and eat the packets of graham crackers I have secreted away in the drawer of the bedside table. When they are gone, I feel a sheer panic, as though my center of gravity is not strong enough to keep me obedient to natural laws. The graham crackers form a doughy mass of proxy in the pit of my stomach, but they are not enough. Perhaps when Dr. Caspian hears of this, I will have to have the shock treatment after all. I don't suppose it matters. I cannot kill myself, I cannot cure myself, I cannot abandon myself to insanity. I can see everything as it is and do nothing as I should, and I am better for it and the world is better for it and it destroys me and it saves everyone.

⬛◆⬛

That evening, I sit on the window ledge in my room and watch the free entities moving on the far side of the glass. They seem not to exist as discrete points but arcs of light and purpose that sear across my visual field, rays of cause and effect radiating from their bodies like serpentine gold threads. They make electromagnetic noises like storms or angry cats where they cross. As night falls, the city beyond the hospital grounds becomes an endless grid of light and karma and darkness. It's one of the most beautiful moments I've ever known, the kind that can only come when you've defeated yourself.

Later, someone comes and stands outside my door. I can see their reflection in the glass. The person watches me for a minute before knocking on the frame. I turn quickly, but it's not Dr. Caspian; it's an Indian woman barely five feet tall. She looks like a child with her smooth caramel skin and curly black hair pulled into a ponytail. She introduces herself as Dr. Ramjerdi, Dr. Caspian's resident.

"Are you new here or something?"

"Yes. How are you feeling today?"

"I've been thinking a lot. A last supper sort of thing, because I'm about to make a decision. Don't ask what, it doesn't matter now. The important part is the dilemma in the abstract. You see, I believe there is an aggregate of three words that expresses the most dangerous sentiment in all of language, but I'm torn between two interpretations."

"And these are?"

"'I love you' and 'I don't care'."

The resident makes a note on her chart, but briefly, so I don't think she's recording my musings for posterity. I think she is checking a box of some kind, turning me into a line or a cross and putting me inside it.

"I understand that you refused the ECT treatment that Dr. Caspian ordered," she says when she is finished. She speaks precisely, as though she would have no trouble rattling off *acrocephalosyndactyly* or *vestibulo-cochlear* despite her foreign lilt and syntax.

"Yes. Where is he?"

"He is busy, and I am seeing you today. Why did you refuse the treatment?"

"I don't know. So you're in medical school, aren't you?

"That is correct."

"Do you like it?"

"I find it a rewarding career path. But Dr. Caspian thinks you are depressed and have psychotic thinking. He recommends, and I agree, that ECT is the best treatment for you." She flicks her hair over her shoulder. Her wrists are so delicate, I could reach out and shatter one so easily. Oddly, it is the fragility that restrains me. Dr. Caspian or one of the male orderlies, I think, I would strike without hesitation now . . . my prefrontal cortex is just so tired of *regulating*. But to hit the resident would be like stomping on a china doll. I wonder if this has saved her before, if it works to her advantage, if people are stopped short, realizing their power.

"Well?" she says. "Will you try again with the ECT treatment?"

"No."

"It is not dangerous, you know. We electrically stimulate the brain, and we do not know exactly why, but it makes people less hopeless and they are able to live again. Sometimes they say colors seem brighter, that they feel more like themselves than they ever have before."

Stop. Just stop making me the unreasonable one, the self-defeating one who wants to lie in her dirty bed.

"I can't."

"This is your decision?"

Flinch. Decision. I choose. I am free.

"It's really better if I don't," I mutter. "A physicist put this cat in a box, you see, and it's neither alive nor dead until someone is watching. The observer is crucial for the formation of reality. And I'm not being observed anymore, so consequently, I am neither alive nor dead but somewhere in between. It changes people, not having a truth value, so perhaps it's best if you leave me alone."

"I will tell this to Dr. Caspian," says the resident, and turns to leave. She is lithe on her feet, but I could easily strike her down from behind if I wanted. I touch glass very softly instead, and for the rest of the night lose myself in that favored childhood thought experiment, the one where you try to become something, anything other than what you are. My hand and the window compromise to become the same temperature after a while, but that's as close as I get to transformation.

———•◆•———

Days or maybe weeks later, I'm summoned to Dr. Caspian's office. As I enter the room, The Doctor's eyes are cast down on my chart. "Good afternoon, Whitney," he says, not looking up. "The nurses report that you have stabilized on your medication, are eating well, and have been participating in groups. We're pleased with your progress."

I have no idea what he's talking about, since I have merely tried to move as liquid through the interminability of days, trickling down a gradual slope along the path of least resistance, guarding my vacant eyes with a passive smile. Or perhaps that is what they mean by progress.

"Since this is a critical care unit, we only keep patients for as long as is medically necessary. I believe Dr. Ramjerdi discussed with you the possibility of being released into a long-term program, here on hospital grounds, that specializes in caring for people with schizophrenia."

I make some kind of movement with my shoulder in response, but he's still not looking at me.

"It's a residential facility, but not a locked unit like this. You'd attend outpatient groups during the day and live in a household with other patients and staff members. Your parents agree that it's not realistic for you to continue living at home."

As he speaks, he pushes some papers across his desk for me to sign. In this worldview, there are always forms to sign before change occurs.

"I don't have a pen," I say. "We're not allowed to have pens here, remember? We might use them for evil instead of good."

He hands me a pen. I sign the form and hand it back to him.

"This is a big step; how do you feel about it?" he asks, shuffling the papers. I look at him blankly, as the question has no semantic relevance.

"Someone from the program should be here soon to pick you up," says Dr. Caspian. "You might want to pack your things."

I search out his eyes, but they keep sliding away.

"I'm sorry, I . . ."

"I wish you the best of luck with your continued treatment." His voice is courteous and impersonal, as though we have had no previous acquaintance.

I go back to my room and gather my things. Soon, a nurse comes in and tells me that someone from the halfway house is here to pick me up. That's what she calls it, a halfway house. Dr. Caspian said it was a residential facility: He knows me well enough to mollify me with precise Latinate polysyllables.

I reach the exit just as Dr. Caspian is leaving on other business, or maybe to go nap in his coffin between appointments. Oh, shut up, he's done his best for you. It's hardly his fault that a vein of sickness runs right to your core, a crumbling fault line that drugs or words can't repair. It's hardly his problem if your fallen image shattered a little on contact with solid ground, if your eyes never came to know themselves in glass except by careful intellect, and your mind is a seditious thing that will claim any compelling sense object as self to escape you.

As we wait beside each other for the atomic age door to release us, Dr. Caspian's gaze is drawn to a sign taped to it that proclaims in letters of fiery red crayon:

Abandon hope, all ye who enter here.

Maybe it's taking too many liberties with the world, to create something with symbols and language and *gestalt*, but I'm not the first to say it, at least, and people must be warned.

"Yours?" Dr. Caspian finally inquires.

"Yes."

The door buzzes and unlocks.

"But it's on the inside. You're warning people who go out, not people who come in. You put it on the wrong side of the door."

"No," I say, and smile with empty courtesy as I step across the threshold to freedom. "I didn't."

CHAPTER TWENTY-FOUR

The halfway house has gray carpets like the rest of the hospital. Institutional gray, and they somehow smell of overcooked oatmeal, in all the rooms, everywhere. The whole complex was built back when it was fashionable for young women of high birth to break down on occasion, to take a soothing holiday for the nerves and the uterus. The building that houses the day program is mazelike, with windows of distorted glass. The walls have the thick-skinned look of many paintings, ribboned with inexplicable stains and poignant with the echoes of a thousand pleas for silence.

Most of the patients fall into one of two categories—the broken ones who trace hieroglyphs on paper and rant about nanotechnology in the rice pudding, and the silent ones who drift like hungry ghosts through a world they can neither escape nor manipulate. When they speak, their voices seem to come from some disembodied place. We're all lost in the same dark wood of error, but so far apart we'll never find each other. People mumble aloud to their demons, to their alien hosts, to their hidden cameras, to their dead mothers, to their gods. We choke on meaning, but it can't be shared, and we're adrift in our respective eternities, simply passing through each other wherever we intersect.

I wonder how many of them were once precocious young people who might have become doctors or lawyers if karma or biology had dealt them a better hand. For example, there's a woman who always watches crime shows from dinner until bedtime—*Law and Order* followed by *NCIS* followed by *CSI*—and she is eerily accurate at picking out the perpetrator within the first five minutes of the episode. The dog, the faulty wiring, the jealous trapeze artist. She spoils every new episode, and sometimes I wonder if she might have been a detective or an FBI agent in one of those alternate universes that physicists say are born in every moment.

The staff are not crude and cruel or even dull and disillusioned. They are genuine, well-educated and respectful. Their only flaw is that we are not equals, we are incompetent beings who must be shepherded and sheltered, spoken to clearly and slowly in simple terms. Some of the patients have part-time jobs at convenience stores or factories. Places where it's OK if your frontal lobes don't work so well.

My parents come dutifully to see me every week, but there is little to say, and their visits are brief. They promise they will not sell Apollo. I tell them to do what they please; I want nothing left in the category of *possession*. They bring me things anyway, clothing that no longer fits me and books I can't read and Pocky that will make me even fatter than I am. They cling to this, the Pocky, that I like it, as one object of knowledge about their daughter that remains to them.

Sometimes I want to run after them and beg them to take me from this place. But I don't, because they are afraid. I can see it in their eyes. Maybe the fear is of finding me bled out on the floor with more cryptic messages smeared on the walls, or even of awakening to see me standing over them with a knife in the dark. The knowledge that I have become a person with whom it is not safe to be alone is like holding some wicked medieval weapon I don't know how to use, or want to, but can't set down. Once you've crossed that line of being a danger-to-self-or-others, are you allowed to come back? Is it a painted traffic line you can cross whenever you've got the nerve, or does a razor-rimmed fence spring up behind you as soon as you've entered the wrong lane?

Here, at least, they give me an excuse for what I've become. They say, your brain is broken. These pills, for as long as you take them, will keep you safe. They are vehement: *You must take the medication.* Your enrollment in the program is contingent on your cooperation. In theory, I agree. Do whatever you must to maintain order. I've violated the social contract in the worst possible way, not in action but in mind and in heart. You've earned the right to tinker with my chemicals. More to the point, they have made me slow, unimaginative, too literal to be seduced by demons or other creatures of poetry and dreaming. Indeed, I am closer to being an inanimate object than I have ever been in my life. Sights enter my mind and die before they are transformed into visions. And I am fat, my hands shake, I drool on the pillow, I slur my words and fall into chairs and stay in them until someone tells me to move. I can't live like this, but I have to. In order to justify my continued existence, I accept their explanation of my experience: I have a disease. My mind transforms things that are into things that aren't—or is it the reverse? But they tell me not to pay attention to these questions. Philosophy kills. Focus on this moment, they say. On being here. They say that a lot, just be here, and probably not one of them knows they are echoing Heidegger and his *Dasein*, the being that simply exists without questioning itself into negation. The Nazi philosopher who would not forsake his brutal ideology, yet who was brilliant enough that history could not forsake him as mad or insignificant. But this kind of knowledge must not be mistaken for insight, nor can I allow my natural gift for rhetoric to make me think myself some kind of mystic or visionary. I do not see the world through a glass darkly, but through a haze of misdirected dopamine, or glutamate, or whatever they say is wrong with us now.

This solution is tolerable as long as I believe this will only happen once, if I do not allow myself to think: *What if some day or night, a demon were to steal after you in your loneliest loneliness and say to you, This life, as you now live it and have lived it, you will have to live once more, and innumerable times more . . .*

I don't imagine it directly, I can't, but whenever I see children passing by on the street or coming to visit their crazy relative, I feel a sick shock and smell the saltiness of dead things decaying in water. Later I realize it was only my fearful sweat, but the dread will not leave me. Every time I want to leave this place, to take up my freedom and comb my hair and not look back, I go outside and listen until I hear the shriek of a child in the world beyond the gates, a sound that carries across a surprising amount of intervening air. An expression of play and not murder, I can only assume, but it's enough to quell my desire to step outside the gates of my chosen prison.

Killer killer wannabe
Cut him up to set you free.

I hear it in my own mindvoice, not his, but it rings like a playground skip rope rhyme on eternal repeat until I wonder if it's possible to give oneself a lobotomy with a plastic spork.

Every day after the insipid lunches we eat with the aforementioned tool—the ultimate symbol of our societal castration, that we are no longer allowed to use metal—the staff coerce the gelatinous patients to take a walk around the hospital grounds. The ginseng tree is a gaunt skeleton, unmindful of those who pass. The inpatient unit lies beyond it, and several times I have seen Dr. Caspian crossing the square with his eyes downcast on some thick sheaf of papers, apparently as reluctant as myself to engage with the outside world.

On one of these walks, a gleeful January wind stirs a pile of dead leaves from beneath the ginseng tree. The sound they make is so full of dry amusement that I fall to stone behind the others and let them swirl around me, certain my demon will speak to me with their voice. That sound of delight in desiccation that could only belong to him, a reminder that things are not necessarily gone when they no longer skim the surface of our minds. I wait for words to form, but the wind quiets and the leaves fall dispossessed to the ground. A small anonymous love note pinned to a high school locker, that's all. No, I need more . . . say something, say anything. Come back to me, I plead him, but they are only dead leaf husks scraping on the ground.

"Stay with the group, Whitney," says Al, who is leading the walk. "Remember, regular exercise is an important part of a healthy lifestyle."

So I keep walking, although I don't think these forced marches are doing anything for my metabolism. I jog to catch up to the others and get quickly breathless, but it's not the right kind of burning I feel. Just once more, I want the heat of his will choking out the air, leaving me to suffer the giddy terror of asphyxiation. What on this earth could I possibly desire now that would not incinerate me on contact? I could burn only for my Other now, but he's left me in cold silence and there will be no conflagration. This is my penance, to remain a sickly flame on a slow-burning candle, undistinguished among the rows of countless others and not permitted to extinguish. I can still see them in the church in my mind's eye, because despite everything the poet in me will not die.

Al calls out again for me to keep up with the group, and I follow obediently toward the sound of my name. I will stay here and I will turn gray. When I die, the energy released by complex things turning simple will be used by consequential beings to do consequential things, and it won't matter that I wasted everything I was given. Chemistry doesn't care, catabolism will set me free, and my brief impact on this aqueous gem of a planet will be absorbed that much sooner by the indifferent universe.

CHAPTER TWENTY-FIVE

Take the life I've described and multiply it by whatever integer you like. The difference between yesterday and today is that the staff are taking the patients to shop at Target. They make this trip weekly, and sometimes go out for a movie after if the CIA seems to be taking the afternoon off from its voyeuristic interest in heavily sedated mental patients and if public freak-outs have remained at a minimum. I've declined these outings until now, but it's become inescapable that I buy certain necessities like shampoo and shirts without little holes in them, each thread plucked away until the hems are like lace.

We go in a big white van with a hospital insignia that screams, "We are either crazy, stupid, or disabled." There is a staff member watching over every two patients, but I get one to myself because, although I am malleable in my silence, they can't quite interpret the glint remaining in my eye. They assign me to Melodie, a twenty-four-year-old night school student who is cheerfully violating the staff dress code by wearing sandals with straps that wrap up to her knees and a skirt that leaves a significant gap of bare thigh above them. She seems delighted to sift through racks of women's clothing, occasionally holding something up for my inspection. If I don't recoil in horror, she adds it to our shopping cart.

"Do you need anything else?" she asks when she's chosen half a dozen shirts for me. I shake my head. I will speak if necessary, but never more than the bare utilitarian minimum, and never for the luxury of social connection. My exoskeleton will remain here, but it will not be permitted to enjoy the experience.

"Well, if you don't mind, I want to look for a new purse."

I shrug and follow her to the accessories department. The designers' inspiration this season seems to have been a hallucinogen-enhanced safari. Everything is covered in rainbow swirls or fake animal fur. Melodie is entranced. "This is totally rad," she says, holding up a scarf that looks like something Picasso might have vomited on after a frolicsome night on the town.

My eyes wander across the store. A small boy stands unaccompanied in the toy aisle, ogling some sort of Power Rangers blaster gun. Melodie is spellbound by the scarf, and the only other adult in sight is hypnotized by a towering wall of electronics. The child wanders away from the toys and stands wistfully in front of the vending machines by the door. Gumballs shaped like wholesome fruits and 25-cent plastic superheroes and blobs of alien goo that glow in the dark. That's what he desires with his wide eyes and moist red mouth formed into an acquisitive O. I do not know his age, but it must be less than five because he has no theory of mind; he does not look around to see if he is observed before reaching his small hand up the chute to illicitly acquire some of this irresistible neon ooze.

Jesus Christ, doesn't anybody watch their children? Don't they know there are people like me, apocalyptic and insane, and they are only spared when we've lost our knives and our wills? The aisle is a straight shot to the door, the cashiers are busy. There are security cameras, but by the time the alarms sound and the film is checked, it could be too late, he could be a little boy trapped in amber forever. In the terrible clarity of my broken mind, I see him preserved in liquid gold. We perceive only the surface of slashing silver and flashing bombs in the night, but elementally chaos is a slow golden resin, entropy is a small boy or a butterfly caught up in sweet sap before it can ever change the world for good or ill. My hell will be to drown in the sewage of my own metaphor and I wish I had let them electrocute me while they had the chance.

I walk over to Melodie. "I want to go to the car," I say, enunciating every word so I will not have to repeat myself.

"The van isn't leaving 'til three-thirty," she says, inspecting a belt made from the hide of a rare pink zebra. "The others will meet us at the registers."

Behind me is a multifaceted display of sunglasses. I spin it around so it totters and squeals and the colors blur kaleidoscopically. Melodie murmurs an absent word of discouragement. She has found a rack of purses coated in the fur of feral cats.

"Ooh, they're so soft. I wonder if they have any that look like white tigers."

Nearby is a lava lamp display. Blobs of yellow wax bubble lasciviously to the surface, then harden and sink. I sweep the lamp off the counter and send it crashing into the mirrored stand. The whole thing explodes into glittering shards. Bits of broken glass rain down and the lava lamp shatters too as it hits the floor. A spray of egg yolk and magenta cascades across the linoleum and makes a satisfying sound, a good proxy of what I wish to say.

There. Proof positive. I am not fit to be in society. Melodie looks at me in frozen horror, clutching a leopard-skin bag. A manager comes over, drawn by the noise.

"What happened here?" he asks warily, one hand on his pager like a cop reaching for a gun. I stand vapidly amid the crime scene until Melodie is forced to stammer an excuse.

"I'm sorry, she's from . . . um, we're . . . on an outing." Being a genuinely decent person, she seems to want to avoid embarrassing me. But in the end, she is more afraid of being detained for vandalism. "She's, uh, mentally not . . . her, ah, residence will pay for the damages."

The manager looks at me but I keep my gaze trained on the fake fur purses.

"No," he says finally. "That won't be necessary. I have a son who's autistic, I know how it is. Maybe you should take her outside."

"Yes, thank you." Melodie stammers some more apologies and propels me toward the exit. I wait for an explosive "What the hell is the matter with you?" when we get outside, but she only nips anxiously at one of her metallic purple fingernails as we walk toward the van.

"I'm sorry," she says. "I should have listened to you. I should have taken you outside." Only when we are in front of the vehicle does she realize she has walked out of the store with the leopard purse. I climb into the van as Melodie flits about uncertainly, holding the purse at arm's length.

"If they ask, say I stole it." Using up tomorrow's ration of words, but she's probably too dumb to figure it out herself and I've caused enough trouble for today. I don't want her to get arrested. I think she would be unhappy in jail without her wraparound sandals, and they wouldn't let her have them because the straps are long enough to choke someone.

CHAPTER TWENTY-SIX

"Today we're going to write a letter," says Al, one of the milieu counselors, sweeping magazine tatters off the table. The inspirational murals we have made for the last group, art therapy, are tacked to the wall for display. Except mine, of course. As you can imagine, the riotous possibilities for perversion of the exercise surged through my consciousness like a thousand radiant suns. But then I caught sight of a back issue of *Seventeen*. The special "Which is Worse?" edition, and my apathy engulfed my cynicism, swallowed it alive. The poster paper remained blank and sunny yellow, full of wholesome motivational potential for someone else.

"This isn't the kind of letter you put in the mail," continues Al, handing out sheets of paper, dull pencils. "It's a chance to write to the most important person in your life. Maybe a parent, a teacher, or a friend." She does not say boyfriend or girlfriend, probably assuming, accurately, that no one here is getting much action. "This letter can say all the things you wished you had told them but were afraid to, or never got the chance."

I look down at the paper in front of me. To make such a lasting mark on the world would be unforgivable arrogance. And yet the pencil moves and the page is filled. And the eyes are filled also, but the writer does not allow them to drip pathetically. She dabs her face with a sleeve and is told that we use tissues to wipe our noses, not our clothing.

"Remember," says Al. "If you make proper hygiene a habit, it becomes a way of life." Sort of like heroin, I guess.

"Would anyone like to share their letter?" says Al after we have been writing for ten minutes. My throat contracts, tries to form speech, but fails.

A woman in aquamarine sweatpants raises her hand. "Dear Sparkles, it's been four years since you died, but you were a great dog. . ."

I bow my head to the scarred table, press my forehead into the cuts and grooves created by pens and plastic safety scissors in restless hands.

Al waits until the woman is finished speaking. "Stay with us, Whitney. You can rest between groups. It's not polite to sleep when people are talking."

I lift my head. The tendons at the back of my neck feel weak and desiccated, reluctant to support the weight of my head. Al is speaking now. I try to make eye contact with her. It's right there on my goal sheet, "maintain eye contact during conversation," but she has no eyes, they are painted on. She is made of primary colors: red lips, yellow hair, blue eyes. Her full name is Allison, it says so on her staff ID. Maybe she thinks Al sounds cozier, but it makes me think of a used car salesman with a greasy toupee. It doesn't matter, words mean nothing. Actions carry the weight of the world. I toss my paper in the trash when the group is over.

"You threw this away," says someone behind me. It's Jared, only forty but gray haired, gray skinned. As he speaks, his face is momentarily turned gargoyle by the spasmodic contractions of tardive dyskinesia. Involuntary facial tics caused by the kind of drugs they gave mental patients twenty years ago, or maybe the ones they give us now, for all I know. He holds out my crumpled paper.

"It doesn't belong in the trash," he says, his skin sliding down his face as the contraction passes. His tongue flickers snakelike at the corners of his mouth.

"Really?"

"Paper goes in the recycle bin." He presses the paper into my hands and shambles off, grimacing. So, I put it in the recycle bin. Actually, I throw it into the recycle bin with such force that it bounces off a stack of newspapers and lands on the floor. The newspapers slump down after it, but I don't bother to pick them up. They probably symbolize the self-defeating nature of the aesthetic or something else I'll never know because I did not take comparative literature when I had the chance.

One of the researchers, Dr. Hunter, is sitting in the hall and marking a stack of papers with a red pen. He wears rumpled suit jackets with no tie, and his office resembles a polar region with flurries of paper accumulating on every surface. He's a comforting presence among the bleached, cheerful uniformity of the day staff. Nice as they are—too nice, in fact—there are shades of Orwell's chilling vision in them. I could imagine most of them doing calisthenics to a video of Big Brother between therapy groups. But Dr. Hunter, he's an academic, adrift in a world of elegant abstraction. Kinda cute, too. Not that I notice such things anymore. I lean against the wall to watch him work, and after a moment, he looks up.

"Hi, Whitney. Do you need help starting your computer?" He has designed a series of computer games that are supposed to improve our executive functioning. I wouldn't tell him so, but they're pretty dull, and I don't think they're making us smarter any more than our daily strolls are shedding the pounds produced by twenty-three and a half hours a day of chairs, graham crackers, and drugs that alter our metabolisms.

I shrug. "How's your research going?"

He looks surprised to hear me speak. "Fine, thank you. But these are actually exams I'm grading for my class."

"You're a professor?"

"Yes, I teach cognitive psychology and neuroscience. How the brain functions and encodes what it learns, basically."

I tilt my head and read the first question on the sheet upside-down.

1. *The first neurotransmitter to be discovered. Plays a key role in cortical associative memory and also has an excitatory effect on skeletal and cardiac muscle.*

The student has circled A., norepinephrine, but that's wrong. It's D., acetylcholine. I sit down at one of the boxy tan computers. Today, I'm supposed to look at numbers that flash on the screen and are then hidden by colored squares, and remember these numbers and provide them on request. Instead I find a more interesting program among the files, a code-breaking game. I've never been good at math or music or anything with rhythm, but these word patterns reveal themselves quite easily. Language and meaning seem to spew from cryptic filler just for me, but unfortunately I don't think the RAND Corporation is hiring.

Dr. Hunter walks up behind me. "How are you coming with the . . . what's this?" He gazes, puzzled, at the screen. "Is that Dan's cryptogram game? Is that the *fourteenth level* of the cryptogram game?"

I *X* out the screen and switch over to the matching program, then pretend to have difficulty remembering which of four colored squares conceals the number seven. Hesitantly, I click the wrong square.

Dr. Hunter runs a hand through his hair so it stands up like he stuck a fork in a wall socket, and gives me an odd bright look. He seems about to say something, but someone calls out that their computer crashed and he is distracted.

I bolt down the gray hall to the outside, ignoring Al's cry of "Whitney, where are you going? You're not supposed to leave the building during group time," as I pass her office. Outside is gray also. Dirty snow, dirty cars on soggy pavement. A bus is pulling up beyond the hospital gates, and I hurry over and get on board before I fully know what I'm doing. I have just enough change in my pocket for the fare.

"Tell me," I ask the driver, "Are there any cultural experiences nearby? Art, dinosaurs, anything?"

"There's an excellent museum a few stops from here. No dinosaurs, I'm afraid, but lots of art."

"Fine. That's fine."

When the bus pulls up in front of the museum, I realize that my remaining three cents are not sufficient monies to gain me entrance. I could tell them my story, maybe, that I'm an escaped mental patient seeking high culture. If they have any poetry in them, they will let me in for free. Or I could just do what I'm better at, which is sneak in. There's a back entrance to the gallery in the gift shop, and it's a simple matter to wait until someone comes in from the exhibit, then slip through the door before it closes behind them.

Inside, I run my hands over the draped red ropes and gulp down the civilized museum air. I can hear people making polite pigeon noises of appreciation in the Thomas Cole exhibit beyond. I stand among them, solemn, moved, and nearly guilty, like a dog that's been let into the parlor during a tea party and allowed the rare luxury of a chocolate or a sprig of grapes. I walk the halls in reverent silence, drinking in the glorious oil landscapes, the bronze deities of Egypt, and the modernist's childlike lamentations of color and blank canvas. This is what humanity has produced, trying to make itself immortal.

At the end of a hall filled with old tea sets, there is a dusty stairwell blocked off with a length of red cord. In the space of a few seconds, I concoct a plan for my future. I will duck under the forbidden rope and live in the storage room above. At night, I will sneak down to the cafeteria and feast on leftover pear and brie salads, I'll borrow Van Gogh starry nightgowns from the gift shop and bathe in Cupid's Fountain on the first floor. I will live among that which is eternally beautiful, no one will tell me to make eye contact or tie my shoes, and nothing I wear or touch or breathe will smell of microwaveable oatmeal and institutional gray carpets.

"Ma'am," says an authoritative voice, and I whirl around to see a security guard standing behind me. "The museum is closing in five minutes. Didn't you hear the announcement? Please make your way to the exit."

Walking across the majestic entrance hall, tiled in white marble and gold, I pause to dip a finger in Cupid's Fountain. The water is much too cold to bathe in. When I get back to the halfway house, they scold me like a child who tried to run away to China on her bike, but got as far as the edge of town before she realized that it's father than it looks on the map. They take away my outing privileges for a week for disobeying the rules of the program. Freedom is to be earned. I'm not entirely sure they're wrong; it *is* farther than it looks on the map. Much farther.

CHAPTER TWENTY-SEVEN

I've reached the zenith of the day, which is to say lunch, surrounded by sleepy patients nodding over their trays. Specifically, I am not really eating but picking the raisins out of a cup of rice pudding and flicking them in the general direction of the trash. When I hear someone approaching, I assume it's Al coming to talk to me about how raisins are an important part of a nutritious diet and healthy lifestyle, and I alter my raisin trajectory accordingly. Too late, I see that it's Dr. Hunter.

"Could I have a word with you, Whitney?" he says, picking the raisin delicately off his shirt front.

"Sorry, I didn't mean . . ."

"No, not about that." A smile flickers across his face. "Would you come into my office?"

I abandon my pudding willingly. In his office, Dr. Hunter shifts a towering stack of journals off a chair for me.

"When you first came here, we gave you tests to assess your level of cognitive functioning. For my research and the program's own purposes."

He waits to see if I will speak. When I don't, he continues.

"On the general intelligence test, your list of the continents failed to include Europe, you couldn't solve a simple mental arithmetic problem, and you were unable to name the current president of the United States."

"I don't really keep up with politics." That was decadent and unnecessary. Irony is above you now, beyond your means to express.

"Yes," says Dr. Hunter quietly, "I thought so." He takes a piece of paper from his pocket and hands it to me. The page is limp and creased, as though it had previously been crushed into a ball.

"This fell out of the recycling bin," he says. "It's yours, isn't it?"

I shrug.

He glances down, and for a moment it appears that he is going to read it aloud. For a moment I want him to. I want to hear my words spoken, resounding, *voiced*. But he just holds out the paper, and I take it automatically. I'm surprised he could read it. The handwriting is disjointed, chaotic.

"A few years ago, there was a young man here who was around your age," says Dr. Hunter. "He talked a lot, and most of it didn't make any sense, but sometimes it did. He stayed here a while, and he started to make more sense, but most people didn't notice because he was talking about physics, and physics all sounds like delusion if you've never studied it. We ended up having a similar conversation to the one I'm having with you now." There is a curious sensation of heat and pressure building around my solar plexus. Possibly it is hope, but I don't dare label it as such.

"What happened to him?"

"He's in graduate school. Studying physics."

"Quantum physics?"

"I believe so."

"Everyone wanted to hear about it when I was in college, more than anything." Now that I've started talking I can't seem to stop. "Maybe because we were questioning the world, seeing disorder in everything. And at the highest levels, physics *is* chaos. And then we have to pretend it can't be true in the real world, that it's somehow separate from us, academic. Because how do you survive otherwise?"

That flicker. That sudden light in Dr. Hunter's eyes when he sees I am an intelligent being is like a drug. That flinty spark of a mind striking a mind. Suddenly, I want that glint of recognition in everyone's eyes, everyone who looks at me. I do not want them telling me to tie my shoes and make eye contact. I want their eyes to blaze when they meet mine because they see something in me that catalyzes, that ignites.

But now, under the directness of Dr. Hunter's gaze, the words coagulate and scab over. I look up at him pleadingly, though I don't know what I'm asking for. Approval. Permission.

Forgiveness.

I swallow hard and enact the potential. "Not . . . not being stupid, OK, being exceptionally unstupid, in terms of, like, facile academics . . . It's not always enough. It's not the only reason people don't survive in the world." My voice sounds dusty and feels raw in my throat from lack of use.

"I'm not here to tell you what to do with your life, Whitney. But

I teach some very bright students, and I think even among them you would be exceptional."

"Please don't . . . I'm not." Please don't offer me the world. I'm not ready to take that weight again.

He holds up his hands. "I'm sorry. I'm not your doctor, and it's not my place."

I get up and move to the exit.

"But Whitney?"

I stop in the doorway.

"Think about it."

I step out of his office and hold the paper in shaking hands. My handwriting really does look like something a serial killer would leave scrawled in blood or lipstick on a corpse or the face of a shattered mirror. And the content.

Dear Sir,

I'm not quite sure how to address you. You never told me your name, and I could take my pick of literary or historic antiheros, since doubtless you had a hand in their formative years, but nothing seems quite right. But as some elder relative has surely told me, just use good manners when in doubt and they will see you through.

I hope you are well. And by that, I mean I hope you are clinging despairingly to a few shattered egos who will ultimately have the courage to reject you, who will choose to destroy themselves or not destroy others if it means you will be cast into the realm of things neither seen nor imagined, existing only as a bleak probability again, waiting for some body in motion to strike you in the dark and once again collapse you into being. I hope you have to wait a long time.

I hear you sometimes, in the messages you send to others. Your silver poetic voice, the one that flashes through the darkness between stars and axons. Sometimes people hear and look up for a moment, hazily, from their cell phones or self-help books. They look around for an insect or a drop of rain, for the thing that has taken them momentarily outside themselves. The things you tell them . . . I don't wonder that they need self-help books. Every one of them is haunted by the ghosts of things unsaid to consciousness, but they are never as open as I was, and you break them down without ever reaching their ears. And you sound so sad. Or maybe I'm projecting, and it's just that the pills make everything sound slow and entropic. Maybe someday I'll scatter them from some high place in a revoltingly symbolic gesture and beg you to come back to me.

This is beginning to sound, disgustingly, like a love letter. I'm not much of a writer, but I know when you've written something and it nauseates you to the core, you've hit upon truth. Is it even possible that I can live in this world, having glimpsed through your eyes all the riotous potentials from which we must look away or blind ourselves? I think if you rolled the dice a dozen times for the outcome of that moment, maybe six times I would be a utilitarian, a hedonist, a psycho killer. Hesitation saved me from *becoming* with you eternally, and I am so glad of physics' inescapable straitjacket keeping time and matter in line, promising that choice will never return to me again. But in such a linear world, I also have no chance of redemption, because I can never unlive that moment in which all things were possible. So if it was only me you were really trying to destroy—well played.

Beyond that, I can only confess that sometimes my deeper structures wish you were still observing, that you could bathe me once more in the pure light of delusion and fill the part of me that was born empty. Sometimes the scar tissue is not enough.

Signed,
Your Other,
the one left real as we reach the end of this.

———◆———

The night nurse is bent over some papers in her office, and my medication is set out on the edge of the desk. As I pop the pill out of its plastic bubble, it seems to leap up out of my grasp like a living thing. It flashes briefly in the air, then falls and rolls away beneath a filing cabinet. The nurse looks up and I take a swallow of water.

"OK," she says, exploring the folds of my oral cavity with a tongue depressor and a small flashlight. "Thank you."

They always thank us for swallowing, because on some level they know what we are giving up. If paranoia is truth, then delusion means you are important enough to be persecuted. The nurse asks if I want a snack. I say yes and she brings me a cup of blue sherbet from the freezer, which is kept padlocked because there is little else to do here but eat blue sherbet. I take the dessert to my room and spoon it up mechanically as I sit on the windowsill, watching the traffic lights change in the distance. Green to yellow to red to green to yellow to red. How quickly my life is ticking away when measured in traffic lights. Flashes of headlights make raindrops on the window glitter briefly, then go dark.

Something crunches between my teeth. I spit out white fragments like eggshell, sticky with saliva. I remember Alexis doing the same innumerable times before. Her favorite spoils from the ice cream truck, a cup of blue raspberry sherbet with a gumball in the center. She always spat the gumball into the grass. I'd see it the next day sometimes, covered in ants. Once she got one without a gumball and complained bitterly until the ice cream guy gave her another one with a gumball in it, which she spat into the grass.

The window is wet on the inside now. I press my face against the glass, but it will not yield to tears. My mouth is sticky with the film that forms when something sweet is left too long in your mouth and begins to decay. I think the acid taste is the excrement of bacteria. I go to the bathroom and brush my teeth hard to erase the intolerable taste of nonexistent fruits and life I can no longer claim. Back in my room, I put on the radio so my mind is filled with something other than itself, but the songs all sound as if they were produced by Orwell's versificator.

click. Rock station. *I gave you my heart and you ripped it out bleeding*
click. Pop. *Baby, I gave you my heart but you just walked away*
click. Country. *I gave you my heart, but you can't have my truck*

I switch to AM radio, some staticky call-in show. With the odd sense that something above or below me has planned this with sinister or tender care, I realize the program host is an ornithologist. He is telling a caller why flamingos stand on one leg.

Because if they lifted the other, they'd fall over.

Staticky laugher from the ornithologist, silence from the caller.

But seriously. Flamingos stand in cold water all day, so raising one foot under their feathers conserves body heat and prevents the delicate webbing between their talons from pruning up, like yours do if you stay in a bath too long. Incidentally, flamingos are pink because shrimp, their favorite food, contain chemicals called carotenoids that pigment the shrimp and the flamingo in turn.

That's interesting, says the caller, I never knew that.

The program fades into white noise.

—•◆•—

For a second time I awaken in the dark, frozen in a night-terror state of arousal and unreality. I feel him breathing, quicksilver knife inhale, forbidden fruit hot copper exhale, and wait trembling for him to speak. But something of my mind is beyond his authority now—the neurons to which he whispers are drugged and stupefied. When I feel him fading away, I am seized by a paroxysm almost as violent as when he came, but of my own making. He isn't squeezing my lachrimal ducts; the tears splashing onto the sheets are those of a free agent.

When my own consciousness starts to slip and spiral, I am not falling asleep but falling away. The center of the earth stops holding me down, and I am suddenly free to spin off into the time and place that almost came together, that might have been if my fingers had tightened over the sticky mouth and refused to let go.

In fact, I am free to go nowhere else. It draws me in like a vortex, and whether in a place of universal truth or only a truth of my own, it *is*.

CHAPTER TWENTY-EIGHT

I am standing in front of the barn where I keep my horse, and the air is thick and sweet and hard to breathe. For no apparent reason it is summer, and the leaves hang limp on the trees, seeming to have ceased respiration. The flowers lining the path smell too strongly of their essence, like cheap perfume. The barn, weathered and gray and knowing, stands impassive before me. The windows are opaque, the door closed. A white cat is sitting in the middle of the path. It looks up at me with the bluest eyes I have ever seen and rolls over to expose its belly, a posture of submission. I kick the animal viciously in the ribs and send it skittering into the rose bushes.

"I've been wanting to do that for a long time," I say. The cat slithers out of the thorns and trots down the path toward the stable. It pauses at the doorway and looks at me archly. The door is cracked to reveal perfect darkness within.

"Why did you bring me here?"

My voice seems too loud and abrasive for this place, like fingernails scraping on flower petals. No answer, and the cat slips through the door. I look around and see that the houses across the street seem to have melted a little, like frosted cakes in the sun. Peripheral things like the numbers on mailboxes are impossible to focus on; they slip away as languidly as the dandelion seeds drifting through the lifeless, pudding-sweet air. Someone has taken great care to get the barn right. Every knot and crack in the wood is as it should be, its shadow is cool and dark. An ant climbs up the wall and disappears between two boards. The only reality is in front of me.

When I step inside, the light from the doorway seems to lose its nerve a few yards in. I scrabble my hand on the wall for a switch and several bulbs flicker to life, but they seem to light only themselves and not the air around them. Waiting halfway down the dim aisle, the white cat is brighter than the lights.

A snort beside me makes my heart skip. A rolling white-rimmed eye stares out at me from the darkness of Apollo's stall. I reach out toward the soft nose, but he retreats with the sound of hooves scuffling through straw. Walking down the aisle, I can feel the other horses watching, but see only silhouettes and the shine of eyes.

The cat turns and trots away when I get within kicking distance again. I follow it through the labyrinth of underground storage rooms. The remnant of sunshine that seeps through the boards above is barely enough to clarify the dimensions of each room. I pause to contemplate the exoskeleton of a rusting carriage, then look around and realize the cat is nowhere in sight.

The splintered door ahead stands ajar, and I don't consider that he could have gone back the way we came. I step into the room and find myself at the edge of some kind of pit or root cellar. A dusty window high above casts the only light in the room. At first, I see only what you might expect: scattered straw, a rusted bucket, some fraying ropes and feed sacks. Then a splash of red catches my eye, a small form crumpled at the base of the ladder. My blood is replaced with liquid panic, adrenaline so pure my muscles shake because I won't let them fight or run.

"How . . . this isn't possible. I didn't bring him here."

The cat only sits by the ladder and washes its paws. A gurgle from below—the boy stirs, his head falling back against the ladder. The red was only from his shirt . . . I don't see blood, but the shaft of light from above make his eye sockets look gaunt and hollow, his face old.

With the mechanical calm that comes when you've used up the raw materials that manufacture fear, I climb down the ladder. The buzz of flies and a rotting smell emanate faintly from the corner. Someone has tied the boy's hands together with loops of baling twine. Anyone who has never been tied up this way might think this method of restraint inadequate, but just try to open a bale of hay without a knife. The boy's skin is ashen pale, blue veins lacing the small wrists. I reach down for the radial pulse, then hesitate. Maybe to avoid putting my fingerprints on him, or because touching him will make this real.

But fingerprints don't trace on skin, and I don't think I'm the one who gets to decide what is real. If everything is a nonzero probability, if every choice creates a world, then it is not only possible but certain that, in some reality, I have caused this to be. Since I am observing it now, it's at least as real as I am. Not a ringing endorsement to be sure, but the burden is on me to act. My Swiss Army knife is lying in the straw several feet away; someone isn't being very subtle. It's strange to see it separated from me, like looking at your own limb lying cut off on the floor. The cat, sitting on the ladder, arches its tail into a question mark.

I think of the leaden doom that has shadowed me since I watched this small catalyst run away home. Butterflies in China, a storm that could have been averted with a little insecticide. I feel no attachment to this ragdoll propped up before me. His eyes are hidden beneath lids that tremble as exquisitely as moth wings in seizure or sleep or dream within another's desolate dream. As long as they stay closed, he is not a boy, just a symbol to be interpreted and acted upon accordingly. The juice stains on his mouth elicit no imagined snack scene in a sunny kitchen, and I've forgotten his name along with my own. He is just a small column of elements that has not yet learned to spew many words, and this decision has the purity of a hypothetical scenario on a philosophy exam. Or is physics the subject in question here? Maybe if I dispose of this variable, this world will remain constant and there will be no more gray carpets, no daily goal sheets, no sedated slow motion basketball games or people painted in primary colors telling me to look them in the eye. Maybe I can spend a quiet eternity with the shadow horses and the cryptic moonlight cat instead. Either way, it's a half-life of one kind or another.

The square of light cast by the window forms a makeshift hourglass, drifting across the floor by imperceptible degrees. There is no ticking down of finite seconds, no maternal cries growing ever closer, no absolute zero when the bomb must be disarmed or the world must end. But I know, I have always known what I would do in the dark and the quiet. I flick the knife open with only a glimmer of taffy-induced hesitation. What is right action in a world without God or judgment?

A quick slash of silver and it's done.

I unwind the severed rope from the boy's wrists. His arm bleeds a little, nicked by the blade. There is a feed sack on the floor, a bucket of water. A gag and a drowning pool. On the ladder, the white cat watches me inscrutably with its impossibly blue eyes.

I dip the sack in the bucket and wipe the cut clean. The cat zigzags down the ladder and slips into the shadows. The hum of flies becomes offended, and I hear the sound of small bones crunching. I form a cup with my hands and trickle water between the child's cracked lips. Most of it runs out the corners, but he splutters and coughs and his eyes move spasmodically beneath the lids. I scoop more water, and this time he swallows properly, and the eyes open. I don't know what I expect—fear, confusion—but there is nothing. He looks at me with the blank eyes of a doll. I notice for the first time that there's a bruise with a bloody center on his temple. Did I . . . ? But guilt is irrelevant in a world formed by the not-chosen of my actions.

Something crackles in my pocket as I crouch to take a closer look at the wound. A starlight mint, of which I always carry a few in my pocket for Apollo. It's a melted Dali pendant, the red bleeding into the white and signifying, no doubt, something I do not care to interpret. Forests of metaphors, and we must cut out their eyes so there is nothing to reflect us. I don't need the Other to be horrible inside, or to show mercy still. This is a heavy conclusion, but a liberating one. If I will suffer for as long as I am, I would rather it be with a clear conscience. I will not kick over sand castles because mine was taken by the tides.

I peel away bits of wrapper and hold the mint out to the child, flat on my hand like you'd feed a horse. His eyes shift from my face to the offering, and after a moment he reaches out and takes the candy, crunches down on it with the same sound as the cat eating a dead something in the corner. When he is finished, his eyes drift closed. At first I think the coolness falling over me is fear, but then I realize the sun has shifted. The light from the window is dissipated, no longer falling in a neat golden square around us. There is no definable danger in this place, but I somehow know I don't want to be here in the dark. I lift the boy and lay him awkwardly across my shoulder. Even half dried up like a raisin, he's almost heavier than I can carry. I feel the bat of eyelashes against my neck, so I know he's awake. I bring him to the ladder and press his body against it.

"You're too heavy for me to carry," I say. I don't know if he can understand me, but I always did at that size, so I speak as if he can. "You have to climb." I press him against the ladder, but his fingers curl like defensive caterpillars. Still unnaturally silent, his only rebellion is to become dead weight in my arms.

"Please, you don't want to stay here." I look around the cellar with its carefully chosen accoutrements. The smell of rotting has gotten stronger. The boy lets his feet slide off the rung and hangs limply in my arms, which begin to shake with fatigue. Maybe I will have to leave him after all.

Something hurtles past my cheek and lands on the ladder above us. The cat licks the pink from its whiskers and emits a bright meow that captures the child's fading attention and consciousness. His hand reaches up to tug the white tail, which waves tantalizingly as the cat springs up out of reach. The boy's clumsy feet find the second rung, then the third. A sticky hand again reaches upward; this time, the cat catches a glancing pat on the ribs before it can slither to higher ground.

Soon the cat is sitting on solid boards, peering down at the child's surprisingly rapid progress. Indeed, he is forced to retreat as acquisitive fingers strain for his whiskers. Now the child is flopping onto the floorboards, having forgotten that a starlight mint is not much sustenance for a growing boy, that his hands were recently tied together. There is a cat to be played with if only he can find where it has gone. His eyes search the perimeter—there, by the door! His legs are clumsy, but he's used to that because he has not yet learned to walk any other way. He chases the cat through the maze of forgotten rooms, out into the cubist nightmare of a world. The girl follows some distance behind them, hoping he will not trip and need to be carried, hoping she will not have to touch him again.

At last they are out in the clear daylight that hurts their eyes. The cat is trotting down the driveway now—he has got to hurry if he wants to catch it. He looks back at the girl. She is awkward, doesn't like looking at him. She strips some pink flowers from a blossoming tree. Instead of being petals, they crumble like moist cake in her hand. She is becoming like the landscape, not quite real. Only the eyes are still right, made of membranes and veins and vitreous humor instead of ideas.

The white cat capers across the street, waving that long tail just right to pull, and the boy follows him home to a time and place that wasn't. The girl stays behind to watch them for as long as she can, holding her crumbled flowers. Her eyes are turning metaphoric too, symbols of eyes drawn with too few shades. The shine is already fading.

Chapter Twenty-Nine

Upon entering the day program one morning, I notice a stack of pamphlets on the front desk, announcing a contest for student research on mental illness. I slip one into my pocket like contraband, glancing around to make sure I haven't been seen.

Over the next several weeks, during the free time between groups, I dash off a 25-page research paper on the history, neurobiology, and causal theories of schizophrenia. It's not particularly original, the tone is robotic, and I'm pretty sure I screwed up my APA references. But there's something about crafting these dry factual sentences, peppering semicolons in all the right places and directing the flow of regurgitated information in a smooth and economical stream that makes me feel more at peace than I have in a long time. Writing this, it's more luxuriant than scented bubble bath and red wine. But don't get used to it, I tell myself. You no longer have the right to derive pleasure from language. And surely you remember what happens when words form where they don't belong.

But instead of falling silent, I keep writing, and it gets worse because I'm getting creative now, encapsulating a small piece of my own story in the paper, and finding poetry and art to put in the margins. Now I'm submitting it to the judges, even though I've promised to forsake any further acts of creation in my life.

A month later, I receive an email from the medical director of the hospital informing me that I've won first prize in the contest, and that I'm cordially invited to present my paper at an award ceremony following grand rounds. When the day program staff find out about this, they are perplexed, and rightly so, for I don't think I have ever given them reason to believe that my cognitive capacity lies much beyond that of your average root vegetable. Only Dr. Hunter seems unsurprised, and he tells me he is looking forward to my presentation when he passes me in the hall.

My parents come and take me shopping for something other than ripped jeans and a Nirvana hoodie to wear to the ceremony. We go out to dinner afterward, to some restaurant with candles melting down the necks of old wine bottles, and little dishes of withered olives on the table. It seems like a fancy sort of place, or maybe I've just gotten used to eating from trays. My parents keep telling me how proud they are, but they look perplexed too. I can't really blame them, because so am I. What was I thinking? I've never told anyone, not even Dr. Caspian, some of the things I put in that paper. When my steak comes, it bleeds red juice onto my plate and I hear malicious laughter sizzling in the hot fat. I look down at the knife in my hand, and suddenly I can't eat a bite. I've made a terrible mistake, letting this thing called desire have its way with me. There's no telling what it will want next, what kinds of dangerous freedom it will demand.

⸻

The award ceremony is held in the conference room where psychiatrists at the hospital do grand rounds. For all I know, Dr. Caspian could have presented my own case here. The other winners are mostly university students, psychology majors from nearby schools presenting their capstone projects and senior theses. They chat easily with each other, they are so full of promise. Maybe one day they'll be therapists or psychiatrists.

When I go up onto the podium to receive my award, heat is shedding from my body like an extra skin and my palms are slick with sweat. I can see my parents in the audience, Dr. Hunter and some of the other day program staff. Then, with a start, I notice a familiar figure in a black suit in the back row—Dr. Caspian. We make eye contact briefly, then I drop my eyes to the printout on which I've marked the passages I want to read. I was just going to do a little of the gruesome history—

insulin comas, lobotomies, et cetera, then concede that things have gotten somewhat better, and talk about transcranial magnetic stimulation, which is what the guest lecturer from Yale is researching. But now my eyes stray down to the last paragraphs, where things get personal.

People are expecting me to talk now, and I find that I can no longer stay silent, or hide behind words that mean little to me. "I wrote this paper on the history of schizophrenia, and how the conception and treatment of the disorder has evolved with the cultural zeitgeist and our understanding of neurobiology," I begin, "But most of you already know that because it's what you research or because those are the patients you work with every day. So I won't tell you what you already know, and I don't think that's why I'm here anyway."

And I go on to explain who I am—a patient here, not a student any longer—and read my account of the first time I heard the Other in the dark: no resolution, no interpretation, just a brief portrait of a brain interrupted. It sounds jarring and out of context in this academic environment—too personal, too literary, too shocking—and I jump in my skin at the sound of applause when I reach the end.

The medical director makes some closing remarks, and everyone gathers in the next room for sandwich triangles and fruit pieces. I mutter thanks, thanks, thank you as people come up to congratulate me, then flee to the bathroom and splash water on my flushed face. My reflection watches accusingly from the mirror and reminds me that I'm only a ghost now—I can only pass through people, I cannot touch or move them.

When I go back out, hoping everyone has left for the tour of the MRI lab, my parents tell me that Dr. Caspian was looking for me, but there was an emergency on his unit and he had to leave. I can imagine from experience what such an emergency might entail, and I don't envy him. But it's too bad, because there are things I might have liked to say to him if I'd had the chance. For example: I'm sorry I was so difficult, that I argued with everything you said, and blamed you when you couldn't restore order to my shattered world despite your Harvard education and paternalistic attitude of material reductionism.

It isn't in my nature to listen to people with more education and experience than myself, but your faith in science and reason was a comfort, even when I couldn't share it.

I never told you this, but there were times when I'd close my eyes and imagine we were in your office with that ridiculous snow globe on the table between us. You'd just look at me without saying anything, observing with a worldview that held no place for entities multiplied beyond necessity, and often the Other would be silenced until I lapsed back into my own chaotic truth.

But if you were here, I may also have been tempted into some false display of bravado. I'd probably have told you I was intending to get a Ph.D. now, or even write a book. Just enough of my obstinacy might have returned that I'd start looking around me longing. So it's probably better that you had to go and talk someone's giant spiders or communist spies into nonexistence, to dispense more of your secular holy water that anesthetizes demons but does not exorcise them.

———◦•◦———

My monthly meeting with the day program clinicians is the following week. Usually, these involve me sitting in petulant silence while the staff give status updates on my recent behavior. "Whitney has seemed unusually tired during group this week. Whitney has been eating too much ice cream and gaining weight."

My parents hang on to every word as if it were a message scrawled inside a bottle that had traversed the Atlantic Ocean. I know it costs a lot of money for me to be here, and I wonder if they are thinking about everything I've taken from them. All the bedtime stories and organic apple juice and handmade dollhouses filled with Victorian replica furniture and occupied by velveteen rabbits and bears. They wanted a simpler and happier life for me. Berry-picking, visits to historic battlefields, no MTV. And all the *lessons*—riding and art and music, tae kwon do and compass navigation and revolver marksmanship. All that and it's come to this. They must be so disgusted. I would be. I'd want a refund.

Today, however, all eyes turn to me and remain there steadily, expecting more. They have seen what I am capable of, and now they expect complete sentences. Progress, that's what they tell me I'm making. I've moved from the Dark Ages into the Enlightenment, chosen reason over superstition, and now I'm going to be OK. But they're going too far, now they're talking about discharge planning, asking how I feel about leaving the program next month, maybe taking an online class or two.

These people are supposed to be experts—don't they see I'm an unstable element, that I need to be contained in an airless place away from direct sunlight or there's no telling what could happen? I want them to put me in ice water and threaten me with leeches. I want my freedom taken from me because it's sharp and dangerous. Stop telling me that my life is mine, that with treatment and support I can have a normal life. I've drowned that future, and now I want to lie here holding my breath.

But there is something in me that's still burning, that will not extinguish. They say the best predictor of the future is the past, and haven't I already made my choice within the confines of a closed system that does not let us pick the color of our eyes or our desires? Maybe I was a demon, but I chose to be good, and perhaps now I have the choice to simply be a girl.

Apparently my paper has been disseminating, because someone has gotten a hold of a copy and the psychiatrist is reading from it. He looks at me over the top with raised eyebrows. He is impressed, but I read accusation in his expression. *What more do you want from us?* And now I see the answer: an excuse. I want to be told how I am broken. But I'm not, I'm only afraid now, and nervously I stroke the cover of my Nietzsche compendium. I've read the words so often that I don't need to look at them, I just like to have them near. Nietzsche died in madness; his biology offered him no second chances. But if time is a circle, this is no defeat because he always comes around again to give the world the graceful imperative that has lodged itself inside me as an antidemon.

I still live, I still think. I still have to live, for I still have to think . . . I want to learn more and more to see as beautiful what is necessary in things; then I shall be one of those who make things beautiful . . . I do not want to wage war against what is ugly, I do not want to accuse those who accuse. . . . All in all and on the whole, some day I wish to be only a Yes-sayer.

And as for sickness: Would we not almost be tempted to ask if we can do without it? . . . It is only great pain, the slow protracted pain that takes its time, as if we are burned with green wood, that compels us philosophers to descend into our ultimate depths and cast away all that is good-hearted, palliated, soft, and average where we previously reposed. I doubt whether such pain "improves"—but I do know it deepens us.

My dear philosopher, my horse-hugging syphilitic mad genius who was possibly even more of a social retard than myself, I will try to live by your words. I am terrified by the possibility of my own violence or mediocrity outside this sheltered place, but I will not pass the dice. And so, as the psychiatrist and the social worker and the occupational therapist delineate the plan for my release into the wild, I do not fight to stay in my cage. I nod, I shrug, I acquiesce. It's not a very noble sort of affirmation, but it's a start.

CHAPTER THIRTY

The laws of our world are such that things naturally decay, but it takes a great deal of energy to make them whole again. My parents have sold the house I grew up in, and moved to a town with an art community that doesn't involve spray paint and railroad bridges. The new house is bleak and modern with not a single stained glass window or spiral staircase to its name. Alexis has moved to Colorado and Evie, having been impregnated by Drake, has fallen out with her family and gone with her. Home again but not really home, I feel like the proverbial cat of the experiment: neither alive nor dead, happy or unhappy, constantly observed yet always alone.

Apollo is my only friend and confidante—with him I explore the wooded trails of his new stable, different woods in which I have not left small pieces of my soul. They are still a treacherous place for me—their ambient sounds so easily form into dangerous voices. But Apollo protects me, he carries me steadfastly through the vales of whispering pine and muttering streams, and the ring of his hooves against small stones are a chime that clears my mind as a Buddhist bell is struck to echo through delusion. Alone with horse and nature, I am closer to being human than I may ever be when surrounded by others of my species, trapped within their dead walls.

But I try. Each day, I write down a series of small tasks to be performed: Buy groceries, make dinner, twenty pushups, fold the laundry. It seems vulgar to break one's life down into a series of mundane accomplishments—surely everyone of consequence has lived a continuous and poetic existence, no need for daily goal sheets—but it succeeds in filling the hours so that each one passes relatively smoothly into the next, so maybe I have learned something from my Life Skills Training after all. I force an act of creativity into each day, dragging out my old craft supplies from the basement. I make beaded chokers, blobby clay horses, layered bottles of colored sand. Things for the alien anthropologists to find in a million billion years as proof that I once existed. In a box of embroidery floss, I find a half-finished collar and a ten-year-old container of Whiskas seafood-flavored cat treats.

My parents are busy with their own lives, and for the most part I am left to my own devices, free to lie in the sun and read my philosophy books or lie in my room and listen to Nirvana CDs on eternal repeat. I do studio work for my mother, I take care of Apollo, I go to doctor's appointments, and that seems to be all anyone expects of me. It's an easy life, a tranquil life, yet I still feel defeated. Symbolically I've chosen the upward path, but I don't feel closer to truth or vitally alive.

Indeed, I am listless and indifferent on the subject of phenomenology, and I don't know if this represents an evolution in my spiritual development or simply a learned helplessness born of my inability to find a solid foundation, to form any opinion about what I've experienced or why. Most philosophers seem to be in agreement that it's happiness, not truth or meaning, that's the highest good in life. Yet it seems almost a vulgar thing to desire, happiness—isn't spiritual terror a much loftier and more meaningful condition? Still, I think I'd settle for it if it didn't seem equally far away, as theoretical as unicorns or quantum foam, existing only in a dream or an equation I can never hope to understand.

In part, I think it's the drugs that are causing this, quite literally turning my world gray. They are not just antipsychotic, but anti-everything. I do not feel scared or violent, but also I do not feel. It may be that their slow drain of my chemicals is the only thing keeping me sane, but there's a reason that many patients stop taking them despite all rational evidence to the contrary. The brain states that produce psychosis are similar to those that get us incredibly, omnisciently high, and the drugs take this away, both the terror and the elation of madness. On the physical plane, there's no doubt they're destroying me. I am swollen and shaking and I drool into the pillow at night. Even my blood is speaking out on my behalf, my liver enzymes, blood sugar, and serum lipids raising their wordless alarm that something is going very wrong inside me.

At the hospital, the doctors told me I would relapse if I ever stopped taking the medication, that I would be a danger to myself and others. And how can I deny this? Yet as the months pass, I begin to choke on this knowledge, to regurgitate it into napkins and flush the slimy pills into the sewers to dispense sanity equitably to all as it leaches into the groundwater. When I get careless and begin to leave them in pockets and behind sofa cushions, my parents raise the alarm. The doctor says you won't outfox me, and switches to liquids. I become adept at carrying on conversations while holding 15 milliliters of cherry-flavored antipsychotic syrup in my mouth. I know I have no moral grounds to exercise my freedom, but I'm rotting from the inside and I simply do not care about the greater good.

Besides, I know by now that the Other and the self have nothing left to say to one another. My mind may not be content to stay in a Newtonian world of order and reason, but my demon will not return. They have their pride, and he knows he won't get what he wants from me. Even now, it almost seems absurd to think of him as a real entity and not some neurochemical mirage. We seekers lust for the inexplicable until it finds us, and then we prefer it be explained in terms we can understand. We throw rocks into the abyss and run like hell when something moves. But even so, I cannot separate my philosophy from my life. When I face the possibility that my every action bears the weight of countless repetitions, I'll take the path of uncertainty and doubt over the simple explanation that my brain is broken and only this patented drug will fix it.

In making this choice, I stand in defiance of scientists with more education than I'll ever have, doctors who speak with despotic certainty, and my weary parents who only want to keep me safe. The people on the Internet who advocate a drug-free approach to recovery often don't sound like they're doing so well, and for once in my life, I'm not filled with the conviction that whatever choice I make is by definition the right one. So I hide it for as long as I can, and when the truth comes out my justifications sound empty and childish. Don't you see I'm only sick in a different way now? Don't you see that things aren't better at all? My arguments crumble against the reasoned, measured, weighted words of the clinicians, and my parents insist that I must take the medication. If I refuse, I'll have to go back to the hospital.

I love and I despise the sinuous nature of words, how they twist to form black into white. Demons love words and I have always had a little demon in me, long before I was ever possessed. Words spill out of me until they erode the better judgment of their opposition, and I do not have to take the medication anymore. My parents do not think this is right, but I continue speaking and for some reason they agree, and I feel like at any moment my tongue will split down the center, like a snake's. But I want to be good. I want to be still inside and not hurt things, and I can only hope this is enough.

The world reacts philosophically enough to the absence of dopamine blockers in my brain. It brightens, gravity stops pinning me to my bed with date-rape force, the characters of objects and plants emerge from their dead state. Things get too clear, crescent moons become malevolent smiles and leaves scrape cryptic equations on the glass of my bedroom window. I try to observe without attachment, to notice without reacting, and these things remain as passing phenomena and do not conspire to topple me from my throne of self and ruler.

In the fall, I enroll in an online social psychology course at my former university, and my papers are returned with glowing comments. I love my glossy textbook, I love videos of students turned into prisoners and gorillas strolling unnoticed through basketball games, I love the game of explaining these things. Psychology comes naturally to me, but "social" still eludes me. Even brief interactions with librarians and post office clerks leave me drained and shaken. People who used to know me are even worse—I can feel their gazes oozing over me like that sludgy filling between the pecans in certain pies, chokingly sweet and sticky with pre-conceptions, binding my tongue to the roof of my mouth because neither they nor I know who I am anymore. At least in my essays, no one needs to know that I could never deliver those words while looking someone in the eye, or that I have no business saying anything about how normal people behave in social situations, because I'm not one of those at all.

———————

Months pass, it's winter again, and on Christmas eve there is a family gathering at my aunt and uncle's. I'd rather stay home and watch little Ralphie shoot his eye out with a BB gun, but that would not be Socializing or Normal.

The house is like a Yankee Candle outlet with sofas, decorated within an inch of its life, tables overburdened with cheese and wine. Small children in tiny suits and dresses stampede underfoot, chasing a dog with a foil bow stuck to its head. Everyone is so prosperous and well coutured. At least on my father's side of the family there are drug addicts and autistic children, but here, all the cousins are in graduate school, are protecting the nation, are saving the whales. The aunts and uncles own businesses, they administrate, they cruise and kayak. The conversations are wrought in terms of "What do you *do?* What have you accomplished this fiscal year?" They tactfully exonerate me from such interrogations—how *glad* we are to see you, what a lovely dress—they are gracious and sincere. They don't disturb me when I go and hide behind a vast pile of wrapped presents with a plate of cheddar cubes and Lindt truffles. But glances sweep discreetly in my direction and the words of a great aunt drift my way:

". . . Ruth and Ken's daughter—schizophrenic. I used to babysit her when she was a little girl. She was in college, had some kind of breakdown. Hardly talks now, been in and out of hospitals for a year. Such a shame . . ."

I set my remaining cheese on the floor for the dog, put on my jacket, and slip out onto the porch. It's snowing, and the scene outside is a postcard of winter suburbia: large houses adorned with tasteful wreaths and strings of gold lights, SUVs slumbering under thick white blankets in the driveways.

The door opens behind me, and I turn to find a little blonde girl of about six, my second niece once removed or something. She's suited up in a pink Barbie snowsuit and purple mittens. "I wanted to play in the snowstorm," she says. "Mommy said I could stay out here as long as you're watching me."

Without waiting for a reply, she flounces past and wades into the waist-deep snow, shields a mitten over her eyes and looks back at me. "Come *on*," she says in the princess tones of an indulged child, "I want to build a snow unicorn."

I stand at the edge of the porch as though it were a precipice filled with writhing snakes. *I can't,* I try to say, *I'm not allowed.* But looking out at the blank canvas of the yard, I realize my hands are already shaping the menagerie. I follow the girl into the snow, good wet packing snow, form a ball between my hands and roll it until it's the size of a yoga ball. Then a second and a third smoothed into shoulders, belly, and haunches, and a fourth on top from which the neck and head are sculpted. I remove my gloves to shape the snow with more finesse, squeezing knees and hooves and crescent ears out of the dense frozen blobs. The girl has fashioned herself a kind of snow throne and is watching me, chewing on an icicle.

"Where did you get that?" I ask. She points to the roof of the house, edged with a row of glittering spines. I knock the largest one off the corner, where it falls like a dagger into a piled drift, then retrieve it and crown the snow horse with his icicle horn.

"Wow," breathes the girl, looking at me like I'm Michelangelo unveiling the roof of the Sistine Chapel.

"Did you know," I say, "that according to Aristotle, the unicorn was already here in the snow. You just have to know what to take away and what to leave behind."

The girl stares at me with woodland creature eyes, then turns and bolts for the house, leaving me alone in the darkening yard. The snow is falling with a seething force, and I am suddenly aware of my cold hands and numb face. I sink down in the snow, the philosopher creep and her pretty unicorn, and watch the panorama of Christmas festivities through the window. Uncle showing off his incongruous tropical fish next to the bejeweled tree, gesticulating, knocking his glass of wine into the tank, red tide diffusing through the electric darting of confused cichlids, a hasty netting of the fish into a bucket of clean water.

I roll another snowball between my fingers and gouge a pair of eyes and a slash of mouth, a kind of disembodied zombie snowman head. I get to my feet and commence a kind of winter free association, fashioning spiny snakes and half-melted jackal creatures and little cats with hollow eye sockets from the snow remaining in the yard. Only when I've scraped down to the frozen grass do I stop to survey the scene, the unicorn now surrounded by a gallery of the dejected and the ghastly. I'm about to start kicking things back to powder when the front door opens and a bar of elongated yellow light spills into the yard. People are streaming out. The girl leading her mother by the hand, my parents, great-aunts and second cousins and goodness knows who else.

". . . looks *just* like a real unicorn, and you *have* to see it," the girl is saying, and everyone gathers round to survey my artisanship. It might not look so bad in sunshine, but here in the blue light of evening it's like someone vomited Dante's inferno onto the yard and coated it in snow, the saintly unicorn beaming in the center of it all.

"It's like . . ." my aunt, always the diplomat, fumbles for polite phrasing. "Like Salvador Dali, with snowmen."

"Very creative," adds a cousin helpfully. "Like a synthesis of the light and dark forces of winter." I believe she is majoring in English at Mount Holyoke.

The elderly great-aunt, the one who declared me Such a Shame, steps forward and puts a hand on my shoulder. "You always were an imaginative child," she says kindly. "When I used to babysit you, you'd pretend your Jell-O cup was an alien slug that was going to eat your brain. You used to hide in my vegetable garden and chase rabbits with your little knife." She chuckles at the memory. "Now why don't you come inside, dear, and have some pie?"

The little girl rushes forward and grabs my hand. "Sit with *me*," she says. "You can help me assemble my Dream Princess riding stable."

"Adrienne is *very* into horses this year," says her mother. "Don't you have a horse? Maybe you can tell her how much work it is." She laughs a dainty bell's laugh and drifts to the house, leaving her daughter adhered to my hand.

"Um, I'll be there in a minute," I say, and hold back while everyone migrates toward the table and warmth.

I believe there are certain events in our lives that can only be described as apocalyptic. Etymologically, it means not an obliteration by fire but a curtain drawn away. Apocalyptic moments are those that if we survive them, can't help but leave us transformed. Sometimes their revelations are quiet and unassuming, snow piling on eyelashes like nuclear fallout, redemption finding its way to the unwilling and afraid. I feel like I owe this snow globe world a prayer or a thanks, but too often we create meaning and metaphor in a world that would prefer to remain mute and self-evident. The hiss of falling snow could be an angel come to me at last to say, "Tabula rasa, my child," and I could read so much into the shadows lurking behind my fractured fairytale snow monsters. But there is no symbolism without consent, and for the moment I am content to leave my grisly menagerie and go eat pie with my family, who have forgiven my strangeness without asking that it be explained.

CHAPTER THIRTY-ONE

One morning in early spring, my father comes into the kitchen while I'm slurping morosely at a mug of twig tea, which is as delicious as it sounds. "The alternative health expo is at the Clarion Hotel this weekend," he says. "Do you want to go?"

"Yeah, OK," I say, gulping down the muddy dregs in my cup. "Janet said I should try meditating with rose quartz to awaken my heart chakra. I bet I can buy some there."

It turns out my parents were quite the hippies back in the day, and since I've decided to seek an alternate route to sanity, they've made appointments for me to see a Chinese herbalist (hence the tea), an acupuncturist, and a naturopathic physician. A couple weeks ago I went to a LuMarian mother goddess healing in which I was informed that I was a serial killer in a prior incarnation—of prostitutes, no less, how unoriginal—and that traces of this violent karma cling to me through my latest rebirth (hence the rose quartz). Maybe she says that to everyone, but I'm not sure I'd be surprised if it were true. I have no disbelief left to suspend in the realm of the spiritual and the sublime, and it seems as reasonable an explanation as any.

"How would you like to see a Peruvian shaman while you're there?" my father continues.

"Um, I guess so." The truth is that I have no idea whether all this chakra clearing and weird tea is doing anything for me. I can't tell if my damp heat is improving or my spleen meridian is circulating more chi. Of course I thought I'd be special, that I'd sense these things, but I don't and it makes me wonder if we're all just drifting in isolated spheres of delusion, that we only intersect in places where particles can be measured and observed.

"He's very good," says my father, "I had a session with him to clear some negative energy as the result of a curse I may have acquired after falling out with a Santeria voodoo priest, back in college."

This is the first I've heard about my father being involved in the occult, but it doesn't really surprise me. I'm not sure anything could, now.

"Why did you fall out with the voodoo priest?" I ask.

"He wanted me to study with him and be his acolyte, but I had realized by then that he was manipulative and evil."

"Are there voodoo priests who aren't?"

"Well, perhaps, but I was young, and dark forces can be very seductive." His words are laced with a certain significance. He's not spoken of his demon again since that night, but I think there is an understanding between us. If there's a genetic predisposition to my peculiar sickness, I have surely acquired it from him.

The alternative health expo does little to assuage my mood of bleak skepticism, however. The rooms are full of vibrational healers, neurolinguistic programmers, maybe some neurolinguistic deprogrammers, crystal workers, and reincarnated Egyptian priests. The only thing more diverse than the healers are the people who have come to see them: college students seeking drug-free enlightenment, people dying of cancer or inexplicably cured of it, people desperately struggling to find their explanation when the gleaming cold idol of science has rung hollow for them. I let myself be swept up in the crowd, jostled past a magpie's hoard of protective amulets and Mother Goddess statues, bins of Chinese herbs and books that promise to help me align my chakras and Find the Goddess Within Me.

All around me, vendors call out to hawk their wares. A lecturer is giving a presentation on ear candling in a curtained-off corner, and someone else is making sample cups of carrot-mangosteen juice with a 1,200-dollar juicing machine. I can get a photo of my aura taken, or for the same price buy what appear to be pieces of glycerin soap embedded with copper wire and bits of shiny foil. A woman draped in gauzy fabric tells me they will saturate my auric field with beneficial orgone energy, but they need to be recharged in the light of each full moon.

I've heard more coherent worldviews expressed in an actual mental hospital, and the Babel of voices surrounding me has the ring of a hundred false prophets crammed into a room that, next weekend, will be full of computer geeks or sadomasochists or aestheticians. I leave for my shamanic healing an hour later with a rose quartz pyramid, a sample cup of carrot-mangosteen juice, and three books that promise to tell me what this all means, each filtered through their strange, implausible, and yet not perfectly improbable lenses.

— ◆ ◆ —

Nightfall finds me standing in the scrubby woods behind the home of a local naturopathic doctor, a friend of my father's who invited us to perform the ceremony at his house, since conflagrations and excessive chanting are looked down upon by the hotel staff. Trees surround us, but I can feel civilization encroaching from all directions. A siren wails in the distance, and the air is suffused with a stomach-churning mixture of hot dogs and gasoline.

The shaman has built a fire ringed with stones on a bare patch of ground. His face is a map of intersecting lines, like an aerial view of a lakebed. He is wearing blue Adidas jogging pants and a woven poncho that smells of smoke and some kind of animal. Marco, his apprentice, translates as the shaman begin to speak in a dying Quechuan dialect.

"The soul is not always like a piece of opal or jade, a solid thing that can be given or taken at will," he says. "Sometimes, it is like a handful of sugar that is poured little by little into the cup of another until there is nothing left but the crystals that cling to the cracks in our hands. Tonight, we will perform a *despacho*, a ritual to call the soul home."

Next to the fire is a paper grocery bag containing an odd assortment of objects: a bouquet of carnations, bottles of perfumed water, dried beans, a container of candy sprinkles, and some plastic toys. Marco pours a pile of coca leaves onto a cloth near the fire and sets a ball of waxy llama fat beside it. As he works, he tells me that the pattern of the llama-wool *mesa* cloth is woven to represent the intersection of sky and forest and river and earth, of all things coming together. He says the llama is a sacred animal in Peru, that it provides food, transportation, and clothing. No family is wealthy without a llama. He gestures for me to sit on a fallen log, and demonstrates how to glue three coca leaves together like a fan with a glob of llama fat.

"Breathe into the leaves," he says. "Everything that does not need to be a part of you. Give it back to the earth."

As I exhale against the leaves, it feels like some spiny exoskeleton is lodged in my esophagus. With every breath that escapes me, I see some sharp fragment in my mind. Blue sky above me and a shadow blocking

— 229 —

out the sun, minnows pecking black specks of decay from my feet. Zoë collapsed beside the toilet, pale as a deep sea fish with glittering spines of *With Teeth*. Blue sky above me and a knife in my hands. And words and words and words, half-formed fetal specimens in jars of murky cerebrospinal fluid, nurtured inside me until they are born. I try to breathe them into the earth, but choke.

I look down and there is a heap of coca-and-llama-fat flowers on the *mesa*. I make a motion to indicate that's all I have to give. The shaman takes the container of rainbow sprinkles and scatters some over the leaves.

"An offering to Pachamama," says Marco. "She likes sweet things."

The shaman adds a handful dried beans and tiny plastic zoo animals to the pile, then pours a cross of red sand over them. He folds the cloth with ritually precise geometry that I can't keep track of, and Marco motions me to stand. As I get unsteadily to my feet, the shaman puts a bouquet of multicolored carnations in my hands. He sets the *mesa* on top of my head. The bundle is heavier than I expected, as though it were filled with something denser than leaves and candy.

The shaman begins to chant, ancient words that raise the hairs on my arms, although I do not understand them. Marco shakes a pair of gourd rattles and whistles a lilting melody. I close my eyes and try to imagine the altitude shifting, the scrawny trees giving way to jagged mountain peaks and condors wheeling in a frozen sky. I open them with a gasp as a cold spray blows across my face. The *mesa* nearly tumbles to the ground, but I steady it with my hand. The shaman tips a bottle of flower essence into his mouth, then spews another fine mist across my face. He takes the bouquet of carnations from my hands and sweeps it across my body, petals sticking to my skin.

I stand obediently motionless and stubbornly self-aware, wanting to lose myself to the ritual but unable to stop wondering exactly what it's going to accomplish. This tradition isn't even my birthright—can people be healed by ceremonies so alien to their native culture? If Pachamama were here, why would she condescend to cure a failed Christian of blue-eyed fascist heritage whose own patron saints have maintained a lofty distance, content to let things play out as they will?

The chanting goes on, and the rattle of the gourds seems to vibrate in every cell of my body. I am liberally coated with flower water and carnation petals . . . it feels as if dozens of butterflies have lit on my bare arms. Eventually, everything stops and I open my eyes. The fire has gone out and there are flowers scattered on the ground, gleaming in the dull bluish void surrounding us.

"That is all," says Marco in the deceptively simple way of mountain shamans.

That is all. My head rings in the silence.

"Before you leave, is there anything you would like to know?"

I look at the men in front of me, poncho-clad silhouettes with glittering eyes. They are medicine men, not philosophers. But somehow I feel they are expecting the question.

"Do you . . ." I try to phrase my words simply. "Do you believe that our selves continue to exist when our bodies decay, or that they're contingent—that they're only illusions that die with us?"

Marco translates for the shaman, then turns back to me.

"Whatever part of you stands here asking if it is real, is real. Every other part of you, not so much."

The smoke that lingers from the fire shimmers around the shaman's head, and he watches me inscrutably with a face of petrified wood.

"Can you see auras?" I ask suddenly. "Like fields of colored light surrounding people's bodies?"

"Yes, these are visible to us."

"What color am I?" I ask, and cringe at how childish the question sounds.

Marco smiles and speaks without consulting the shaman. "When people come to us, we tell them they have rainbow auras. They like that. Rainbows are very popular in America."

"I see."

"And you, you have a rainbow aura. You shine all colors. Red with passion, orange with courage, yellow with optimism, green with generosity, indigo with creativity, and violet with insight."

"Oh."

The shaman says something, and Marco looks at me with interest. "Don Martín says your energy body is full of light and shadow, that you stand between this world and Uku Pacha, beneath. Spirits speak to you, they attach themselves and drain your luminous body, your *runa k'urku k'anchay*."

"How do I make them stop?"

"Oh, you can't do that. But maybe if their stories are told they will not play such cruel games with you." Marco pauses to let the shaman speak again. "Don Martín says you would excel in a profession of exposing that which is hidden: a writer or a social worker or a detective, perhaps. You could even be a shaman. He also says you eat too many heat-forming foods, and that you should drink garbanzo bean water."

"*Garbanzo* bean water?"

"Yes, for your digestion," says Marco. It seems there is a glint of amusement in his eyes, although it's hard to tell. "Before you go, do you have any more questions?"

I don't even know where to begin, and my mind still seems to be stuck on the garbanzo beans. Aren't those chickpeas? What does chickpea water have to do with any of this?

"These demons, these spirits," I finally ask, "are they just out there in the world, waiting for souls to possess, or are they born inside us?"

Marco gazes beyond me for a moment, and I wonder if he did not understand the question. But eventually he says, "The distinction between these, that is not real."

So much for Peruvian shamans not being philosophers. I feel something tingling in my hand and look down to see a small brown spider scurrying across my palm. The clouds shift above and the forest brightens from shadow to silver. Everything is beautiful and symbolic under the ancient sky: the spider, the moment, and moonlight between the trees. Everything is a circle, and the demon is gone. I flick the spider away with my fingernail, send it spinning off into the dark.

"What will you do with the *mesa*?" I ask.

"If we were in Peru, we would let the water carry it away," says Marco. "But the rivers here are not clean, so we will bury it in the earth. This is a slower release, but everything becomes earth in the end."

I look around us. The sky glows orange with light pollution and there are fast-food wrappers half buried in the carpet of pine needles.

"Not everything," I tell him. "We've created things that can never be broken down."

"Yes, we would like to think so," says Marco with a peculiar half-smile.

The shaman is sweeping the leftover coca leaves into a sandwich bag, wrapping the blob of llama fat in tin foil. I give Marco the money for the ritual and his smile broadens. "Other people, they come to us because they are afraid of ghosts and curses," he says. "We are only afraid of the bills coming in at the end of the month."

He holds out the disheveled remnants of the carnations. "Tonight you should take a bath with these flowers in the water." He rummages in the paper bag and hands me what looks like a cough syrup bottle filled with clear liquid. "Blessed water," he says. "Drink it up and add more, a little bit at a time. What is added will become blessed too."

I thank him and crunch awkwardly away through the woods. I have long since lost the skill of walking in forests at night without a sound.

"One more thing," Marco calls, and I turn back quickly.

"Yes?"

"Do not forget to drink your garbanzo bean water. It is very important." His eyes are full of mirth again. Maybe he is telling me that I'm trying to understand too much, that I should put more faith in ritual. But that isn't how my generation sees the world. Nonetheless, I run a bath when I get home and scatter the red, white, and yellow petals on the surface of the water. It's like a combination of a funeral and a baptism with my body trapped in its prime between. Already it's returned to a state of sleek homeostasis after a year of bloating drugs. How naturally it would mate, reproduce, and slowly wither like any fruit of the vine if left to its own devices. It's only when we know ourselves that things begin to fall apart, when ghosts form in the electrical storm of our machinery and build palace upon concrete palace to prove their mastery over all things. Despite its lonely outcome, sometimes this cold reductionism seems the most poetic explanation of all, and it's not so philosophically problematic if things go wrong, if an extra *I* is formed or the self is entirely lost—it was only accidental to begin with.

I drain my bath and disperse the sodden flowers in the moonlit yard as I've been instructed. I drink my blessed water and add garbanzo beans to the shopping list. Then I go to my room and rummage through the chaos of my desk until I find a pen and a legal pad. My arm is crisscrossed with pale lines of scar tissue, and the irony is far from lost on me as I touch pen to page to forever mark it in my image. What conceit, all the things we do to paper and words, just because their alloy is slightly more eternal than ourselves. It would be so easy and probably better to stay silent. To write of this will surely make me more real than I am, and necessarily him as well. It's an indefensible risk to be sure. And yet the paper fills with words, the demon has a voice again, and the world, so serenely devoid just moments before, shatters into meaning.

CHAPTER THIRTY-TWO

I stop outside the door to my classroom while students stream past me with mindless grace, stumble past me with unbearable lightness and hard lemonade hangovers. Time has swept away more hesitant days, static months of online classes, pills sometimes taken and sometimes spit into tissues, and a book, this one, written in notebooks late at night in the glow of a lamp that is always kept burning so I'm never alone in the dark. Now it's September and it's been a month since I emerged from my room, shouldered again the weight of my backpack, my freedom, my possibility to shift the world toward good or evil or nothing at all.

We get our first exams back today: cognitive psychology, neuroscience, linguistics, and ethics. It's hard to take sometimes . . . not the classes, all bite-sized memes considerately designed so even those in the throes of alcohol poisoning and erotic fantasy can retain something. I mean the students, the others. They are so tan, so insouciant, so vitally alive. They take notes but they don't listen, and they have no idea how free they are, or how bound. They smell overwhelmingly of AXE body spray and tropical lip gloss, and they have no idea what I would give to be like them.

I passed Scott one day, talking to some girl in the hall. Their conversation was obscured by the hum of nearby vending machines, but she flashed a coy smile as Scott reached out to brush back her hair. I think she must have made some comment about her hair to see if Scott would touch it, as this seems to be the easiest way to determine the balance of attraction between two people. The girl's skin glowed radiant blue in the refracted light of the Gatorade machine, and there was a giddy electric charge to their movements. Their flickering eyes and half-suppressed smiles told me they weren't dating yet, that maybe this was the first time they'd touched.

I kept my head down as I passed. The world is full of others, after all, and in the end there is only so much we can explain to them when their eyes are so close to ours and so full of reactions, like chemistry sets changing their color and acidity in response to every word. Everything is changing, changing, falling apart, putting itself back together again. Suddenly I'm afraid, and I want to go home. I want to have a disease, to be exempt. If I said I can't take this, I can never be one of these bright and normal creatures, if I were to collapse and fetally regress and watch the world pass by from a room that still holds too many mementos of childhood, people would understand. It's shocking how easily everyone accepts excuses from me now. But after all this it just wouldn't be a very poetic ending, and I don't know of any better criteria by which I should determine how to live. So in a fairly inconsequential action that nonetheless requires more of me than anything yet, I enter the room and find a seat among my classmates.

Afterword

Ifinished the first draft of this book in 2007, when I was twenty. I wrote it hoping to interpret my experience, to force it into meaning. What did I believe in, the demon or the disease? Unable to arrive at a clear answer, I doubted the story would even be published. If I had reached no conclusions about life and the meaning of everything, why would people care what I had to say?

Furthermore, since people with mental illness must constantly battle the stereotype that they are unpredictable and violent, it seemed unfair to bring my own murky case to light. People might not blame me for hearing voices—genetics, you were dealt a bad hand—but we don't like to exonerate people of their darker desires, even though it follows that they were created by the same fickle union of nucleotide base pairs. Although I'm far from a reductionist, I believe that some people are simply better at being human than others, and that free will is a conditional state. But I think that as long as we work in good faith with what we've been given and take up our freedom wherever we find it, *arête* is never beyond our reach.

It does, however, prove elusive. I've been hospitalized since I've written this book. I've been paranoid and agitated and anxious and depressed. I've taken medications and not taken them; I graduated from college but dropped out of graduate school. I decided to have my book published, but I still feared judgment or maybe desired it, and I've come close to obliterating myself and every word I've written. All things considered I am not a resounding success, but I've found what compels me and so far that has been enough. Words burn in me and I try to express them. I may desire silence, but that's not the hand I was dealt. Throughout this I've remained carefully agnostic, but if you caught me in the right moment, maybe with my back against a rock, looking out over a gray river while Apollo grazes on wild grape leaves beside me, I might confess a belief:

Demons surround us. In this way, they are much like words, omnipresent—in lecture halls, in chatrooms, in pine forests, in bus terminals . . . we never escape them. They occupy no physical space, they have no meaning independent of their hosts. Parasitic, without mercy, our constant shadows . . . they force us to fall, stagnate, become. They make us interesting, they make us doubt. They form our souls from an undifferentiated light.